D0203955

THE HISTORY OF THE CENTRAL ASIAN REPUBLICS

ADVISORY BOARD

THE HISTORY OF THE CENTRAL ASIAN REPUBLICS

Peter L. Roudik

The Greenwood Histories of the Modern Nations
Frank W. Thackeray and John E. Findling, Series Editors

Greenwood Press
Westport, Connecticut • London

Library of Congress Cataloging-in-Publication Data

Roudik, Peter.
   The history of the Central Asian republics / Peter Roudik.
      p. cm. — (Greenwood histories of the modern nations, ISSN 1096–2905)
   Includes bibliographical references and index.
   ISBN 978–0–313–34013–0 (alk. paper)
   1. Asia, Central—History.   I. Title.
   DK856.R68   2007
   958—dc22   2007026941

British Library Cataloguing in Publication Data is available.

Library of Congress Catalog Card Number: 2007026941
ISBN-13: 978–0–313–34013–0
ISSN: 1096–2905

First published in 2007

Greenwood Press, 88 Post Road West, Westport, CT 06881
An imprint of Greenwood Publishing Group, Inc.
www.greenwood.com

Printed in the United States of America

The paper used in this book complies with the
Permanent Paper Standard issued by the National
Information Standards Organization (Z39.48–1984).

10 9 8 7 6 5 4 3 2 1

Contents

Series Foreword

The *Greenwood Histories of the Modern Nations* series is intended to provide students and interested laypeople with up-to-date, concise, and analytical histories of many of the nations of the contemporary world. Not since the 1960s has there been a systematic attempt to publish a series of national histories, and, as editors, we believe that this series will prove to be a valuable contribution to our understanding of other countries in our increasingly interdependent world.

More than 30 years ago, at the end of the 1960s, the cold war was an accepted reality of global politics, the process of decolonization was still in progress, the idea of a unified Europe with a single currency was unheard of, the United States was mired in a war in Vietnam, and the economic boom in Asia was still years in the future. Richard Nixon was president of the United States, Mao Tsetung (not yet Mao Zedong) ruled China, Leonid Brezhnev guided the Soviet Union, and Harold Wilson was prime minister of the United Kingdom. Authoritarian dictators still ruled most of Latin America, the Middle East was reeling in the wake of the Six-Day War, and Shah Reza Pahlavi was at the height of his power in Iran. Clearly, the last 30 years have been witness to a great deal of historical change, and it is to this change that this series is primarily addressed.

With the help of a distinguished advisory board, we have selected nations whose political, economic, and social affairs mark them as among the most important in the waning years of the twentieth century, and for each nation we have found an author who is recognized as a specialist in the history of that nation. These authors have worked most cooperatively with us and with Greenwood Press to produce volumes that reflect current research on their nations and that are interesting and informative to their prospective readers.

The importance of a series such as this cannot be underestimated. As a superpower whose influence is felt all over the world, the United States can claim a "special" relationship with almost every other nation. Yet many Americans know very little about the histories of the nations with which the United States relates. How did they get to be the way they are? What kind of political systems have evolved there? What kind of influence do they have in their own region? What are the dominant political, religious, and cultural forces that move their leaders? These and many other questions are answered in the volumes of this series.

The authors who have contributed to this series have written comprehensive histories of their nations, dating back to prehistoric times in some cases. Each of them, however, has devoted a significant portion of the book to events of the last thirty years, because the modern era has contributed the most to contemporary issues that have an impact on U.S. policy. Authors have made an effort to be as up-to-date as possible so that readers can benefit from the most recent scholarship and a narrative that includes very recent events.

In addition to the historical narrative, each volume in this series contains an introductory overview of the country's geography, political institutions, economic structure, and cultural attributes. This is designed to give readers a picture of the nation as it exists in the contemporary world. Each volume also contains additional chapters that add interesting and useful detail to the historical narrative. One chapter is a thorough chronology of important historical events, making it easy for readers to follow the flow of a particular nation's history. Another chapter features biographical sketches of the nation's most important figures in order to humanize some of the individuals who have contributed to the historical development of their nation. Each volume also contains a comprehensive bibliography, so that those readers whose interest has been sparked may find out more about the nation and its history. Finally, there is a carefully prepared topic and person index.

Readers of these volumes will find them fascinating to read and useful in understanding the contemporary world and the nations that comprise it. As series editors, it is our hope that this series will contribute to a heightened sense of global understanding as we embark on a new century.

Frank W. Thackeray and John E. Findling
Indiana University Southeast

Preface

The history of Central Asia is full of secrets and mysteries. Legends, poems, and anecdotes supplement rich archeological findings and historical documents. The region is home to ancient societies but relatively new state structures. Being located at the crossroad of economies, cultures, and languages, the newly established states of Kazakhstan, Kyrgyzstan, Tajikistan, Turkmenistan, and Uzbekistan demonstrate a unique example of intertwining histories of people who for thousands of years kept their traditions in these isolated steppes, deserts, and mountains; struggled for their national identities; and fought against foreign political and religious influences.

I first visited the area in autumn of 1984, before completing my doctorate in history of Soviet electoral law. At that time, the Soviet Empire was at the peak of its might, and it was surprisingly striking to see how modern office buildings were standing next to medieval windowless houses from clay decorated with portraits of Karl Marx and Ayatollah Khomeini. Later, I had several chances to return to these states to study their turbulent legal and political developments and observe how local people are adjusting their centuries-old traditions to constantly changing political circumstances. This book describes the process of creating independent nations of Central Asia; analyzes numerous state formations that existed on this territory and their relations with the neighbors and conquering great powers; reviews major legal, political, and cultural views and theories developed by influential local scholars and public figures; demonstrates that these states flourished only in the periods when government structures suppressed fundamentalist Islam and provided for secular development; and details efforts to reform these independent nations into modern states. Being a desolate and almost inaccessible area of Asia for thousands of years, this region always was of interest to the great powers. Alexander the Great, Genghis Khan, the British crown, and Russian emperors are just a few who attempted to establish control over this territory. The ongoing war against terrorism together with recent developments in oil and gas explorations have made Central Asia the object of great political games again. However, this part of the world squeezed between China, Iran, Pakistan, and Russia remains largely unknown to the general public despite the fact that the history of this region can provide positive examples of combating radical Islam and demonstrate how to build modern secular regimes in Eastern countries.

The meaning of the term *Central Asia* has been the subject of scholarly discussions, and any attempt to define it can be considered controversial. For the purpose of this book, by Central Asia I mean five newly independent former Soviet republics joined by ancient cultural, economic, and political bonds and a shared history. The word *Turkistan* is applied to Russian and early Soviet possessions in the region in the nineteenth century and in the first quarter of the twentieth century. Hundreds of volumes were written on different aspects of the history of Central Asian states. I have not attempted serious archival research and have been able to rely on the publications—and in important cases the advice, insight, and suggestions—of Western, Central Asian, and Russian scholars in preparation of this book, which is unique because it tells the general history of five different nations in a narrative form for the general public from a Western academic point of view and integrates the region's history into a review of its contemporary political developments. A full understanding of Central Asian heritage is impossible without a study of legal, political, and philosophical views expressed by leading politicians and intellectuals of these counties. For better comprehension of the ideas popular in the region during the entire course of its history since the sixth century B.C. until modern day, the history of political thought is analyzed in a separate chapter in chronological order. Because of that, views of leading Central Asian figures mentioned in this study are not analyzed in other parts of the book.

Library of Congress rules of transliteration were used in this book because there is no universally accepted system for transliterating Central Asian Turkic and Persian languages into the Latin script. The same rule applies to personal names, with the exception of well-known names (e.g., Yeltsin). Personal names took many forms in Central Asia. Some people used Russian-style last names (e.g., Rashidov), others adopted Arabic-style names (e.g., al-Biruni), and some were known under their pseudonyms (e.g., Avitsenna) or by their first names (e.g., Nasrullah). The name most commonly used by the person in question is the one used in this book. The name of a dynasty founder is often used to describe the rule of his successors (e.g., Genghis—Genghisids—Genghisid dynasty). Dates of birth and death are provided for all major figures. All pre–Common Era dates are given with the B.C. notification. The A.D. notification is used only when the identification of a date can be confusing. Most of the Common Era dates have no notification. Before February 1918, the Julian calendar was used in the Russian Empire. Therefore, dates related to the period of Russian colonization between 1867 and 1918 are given in the Julian calendar. All dates outside this time period are in the Gregorian calendar.

I would like to thank many people who have helped me in preparation of this manuscript, but first of all my parents, Bella and Leonid Roudik, whose moral and intellectual influence on my development I appreciate greatly. Special thanks to my colleagues at the Library of Congress, Bryan Bachner, Christopher Murphy, Gholam Vafai, and Nina Zanegina, who took time to discuss this book with me and provided me with invaluable advice.

I am grateful to Greenwood Press editors Sarah Colwell and Kaitlin Ciarmiello for their support and encouragement throughout the writing of this book. Special thanks to my colleagues at the Library of Congress, Bryan Bachner, Christopher Murphy, Gholam Vafai, and Nina Zanegina, who took time to discuss this book with me and provided me with invaluable advice.

I am especially thankful to friends and scholars Olena Yatsunska and Adalyat Issiyeva for their numerous professional consultations and tips on sources, and to Robert Roudik, who helped me with editorial review.

I am grateful to Greenwood Press editors Sarah Colwell and Kaitlin Ciarmiello for their support and encouragement throughout the writing of this book and Apex Publishing for their assistance and cooperation.

It is to my wife, Svetlana, who, for the last twenty years, has offered me her boundless understanding, encouragement, and support, that I dedicate this book.

Timeline of Historical Events

6000 B.C.	First farming and cattle-raising settlements on the territory of modern-day Turkmenistan
2000 B.C.	Complete transition to agricultural communes throughout Transoxiana
1000 B.C.	Construction of first large and long irrigation systems
1000 B.C.	City of Khorezm mentioned in ancient chronicles
750 B.C.	Formation of the ancient Bactrian state
545 B.C.	City of Samarkand is established
Fifth century B.C.	Bactrian and Sogdian states dominate area of present-day Uzbekistan
Fourth century B.C.	Kyrgyz tribes invade northern China
334 B.C.	Troops of Alexander the Great entered Central Asia
Third century B.C.	Ancient city of Merv founded
230 B.C.	Bokhara oasis established in the Bactrian state

Second century B.C.	Silk Road started to function
105–250 A.D.	Power period of the Buddhist Kushan Empire in modern-day Tajikistan
305	Khorezm is established as an independent state
500	Feudal society emerges in present-day Kyrgyzstan
551–774	Existence of the Turkic Khanate
651	First Arab attack on Merv
705	Establishment of the Caliphate rule over Central Asia
750	Arabs complete conquest of Central Asia, imposing Islam
766	Turkic Quarluq confederation establishes state in present-day eastern Kazakhstan
776–783	Uprising under Mukanna leadership
Eighth to ninth centuries	Turkic Oguz tribes migrate into Central Asia
875–999	Samanid Empire is established, the first centralized bureaucratic local monarchy with centers in Bokhara and Samarkand
999	Turkic Qarakhanids overthrow Samanids, ending last major Persian state in Central Asia
1220	Genghis Khan appears in Central Asia, and Mongol invasion begins
1312	Partial conversion of the Golden Horde into Islam
1336–1405	Life of Emir Timur (Tamerlane)
1379	Khorezm becomes a part of the Timur's state
1505	Capture of Khorezm by Sheibani Khan
1558	Visit of Anthony Jenkins, first British traveler and agent of the British-Russian trade company, to Bokhara and Khiva
1601–1763	Rule of the Ashtarkhanid dynasty in Bokhara
1619–1621	First diplomatic contacts between Moscow and Bokhara

1677	Some Turkmen tribes come under Russian protection
1717	First Russian mission to Central Asia slaughtered in Khiva
1730	First Kazakh mission to Russia
1731	Kazakh Lesser Horde accepts Russian protection
1740	Nadir Shah of Iran invades Bokhara
1798	Uzbek Khanate of Kokand established
1822–1824	Kazakh khanates are abolished by Russia
1838–1847	Anti-Russian movement in Kazakhstan under Khan Kenesary
1839–1842	First Russian expedition to Khiva
1842	Murder of British agents Charles Stoddart and Arthur Conolly in Bokhara
1854	City of Almaty (Fortress Vernyi) established by the Russians
1855	Acquisition of Russian citizenship by northern Kyrgyz tribes
1865	Tashkent is taken by Russian troops, Russian province of Turkistan created
1868	Samarkand captured by the Russians
	The Khanate of Bokhara becomes a protectorate of Russia
1873	The Khanate of Khiva accepts Russian protectorate
1876	Russia annexes and eliminates the Khanate of Kokand
1877	Russian advancement to Afghanistan is stopped by the Congress of Berlin
1885	Muslim revolt in the Fergana Valley against the Tsarist rule
1886	Adoption of a permanent Statute on Turkistan
1887	The border between Afghanistan and Russian Central Asia is determined by the British and the Russians

1890–1892	Mass migration of peasants from the European part of Russia to Kazakhstan
1895	Convention on division of spheres of influence concluded between Great Britain and Russia
	Nobel brothers started to extract oil in present-day Turkmenistan
1906	Publication of the first Uzbek newspaper
1909	The Young Bokharan Party is founded in Bokhara
1916	Central Asian anti-Russian uprising
1917	March 2: Abdication of Tsar Nicholas II
	April: Turkistan governorship general abolished, Turkistan Committee of the Provisional Government established in Tashkent
	October 25: Bolshevik Revolution in St. Petersburg
	November 1: Bolsheviks came to power in Tashkent
	November 29: Turkistan autonomy in Kokand established
1918	April 30: Turkistan ASSR formed within the RSFSR
1919 Front	August 14: Bolshevik Army opened the Turkistan
1920	April 26: Khorezm People's Soviet Republic created
	May 7: First military mobilization of native Central Asian people conducted by the Bolsheviks
	September: Turkistan State University opened in Tashkent
	October 8: Bokharan People's Soviet Republic established
1922	March 26: Mountainous Kyrgyz Province created within the Turkistan ASSR
	December 30: The USSR formed
1924	April 28: Soviet decision on creation of national states in Central Asia

	October 14: Kyrgyz AO established within the RSFSR
	October 27: Turkmen SSR established
1925	Kazakh ASSR established within the RSFSR
	February 11: Uzbek SSR replaced Turkistan ASSR
	May 25: Tajik ASSR formed within the Uzbek SSR
	May: Official incorporation of Uzbek and Turkmen SSR in the USSR
1927	Antireligious campaign conducted
1928	Arabic script is replaced by Latin alphabet
1928–1932	Forced collectivization of agriculture and settlement
1929	Tajik ASSR became the Tajik SSR
1931	End of the Basmachi movement
1936	Kazakh and Kyrgyz SSR created
1937	New constitutions of Central Asian republics passed
	Soviet military intervention in Xinjiang Province to support Muslim uprising
1937–1938	Stalin purges of Muslim communists
1940	Conversion of Latin alphabet to Cyrillic
1941–1945	German invasion to the Soviet Union
1942	Status of official religion is given to Islam by the Soviet government
1948	Earthquake in Ashgabat, Turkmenistan; thousands of people killed
1953	Death of Stalin, political liberalization
1954–1960	Virgin Land campaign
1966	Devastating earthquake in Tashkent, Uzbekistan
1979–1988	Soviet invasion in Afghanistan
1985	Mikhail Gorbachev comes to power
1986	Popular unrest in Kazakhstan, first ethnic riots in the Soviet Union

1989	Native languages are recognized as official languages by the legislatures of Central Asian states
1990	Office of the president established in Uzbekistan, the first among the Soviet Union republics
1991	Central Asian states declare their independence
	Central Asian republics admitted to the UN
	December 26: Dissolution of the Soviet Union
1992	Five Central Asian states take over Soviet military installations on their respective territories
	February 1: First U.S. Embassy in Central Asia opened in Bishkek
1992–1997	Civil war in Tajikistan
1993	Central Asian Economic Union created, borders between Central Asian states became customs free
1994	Kazakhstan, Kyrgyzstan, Turkmenistan, and Uzbekistan join NATO Partnership for Peace
1995	Permanent neutral status of Turkmenistan endorsed by the UN
1996	April 25: Shanghai Cooperation Organization established
1996	Kazakhstan, Kyrgyzstan, and Tajikistan pledged assistance to China against separatist Xinjiang Uighur Autonomous Region
1997	First joint U.S.–Central Asian military exercise
1998	Kyrgyz astronaut participated in a space flight with a U.S. space expedition
1999	The term of office of the Turkmen President Niyazov extended for life
	Islamic movement of Uzbekistan conducted military raids on villages in Tajikistan and Kyrgyzstan
	Series of terrorist attacks in Tashkent
2000	UN military contingent removed from Tajikistan

2001	U.S. military bases established in Uzbekistan and Kyrgyzstan
2002	Assassination attempts on president of Turkmenistan
2003	Russia established its first military base in Kyrgyzstan
2004	Kyrgyz Parliament granted a lifelong immunity from prosecution to President Akaev
	Apprehension of a large group of Islamic terrorists with ties to Al Qaeda in Kazakhstan
2005	Following mass public protests, President Akaev left the country and resigned
	During antigovernment riots in Andijon, Uzbekistan, the army was used against demonstrators
2006	Political reform in Uzbekistan, liberalization of political activities
	FBI involved in investigation of a murder of the Kazakhstan's opposition leader
	Death of Turkmen President Niyazov, expectations of political reforms and democratization
2007	Tight control over mass media introduced in Uzbekistan
	Kyrgyzstan joined Global Legal Information Network, a cooperative project supported by the U.S. Congress

1

The Stans: New States, Old Societies

In 1991, five Central Asian republics of the Soviet Union—Kazakhstan, Kyrgyzstan, Tajikistan, Turkmenistan, and Uzbekistan, commonly known as *the Stans*—declared their independence and became sovereign states.

Central Asia is the land where world civilizations existed since ancient times. It was the crossroad for invaders, a place of historic coexistence of nomads and settled people, and the area of migration movements, from the Scythians in the eighth century B.C. to the Mongols and Uzbeks in the thirteenth to sixteenth centuries. More than a thousand years before the Common Era, Hindu-European tribes traversed these lands, and armies of Alexander the Great were here in the fourth century B.C. Later, nomads of the Turkic Khanate, Arabs, and Mongols populated these lands. Large states that affected world history fought each other endlessly in this region, which is why so few historical sources are preserved here. Major historical sources include Assyrian chronicles, Persian histories, reports of Western travelers, and recent data discovered by Soviet archeologists. For most of its history, Central Asia was a bridge between the Muslim and non-Muslim parts of Asia. This land was populated by people of different races and religions, including Buddhists, Muslims, Zoroastrians, Shamanists, Jews, Christians, and many others who met here. Social engineering experiments conducted in Central Asia during the twentieth century made this region a model for speedy modernization.

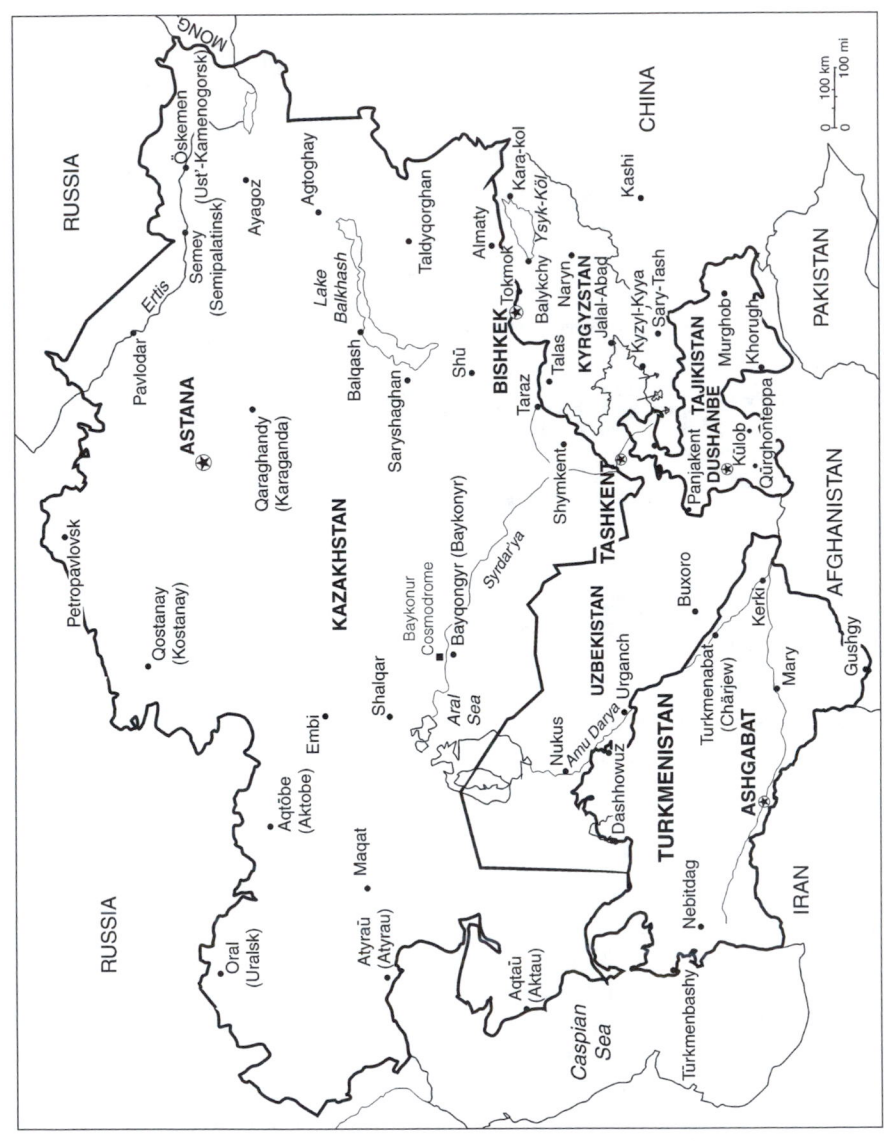

The Central Asian Republics. Cartography by Bookcomp, Inc.

The tolerant version of Islam professed by the local people together with vast unexplored natural resources and the region's proximity to the area of major antiterrorist operations make these countries the center of global strategic interest for the international community.

GEOGRAPHY

The definition of Central Asia is attributed to Alexander Humboldt, and the term is used to describe inner parts of the Asian continent. As the name implies, Central Asia is located in the middle of the Eurasian continent. From a geographical point of view, the term Central Asia has no precise definition. The currently accepted definition includes the five newly independent Muslim states of the former Soviet Union, although geographically this area includes Afghanistan, northern parts of Iran, and some parts of Siberia. Central Asia expands from the Caspian Sea and Ural Mountains in the west to China in the east and from Siberia in the north to Afghanistan, Iran, and Pakistan in the south. Central Asia is an area of almost two million square miles, equal to the size of Great Britain, France, Germany, Spain, and Greece combined. Its external boundaries are approximately 8,000 miles long, and the total population is more than 58 million.

Central Asia is a landlocked area of deserts, steppes, and mountains. The area contains the world's tallest peaks (e.g., Victory Summit, 24,409 feet), which are covered with snow and glaciers. Many parts of the deserts are below sea level. Kazakhstan and Turkmenistan are primarily flat and have deserts. Tajikistan and Kyrgyzstan are mountainous. The dry continental climate is characterized by high temperatures of over 100 degrees in the extremely dry summers and snowy winters as cold as 15 degrees below zero. The major bodies of water in Central Asia are the Aral Sea and the Balkhash Lake in Kazakhstan. The smaller streams were gradually reduced through seepage, evaporation, or diversion for irrigation and consequently disappeared in the deserts. Because of the low precipitation in this area (about 10 inches per year), evaporation exceeds supply. Dry lakebeds make the sand dunes, and the drying Aral Sea is heading toward a major environmental catastrophe. Amu Darya (called Oxus in ancient times, and, subsequently, the entire territory was called Transoxiana), Syr Darya (the Jaxartes River in ancient sources), and Zerafshan are the major rivers of Central Asia, which are fed by glaciers and melting snow in the mountains. Main mountain ranges run west to east; the climate and vegetation vary greatly with altitude and exposure; and agriculture, the main industry, depends on artificial irrigation.

The landscape has played a major role in the politics, economy, and culture of Central Asia. Deserts prevented trade and effective control over nomads; however, they did not provide protection from the Arabs, Mongols, and

Uzbeks, who invaded the region seeking refuge from even harsher deserts. Because of the deserts and isolation, the nomadic and seminomadic way of life in Central Asia persisted for a long time. Plundering bands, which disrupted trade and frightened travelers, operated in the desert, and the inhabitants of these deserts were forced to migrate constantly in search of safety. Medieval chronicles describe these deserts as impassable for horses and even camels because of the scarcity of fodder and exceedingly hot sands. Travelers could find neither habitation nor water in the course of several days' journey. Before the twentieth century, a two-week journey was required to cross the desert between the two major Central Asian cities of Khorezm and Bokhara.

PEOPLE

Geographical factors have impacted the people as well. Due to the aridity of the soil, settlements were concentrated in oases; however, large distances between the oases complicated the communication between them. Because of a lack of natural barriers, the region had been the subject of frequent foreign invasions. Surrounded on three sides by steppes and deserts, the area was open to the influx of nomads who regularly entered the area in search of pastures and trophies.

Contacts with various races exposed local people to external influences and shaped Central Asia into a multilingual country of heterogeneous people. The first known inhabitants of Central Asia were of the Caucasian race. Some tribal groups with Mongoloid characteristics began to appear during the first millennium A.D., but the Mongoloid type did not become noticeable in the population until the thirteenth century, when large numbers of Mongols followed Genghis Khan's armies into western Central Asia. Tajiks, Uzbeks, and Turkmens are Caucasian. Kyrgyz and Kazakhs are of Mongoloid type.

Tajiks, the original inhabitants of the oases, attribute their culture and language to strong Persian influences. Those Tajiks, who, in the twelfth and thirteenth centuries, submitted to the customs of the Turks, adopted their language, and trace descent from an ancestor named Uzbek, are now called Uzbeks. Subsequently, the name Uzbek was applied to all groups speaking the related Turkic dialects, ranging from fully sedentary merchants and craftspeople to seminomadic tribal communities. Turkmens, who occupy the southwestern part of Central Asia, are descendants from the Oghuz Turks who remained in Central Asia after most of their community moved to southwestern Asia in the eleventh century; their language is close to the northern Iranian dialect. The Kazakhs established an ethnos in the fifteenth century as fragments of those Turko-Mongol tribes in the steppes of northern Central Asia who had rejected attempts of Uzbek accedence. Kazakhs retained their nomadic way of life longer than all other pastoral tribes of Central Asia but were the first

Central Asians to establish contacts with Russian colonization forces. Kazakhs speak the Turkic language, distinct from Uzbek and Turkmen. The Kyrgyz came to their present home in the tenth century A.D. from Siberia with a language closely related to that of the Kazakhs, while cultural differences reflect habitual distinctions. Karakalpaks, a group of mixed origin, lived along the lower Syr Darya in the sixteenth and seventeenth centuries. In the eighteenth century, a group of Karakalpaks became vassals of the Kazakhs, while another large group moved toward Bokhara. Eventually, both groups settled along the southern shores of the Aral Sea. Those who moved eastward toward the Fergana Valley came under Uzbek influence. Language similarities evidence close ties of Karakalpaks with the Kazakhs.

Representatives of all Central Asian ethnic groups reside on the territory of modern China. Since ancient times, this territory was the traditional migration area for local nomads. In the eighteenth and early nineteenth centuries, due to border treaties concluded between China and Russia, these lands became part of China. However, in the earlier periods, these tribes remained legally independent from both neighboring powers. Today, the legal status of Muslim Central Asian people in China remains an acute problem. Uighurs constitute the major ethnic group among the Central Asians living in China's Xinjiang province.

Before the dissolution of the Soviet Union, slightly less than half of the region's population consisted of Slavic people, mostly Russians and Ukrainians. First settlers from the European part of Russia arrived in the early twentieth century during the Russian colonization. Russian peasants were attracted by large land plots granted to them. Another wave of Russian migrants was forced by the industrialization of the region during the Soviet period, mass evacuation during World War II, and forced resettlements of entire nations according to Stalin's orders. Since 1991, the Russian-speaking population has steadily decreased, unable to integrate themselves into Muslim societies.

The majority of people in all five republics profess Sunni Islam; a significant religious revival became common in the 1990s. The Central Asian republics remain secular and maintain separation between state and religion; however, in Tajikistan, Islam is becoming a strong political force. In Kazakhstan, Kyrgyzstan, and Turkmenistan—where society is based on cultural traditions preserved since nomadic times—Islam does not have a strong influence, unlike among the sedentary Tajiks and Uzbeks.

The typical Central Asian family, especially in rural areas, has five or six children on average. Children and youth account for approximately seventy percent of the region's population. Slightly more than forty percent of the region's population is children and young adults under the age of 14, and about one-third are young people between the ages of 15 and 29. Clothing styles in the region have been developed according to climatic characteristics;

historical, ethnic, and regional features; and vary among the republics. Central Asians tend to wear European-style dress; however, traditional clothes are preserved for particular ceremonies and often appear in remote areas. While rural women tend to wear traditional clothes made of local fabrics, robes and hats are popular among men. Although the cuisine is somewhat different in each republic, it also has some commonalities. Plov—made of rice, meat, oil, carrots, onions, and various spices—is the most popular and festive dish all over the region. While fruits, vegetables, nuts, sweets, cookies, and hot tea are consumed in all parts of Central Asia, lamb and horse meat are especially popular in Kazakhstan.

Poetic creativity is probably the most distinct feature of Central Asian culture. A large part of local literature consists of household stories and fairy tales with animal, magical, and fantastic themes. The oldest genre of folklore is poetry performed with the accompaniment of a musical instrument. Pre-Islamic culture is represented by an insignificant number of written texts in Old Turkic languages. Since the fourteenth century, literature intensely developed in Uzbekistan with different nonreligious epic and lyric forms. The most ancient monuments of art are rock paintings of animals and hunting scenes of the Paleolithic period. Sculptures made of clay, fashioned in gypsum (rarely of stone) have Hellenic and Indian roots. The region is known for its achievements in manuscript art and bookbinding. All major cities had their individual schools of book miniatures. Contemporary works of Central Asian artists depict modern life of local people and follow common international trends.

HISTORY

The 2,500-year history of Central Asia, which is centered on empires and tribes, contains cyclical periods of highly developed cultures followed by periods of destruction. This pattern was repeated many times. Village settlements first appeared along the southern foothills of Central Asia in the second millennium B.C., and oases in the delta of Amu Darya (River Oxus) spread south to the Aral Sea to the borders with China. Further Chinese explorations opened caravan routes that linked China with India and the West. These agricultural settlements had well-developed irrigation practices and animal husbandry and were populated by ethnic Iranians who arrived in the area during the course of the Persian kings' invasions. Cities, such as Samarkand and Bokhara founded by Iranians, became powerful commercial and cultural centers as East-West trade increased. In ancient and early medieval times, Asia was wealthier than Europe. It had larger states, more goods to offer, and stronger military powers. This prosperity made the region the object of many conquests by Arabs, Turks, and Mongols.

In the sixteenth century, three states were established in Central Asia: the khanates of Bokhara, Khiva, and Kokand along the Silk Road. These states prospered until the colonizing Russian Empire—which competed geopolitically with Great Britain—overtook them. Russia, deprived of cotton due to the American Civil War and in search of new markets and sources of raw materials, started its invasion of the region in the 1860s. In 1917, the Russian Empire collapsed, and the region survived a short period of semi-independence, retaining much of its customary political shape and most of its earlier cultural content before its formal inclusion in the Soviet Union. The republics were defined by arbitrary borders created without consideration of ethnic and linguistic situations in the region. In the 1930s, the region survived a massive disruption of traditional life-styles through agricultural collectivization, industrialization campaigns, episodes of widespread famine, and ideological attacks on religion and traditions. Despite the fact that the region did not play any significant role in the Soviet political process, leaders of Uzbekistan and Kazakhstan were always included in the highest political institutions of the Soviet Union. However, they could not protect their republics from communist purges, and Central Asian elites were affected by the Soviet rule in the same way as were elites in other parts of the country.

CURRENT DEVELOPMENTS

After the breakup of the Soviet Union in 1991, these countries became independent and were unprepared for such an event. Without a tradition of national political institutions, these countries decided to keep and gradually reform the outdated Soviet-era political structures with communist leaders renaming themselves into presidents. Currently, all governments have strong executive branches with presidents as heads of states. Until 2003, constitutions of all of these countries gave the presidents the power to rule by decree with the force of constitutional law. While all of the countries have held elections, none have been recognized as free and fair in conformity with international standards. Two of the governments have former communist leaders who have extended their mandate in extraconstitutional ways. None of the governments has a truly independent judiciary and deliberative legislature with powers to control the executive branch. None of the countries has a vibrant political opposition poised to assume power at the next election. In all of the countries, the rule of law is interpreted to mean the rule of the president and the law enforcement authorities. The gap between the expectations of reform and what has actually been accomplished is growing and leads to public protests and local disorder. All Central Asian republics have acquired memberships in many international organizations and have built their national armed forces on the basis of the fragmented military units of the former Soviet Union that have remained on the republics' territory. All five governments have pledged radical political, social, and economic reforms, but obstacles such as inefficient government bureaucracies, ethnic conflicts, social tensions, and the threat of Islamic radicalism make them proceed cautiously.

Dramatic changes came to Central Asia in 2001, after the terrorist attacks on the United States. As soon as the United States made a decision to fight terrorist networks in Afghanistan, the U.S. government recognized that the successful anti-Taliban operation would require close U.S. cooperation with the Central Asian states. In a development that would have seemed impossible a few years earlier, U.S. military troops were stationed at Kyrgyz and Uzbek air bases. Soon, many other governments around the world began revising their beliefs about Central Asia as a region of strategic importance. Oil and gas resources played an important role in such reassessments.

The region has rich natural and agricultural resources. Reserves of minerals and fuels are enormous, and irrigation techniques have been familiar to the people of the region for thousands of years. Trained workers and a highly educated population with a 96 percent literacy rate add to the region's investment attractiveness. Major industries are metallurgical, chemical, machine building, food processing, textiles, and mining. All republics have a relatively similar range of commodities for trade, including deposits of coal, precious nonferrous and rare metals, and construction materials. Their common emphasis on cotton, oil, and natural gas limits the opportunity for regional cooperation and contributes to competition for trade with other regions and countries. Kyrgyzstan and Tajikistan have fewer fuel resources; however, they control water flow for irrigation in the Uzbekistan and Turkmenistan lowlands.

Relations between the Central Asian states and their neighbors are dualistic: they aim to establish a greater regional unity on one hand and building effective bilateral relations on the other. Thanks to this policy, the newly established states of Central Asia were able to find new markets, secure transportation corridors for exporting their petroleum resources, and substitute broken ties with the former Soviet Union—although Russia preserves its dominant position in Central Asia and easily outplays its major rivals, Iran and Turkey, for regional influence. In the early 1990s, Iran attempted to expand its involvement in Central Asian affairs using the long historical roots of the Iranian culture in the region; however, local people with a European education and moderate religious views did not accept the Islamic fanaticism.

All Central Asian neighbors—Afghanistan, China, Iran, and Russia—influence political developments in the region. Afghanistan remains a constant threat of Islamic radicalization and drug trafficking. The existence of the Taliban on the southern borders of Central Asia immediately alarmed all Central Asian governments and forced them to reestablish a close military cooperation with Russia. In addition to a number of security treaties concluded

Table 1.1 Statistical Profile of Central Asia (2005)

	Capital City	Size in Square Miles(U.S. equivalent)	Population (in millions)	Median Age/Life Expectancy (years)	Gross Domestic Product per Capita/Annual Growth Rate	Natural Resources
Kazakhstan	Astana	1,049,155 (four times the size of Texas)	15.224	29/69	$8,200/9.2%	Petroleum, natural gas, iron ore, grain
Kyrgyzstan	Bishkek	76,641 (South Dakota)	5.214	24/68	$2,100/2%	Hydropower, gold, coal, oil, tobacco, wool
Tajikistan	Dushanbe	55,251 (Wisconsin)	7.321	20/65	$1,200/8%	Hydropower, uranium, silver, gold, cotton
Turkmenistan	Ashgabat	188,456 (larger than California)	5.043	22/62	$8,000/4%	Natural gas, hydrocarbon reserves
Uzbekistan	Tashkent	172,742 (California)	27.307	23/64	$1,800/7.2%	Natural gas, petroleum, gold, uranium, copper, lead, cotton

Note: The statistics in this table are based on information included in the CIA World Fact Book, at https://www.cia.gov/cia/publications/factbook/index.html.

between Russia and these states, specific plans of joint operations against the warlords who refused to disarm after the Tajik civil war were prepared by the Russian General Staff.

China also plays a leading role in the region, mostly through coordinating regional political and economic processes, a goal of the Shanghai Cooperation Organization consisting of China, Russia, and the five Central Asian republics. China supports the existing regimes in Central Asia and does not dispute Russia's active involvement in Central Asian affairs. Beijing appreciates Central Asian regimes' reluctance in supporting Uighur nationalism in the neighboring Chinese province of Xinjang and their refusal to provide outside support to Muslim separatists from Xinjang. It is estimated that between 500,000 and 600,000 Uighurs now live in post-Soviet Central Asia.

After being a relatively unknown part of Asia for many years, Central Asia has reemerged on the world map as a region of global strategic importance. It has become a subject of scholarly interest, and, because of its vast energy resources and security threats (in the form of drug and human trafficking, terrorism, and potential for instability in its ruling regimes), special attention is paid to this region by informed people and by the general public.

In the twenty-first century, two factors will determine the growing role of the Central Asian states in geopolitical affairs: their strategic location between China, Russia, India, and a number of major Islamic countries and their transformation into major suppliers of oil and gas to the world. Understanding their historic role, these countries are trying to shed their historic legacy of Russian/Soviet domination and avoid subordination to their immediate neighbors in the Islamic world. Although in early 2007, the future of the region remains as unclear as it was in previous years, this book attempts to analyze the fascinating past of Central Asian people and their path from ancient times to the twenty-first century in the hope that the history of Central Asia may shed light on current developments not only in the post-Soviet sphere but in Asia and in the Middle East.

2

Ancient State Formations

Early state formations on the territory of Central Asia remain a topic of speculation. Scholars think that agriculture based on irrigation was the basis for the economic development of the region, which started in southern Turkmenistan, Tajikistan, and southern Uzbekistan during the Bronze Age and in Tashkent and the Fergana Valleys in the early Iron Age.[1] The first permanent settlements were established in the sixth millennium B.C., in the area around present-day Ashgabat city; however, the variety of tools made of red jasper and igneous rock excavated on the territory of Tajikistan allows one to observe the traces of human activity in the region since the Upper Paleolithic period.

FIRST SETTLEMENTS

The mountainous cave sites that were occupied in the Middle Paleolithic period show that people at that time lived in stable communities and returned regularly to the same places during seasonal migrations. Flint tools, such as thin blades of accurate contours capable of being inserted in handles made of horn or wood with effective working edges, were typical of that period. Starting some 10,000 years ago, fishing, hunting, and gathering became secondary to cultivating land and animal domestication. Seasonal camps, caves, and rock shelters were precursors to the first permanent settlements with houses built of sun-baked bricks. The gradual domestication of sheep and goats and the growing of cultivated wheat and barley provided reliable food resources needed for a settled way of life. Food-storing pots made initially of stone and then of clay characterized the transition to the Neolithic period.

It appears that farming settlements of the sixth millennium B.C. applied the catchment technique of irrigation, which used simple banks to retain floodwater or channels to divert it, and required minimal labor. Settlements consisted of 30 to 35 rectangular houses built of clay cylinders. The houses often had fireplaces and lime-plastered floors and sheltered nuclear families of five to six members. Settlements with about 200 inhabitants were the foundation for further tribal formations. Major sources of food were wheat and barley harvested with wooden and bone reaping knives with stone blades. These people adorned themselves with bones or stone beads cut into pierced segments. For amulets they created clay figurines of humans and animals, which often bore tiny "stab wounds," most probably the result of magic hunting rites. The dead were buried within settlements. About a third of the excavated pottery of this region shows large black geometric elements, mostly triangles, on a red or yellow background.[2]

In the third and second millennia B.C., herding tribes in northern Kazakhstan transitioned to pastoralism, hunting hoofed animals and beginning to domesticate horses. The Iron Age was characterized by the development of agricultural communes throughout Transoxiana, while in the late second and early first millennia B.C., a sedentary farming culture emerged in the Fergana Valley. Its characteristics included handmade and decorated pottery, advanced bronze metallurgy, and a wide range of secondary stone artifacts. Settlements were located in the valleys of small streams. In these early settlements, the main form of housing was a dugout or pit dwelling with many grain storage pits. Later, houses were built above ground level using rectangular raw clay bricks. The houses were up to 3,000 square feet, and large families of about 30 resided in each. Because irrigated farming and building irrigation systems were very laborious, a consolidation of isolated clans and tribal communities became a necessity.

At the start of the first millennium B.C., the entire region became the northern part of Parthia, under whose influence the Iranian-speaking population in the valleys and oases of northern Central Asia became more localized and stable. Tribal distribution of this period determined future ethnic developments in the region. The Khorezmian people emerged on the southern Aral shores and in the Amu Darya delta, the Sogdian community arose along the Syr Darya, and a part of the Sogdian population later established the Fergana oasis. The formation of these groups was based on the emergence of sedentary agricultural regions and the beginning of urbanization. Members of these communities shared many ethnic traits with other peoples and tribes of Central Asia and were almost indistinguishable in clothing (short tunic, broad belt, and narrow trousers), headgear, and armaments. Ancient Greek and Persian accounts do not distinguish between the Central Asians. Greek historian Strabo, who lived in the first century B.C., said that settlers differed little from the nomads in life-style and customs.[3]

STATES OF TRIBES

Before the middle of the sixth century B.C., the area between Amu Darya and Syr Darya was occupied by nomadic Massagetae tribes. It was during this period that the first large political conglomerates were established— usually in the form of oases states and military democracies controlled by aristocracies and tribal leaders. They were amorphous and survived several cycles of creation and collapse. These state formations were located mostly on the territory of contemporary Afghanistan and Turkmenistan. Bactria, Margiana, and Khorezm were probably the largest and most stable state formations. Balkh was the capital of Bactria, Merv was the capital of Margiana, and Khorezm was located at the mouth of the Amu Darya. One of the largest state formations was Sogdiana, which included central and northern territories of the region. During the early medieval period, this name was applied to the entire region regardless of the ruling dynasty.

The necessity to construct and maintain large canals caused labor shortages, which was one of the economic factors for the creation of states. External factors, such as a threat from militant states of Mesopotamia, played an important role in the unification process. Big Khorezm was one of the earliest states and covered the territory from the Aral Sea to the mountains in the south. The state of Bactria located in southern areas of modern Tajikistan was the most established and stable state organization. In the seventh and sixth centuries B.C., the populations of these state formations kept close blood relations with each other, spoke similar languages, and had identical cultural customs and traditions. Central Asian states were known to the contemporary Greek and Roman historians. In the fifth century B.C., Herodotus, who is regarded as the father of history, based his writings on stories told to him by visitors to the region. In his major work, *The History,* Bactria is mentioned 13 times, Sogdiana twice, and Khorezm thrice, although his writings contain some inaccuracies, especially in regard to the borders.

The cities also were established around the eighth to sixth centuries B.C. With powerful fortifications aimed at protecting oases' inhabitants from nomads' attacks, agrarian settlements gradually became crafts centers with administrative and political authority. Usually, these settlements were established on crossroads of trade routes, around the rulers' settlements, and in centers of irrigation. Ancient Central Asian geographic and ethnic names, social and economic information, facts of political history, philosophy, and religion are mentioned in the Avesta, the sacred Zoroastrian text written presumably in the seventh century B.C. The Avesta is the oldest written source that describes the first statehoods in Central Asia.[4]

PERSIAN RULE

Cyrus II, who became Persian king in 559 B.C., included the territories of Central Asia (Eastern Iran, Khorezm, Bactria, Sogdiana, and Margiana) in the Akhaemenid Empire and, according to Herodotus, placed them under his command in 545–539 B.C. Cyrus brought several thousand people to erect fortresses along the western bank of the Syr Darya and to guard his newly acquired territory from the nomadic tribes. One of the newly built fortresses was Samarkand, probably the most important and historic Central Asian city, established in 545 B.C. During the reign of the Persian Empire, Samarkand was the seat of the governor, who ruled Central Asia on behalf of the king. According to archeological excavations, the area within the Samarkand city wall was about one and a third square miles.[5]

After Cyrus was killed in a battle on the shores of the Syr Darya in 529 B.C., his son Bardiya was left to rule the eastern part of the Persian Empire. During the rule of Persian King Darius I (522–486 B.C.), centralized government was introduced in the empire. All territories conquered by the Akhaemenids were divided into satrapies and ruled by satraps, governors appointed by Persian kings, usually from among relatives or trusted officers. The satraps were responsible for maintaining order, collecting taxes, administering justice, and supervising the territory. An assigned military garrison prevented rebellions and recruited locals for the emperor's army. There were three satrapies in Central Asia: Bactria, Khorezmia, and Sogdiana. Each Central Asian satrapy paid between 250 and 300 silver talants in tribute to the imperial treasury every year.[6] The Akhaemenids ruled Central Asia for more than 200 years.

Control of local areas was in the hands of the satrap and his officers, who collected taxes paid in grain, wine, and livestock. The rivers were the king's property; when water was needed for irrigation, a state officer supervised the opening of locks and regulated the amount of water taken by each tribe or settlement. For the opening of the locks, a large sum was paid to the officer, who was supposed to transfer this money into state coffers. This system of government was beneficial to the Sogdians because it protected them from the foreign aggression involved in commerce associated with the outposts, some of which were located along the ancient caravan routes. Farming had benefited from the construction of irrigation canals, and education was enhanced by the satrap's need for record keeping. The territories were gradually losing their importance, and there is no historic evidence that the kings, except Darius, visited the area, which was considered a source of taxes and military recruitment. Information on Central Asian people and territories of this period is preserved in Persian cuneiform writings.

Socioeconomic development during the Akhaemenid period resulted in the introduction of currency. It appears that money did not originate in Central Asia because of the mostly undeveloped trade and exchange relations. Coins arrived to the region as a form of treasury; later, some local money was coined as an imitation of foreign coins and was used for original monetary exchange in neighboring territories that had monetary systems. Own money was issued in Sogdiana much later. However, it is unclear if Greek coins could be considered foreign to Central Asia since these provinces were included in the Hellenistic states. Of all the provinces, the most highly developed from an economic perspective was the province of Margiana. Bronze and silver coins circulated there before the third century B.C. The high level of Margiana cultural development is confirmed by excavated pottery pieces attributed to the fourth century B.C. These conical and cylindrical dishes with a flat bottom were made by a pottery wheel and were fired at high temperatures. The fact that the pottery was of such high quality shows connections with other highly civilized societies.[7] In Parthia, another province on the territory of present-day Turkmenistan, copper coins of its own were not found. This indicates that Parthia was less advanced than Margiana in the matter of trading and economic development. The valley of Zerafshan was an area of intensive trade; several domains issued their own coins.

THE GREEKS IN CENTRAL ASIA

In 338 B.C., Macedonian Tsar Phillip II started a war against the Akhaemenids. He did not finish this war because of his death, and his 20-year-old son Alexander succeeded him on the throne. In the next three years, Macedonian troops defeated the Akhaemenids in several battles. Alexander the Great in 334 B.C. advanced into Central Asia (which had been known to the ancient Greeks for a long time) in a follow-up operation against the last Akhaemenid monarch Darius III. Darius III fled to Bactria, where he was killed in a plot initiated by Satrap Bess, who declared himself a tsar and took the name of Artaxerx. In the spring of 329 B.C., Alexander the Great of Macedonia reached the shores of the Amu Darya and started his Central Asian conquest, hoping to put an end to Akhaemenid power by crushing the remaining source of its strength in Central Asia. Despite an eight-mile wall, Alexander took Samarkand, the main Persian city in Central Asia, without resistance. As soon as the Greeks moved east, Sogdian rebels inspired guerilla warfare so effective that Alexander was forced to use the most brutal fighting methods known as the scorched earth policy.

The entire region of Central Asia resisted Alexander's march at every stage. The Akhaemenids had built a strong empire, and much of Central Asia shared their cultural heritage for two centuries. It was in defense of this heritage that local people rallied against the invaders. Spitamen, a native military commander, led popular resistance. He was successful at early stages of the revolt and defeated Alexander's troops. Alexander was forced to arrive in Central Asia and personally lead efforts to pacify local people. Because of the strength and courage of the resistance, Alexander was forced to retreat to Bactria while Sogdiana celebrated its victory.

After consolidating his position in Bactria, receiving reinforcements from his home country and from the satraps he had appointed in western provinces, and building fortified garrisons at varied points, in the winter of 328 B.C., Alexander attacked western Sogdiana with two battalions of the phalanx, two squadrons of his personal bodyguards, and some local support. The entire force included approximately 30,000 men. Most of the fortresses were taken after water supplies were cut off and people surrendered because of the lack of drinking water—including Spitamen, who went into hiding in the Zerafshan oasis. Later that year, Alexander advanced to Transoxiana.

Despite numerous losses among the Sogdians, they did not stop their resistance. In 328 B.C., Alexander met a new wave of insurrection and sent an additional 20,000 troops to fight the resistance. About 120,000 Sogdians were killed during the first year of Alexander's campaign. In response to Alexander's new attacks, Spitamen formed an army of 3,000 men and moved toward Samarkand. Both sides suffered heavy losses, and, after changing hands several times, Samarkand was completely destroyed. Spitamen was defeated by his enemy and retreated into the desert, where leaders of nomadic tribes caught and murdered him. His head was cut off and sent to Alexander. Even without Spitamen, the resistance of the Bactrians and Sogdians did not slow down, and Alexander of Macedonia changed his tactics. He began to build better relations with local elites, agreed to some demands of the local population, and changed his position toward Zoroastrianism.[8]

Initially, the invasion of Alexander the Great destroyed the prosperity of Sogdiana, where farms and cities were plundered. Later, however, Greek rule furthered unprecedented urban growth in Central Asia, which, according to Strabo, was famous as "the land of a thousand cities." The cities were necessary instruments for colonization, fulfilling many different roles. They served as military, administrative, communication, and economic centers of the varied regional units as well as trading posts along the international and local trading roads. Some towns were newly built, while others were built around preexisting fortified sites or on sites of former towns. Some towns were surrounded by defense walls 20 feet thick with rectangular towers.

At the end of Alexander's rule, Central Asia was a home for people who professed numerous beliefs and followed cults of different origins. Zoroastrianism was popular among the Iranian-speaking population, and the Zoroastrian calendar was adopted in Parthia, Bactria, and Khorezm. Many Greek settlers living in Bactria formed religious communities, worshipping their own gods and practicing their own cults. The first Buddhist missionaries appeared in Bactria in the third century B.C. Indian merchants and craftspeople who migrated to the cities of Bactria spread Buddhism and Brahmanism. Local cults were important for other native populations.

It appears that the administration of Alexander the Great was more concerned with Bactria than Sogdiana. During Alexander's invasion, many fled the ruined cities of Sogdiana and settled to the east in the Fergana Valley between Lake Balkhash and Lake Issyk-Kul, near present-day Almaty in Kazakhstan. Others went west to Khorezm near the Aral Sea and to the area of present-day Ashgabat. Alexander's empire did not exist long after his death and ceased to exist because of internal fighting. The empire of Alexander the Great was also the destination for large groups of cattle-breeding nomadic tribes. During their relocations, the ancient states of Kangha, Davan', and Kushan were established. The state of Davan', established in the fourth century B.C., was the first state that formed in the western part of the Fergana Valley. In the second century B.C., Davan' fell to Chinese attacks, resulting in a loss of 3,000 horses.

One of the newly established states on the ruins of Alexander's empire was the Selevkid kingdom. Selevk was one of the commanders in the Macedonian army who received lands in the Syr Darya basin and married Spitamen's daughter Apama. His state existed until 64 A.D., when it was conquered by Rome; however, with the help of military personnel located in Greek settlements, the Selevkids ruled in Central Asia between 312 B.C. and 250 A.D. In the fourth and third centuries B.C., Bactria and Sogdiana were included in the state ruled by Selevk. Although these lands were far from the center of the empire, these territories were of great military, strategic, and economic significance. In 293 B.C., Selevk appointed his son Antiokhus I (280–261 B.C.) to rule the lands in the east of his kingdom.

In the early third century B.C., nomadic tribes attacked Central Asia and destroyed its cities. Selevkids restored the cities and surrounded the Margiana oasis with a 150-mile wall. The rule of Selevk I and Antiokhus I was characterized by important political and economic events: the state expanded westward, and crafts and trade were developing in the new cities and settlements along the major trade routes. Gold and silver coins were minted at this time in the Bactrian part of the empire. Later, Samarkand began producing silver coins with the bust of the king on one side and an image of an archer on the reverse. Originally, these coins bore legends in both Sogdian and Greek, but the Greek was eventually replaced by legends in local language.

In the middle of the third century B.C., two independent states, Bactria and Parthia, were established in the Central Asian part of the disintegrating Selevkid Empire. In 247 B.C., Parthian tribes under the rule of Arshak separated from the Selevkids and created the Parthian state on the territory of modern-day Turkmenistan. The Parthian state existed for 550 years and influenced political developments in Central Asia and the Middle East. It appears that different forms of land property existed in the Parthian state, and slave labor was used in agriculture.

The founder and first ruler of the Bactrian state on the territory of modern Uzbekistan and Tajikistan was Diodotus I, who pronounced himself king in 255 B.C. Before, he was a satrap of Bactria in the Selevkid Empire and rebelled against king Antiokhus II. From time to time, the northwestern part of India was included in the Bactrian state, whose capital city was Bactra, present-day Balkh in Afghanistan. Former Selevkid satrap Euthydemus overthrew Diodotus II around 230 B.C. and united the Bactrian and Sogdian states into one large and powerful state union, which existed until the middle of the second century B.C.

Rich nomads who lived along the Syr Darya were ruling the Kangha state, which included Khorezm as one of the subordinate provinces. Kangha reached its peak between the late second century B.C. and early first century A.D. At this time, the nomads began to coin their own money and build fortresses. Since the end of the third century B.C., the region maintained contacts with China. The trade system in Sogdiana was established in the second century B.C. under Chinese influence. In an attempt to find support in its fight against nomadic tribes, China developed commerce parallel to diplomatic activities. The people of Central Asia accepted payments for their services in silk because representatives of the Chinese court used silk as a form of payment for goods. At that time, the demand and market for Chinese goods were created in Central Asia.

SILK ROAD

The second half of the second century B.C. was the period when the Great Silk Road, an intriguing phenomenon in human history, started to function. German geographer Ferdinand von Richthofen coined the phrase *Silk Road* in the nineteenth century. The Sogdians in the second century B.C. defended China from attacks by nomadic tribes, and the Chinese used silk as a form of payment for this service. The road subsequently became an active trade artery. A constant struggle existed between the Chinese and the Central Asians and between the Parthians and the Romans for control over the Silk Route and international trade domination. As early as the first century B.C., Han China took control over the eastern section and launched a military campaign against Fergana. From that time onward, China had direct trade relations with Bactria. From the year 115 B.C. onward, more than ten expeditions a year were sent from Fergana to the west. Caravans made their way unimpeded to Bactria, India, and Sogdiana, reached Parthia, and penetrated even further west.

Because of the easy exchange of local goods for Chinese silk all over Central Asia and because Chinese soldiers and officials, who, in the first century A.D. controlled the basin of the Tarim River, were paid by silk (which was easier to transport than metallic coins) a silk market was formed. Trade along the Silk Road was conducted through the nonmonetary exchange of goods. Silk was exchanged for precious metals, herbs, and spices. There was never a single, static Silk Road, but rather an evolving network of routes across the continent. Central Asia hosted the key stretch of this long haul. The two main routes came from the Fergana Valley to Samarkand or alternatively through the mountains to Tashkent. Routes westward converged at Bokhara and then split west to Persia and the Mediterranean, south to Kabul and India, or north to the Volga River. The choice of routes depended on the time of year, snowfall, conditions of passes, political considerations, and the regional differences in tax rates and piracy. Routes were constantly changing, as traders were joined by diplomats, invaders, refugees, pilgrims, and proselytizers. Traversing the Silk Road had never been easy. Thieves and slave traders en route added to the physical dangers of crossing the great deserts and mountains. Merchants would gather safely in numbers, often traveling at night to avoid heat in caravans of up to 1,000 camels. The load was also transported on horses, mules, and donkeys. Remote caravansaries dotted the route at about 15-mile intervals, the average daily distance traveled, and offered living quarters under the stars, stables for animals, and secure storage for valuable cargo. Larger city caravansaries were to become luxuriant points of transit, where goods changed hands; fresh animals were procured; and guides, mercenaries, and resident craftsmen were hired.

The Silk Road was the foundation for cultural and trade exchanges. Silk comprised only a fraction of the goods carried on the Silk Road. Gold, textiles, food, and colored glass were all carried into China along with alluring exotica—golden peaches from Samarkand, blood-sweating heavenly horses from Fergana, dwarf jugglers from Persia, and the prized magical "camel bird" ostrich. From the east came ceramics, cinnamon, bronze, paper, printing, and gunpowder. The Silk Road served not only as a trade route but as an ancient information highway. It enabled people of different cultures to meet and exchange ideas and then to carry these new art forms and religious doctrines back home. For instance, Manichaeism and Nestorian Christianity

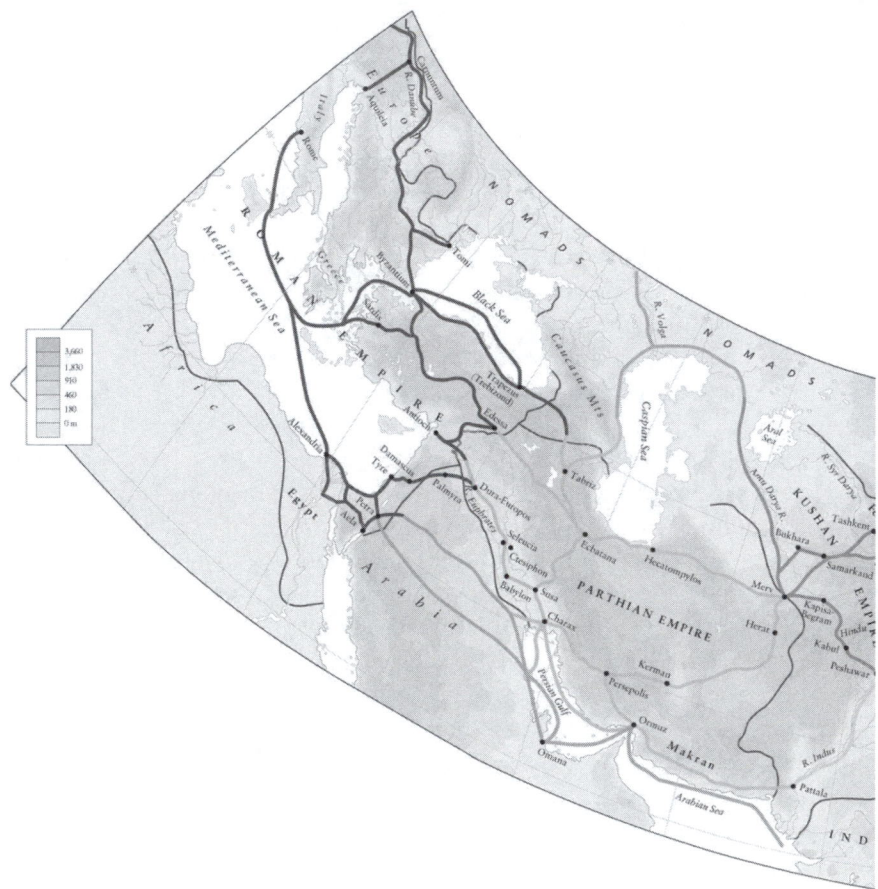

The Silk Road, 112 B.C. to 100 A.D.

developed along the Silk Road. After a network of Sogdian trade communities was destroyed by the Arabs, the trade routes disintegrated.[9]

KUSHAN EMPIRE

Yuchjey tribes penetrated the Bactrian state from the east in 140–120 B.C. They destroyed Greek urban civilization in Fergana and settled in the northern part of the Greco-Bactrian territory along the Amu Darya (modern-day Kazakhstan and Uzbekistan).

The Yuchjey expanded southward into Bactria around 125 B.C., forcing Bactrian King Heliocles to leave the country and move his capital to the Kabul area, from where he ruled his Indian possessions. Because of Yuchjey's attacks, Davan' and Sogd were destroyed, and the Bactrian state collapsed in

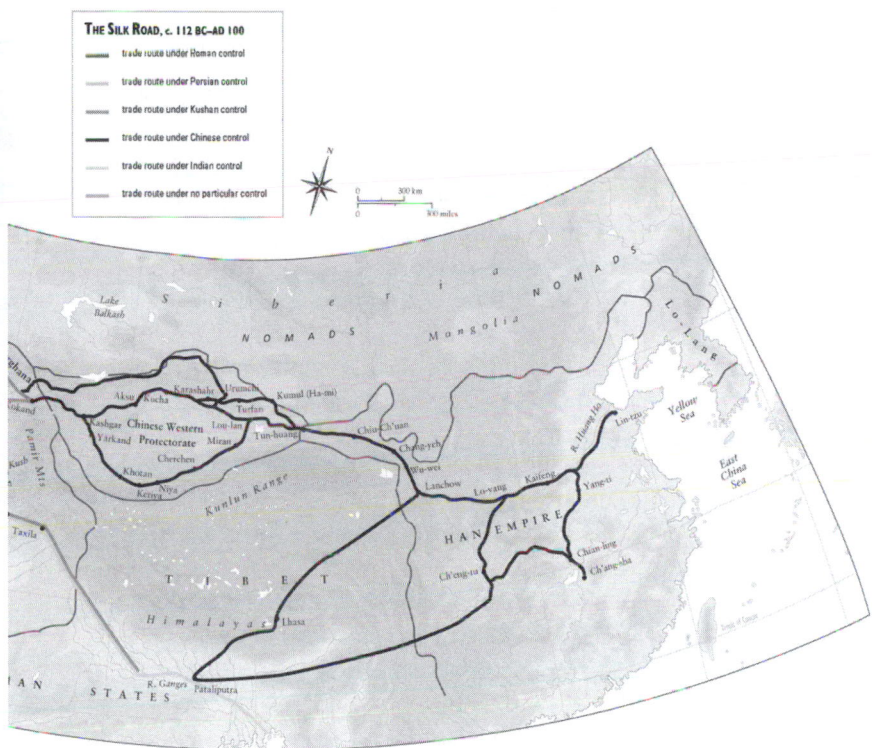

120 B.C. Yuchjey tribes became strong and powerful in the first century B.C. under ruler Kadfiz, who expanded the territory of the state to include a large part of Afghanistan and India. He declared himself the ruler of a newly formed state named the Kushan Empire, which included northern Bactria and regions along the Amu Darya. Other former Bactrian provinces constituted separate domains with different social structures and were bound to the Kushan state by a vassal relationship. Their independence is confirmed by the variety of coins minted before the appearance of the specific Kushan coinage in the first century A.D. One of the semi-independent provinces was Khorezm, located near the Aral Sea in an ancient farming area. The nomadic people came to Khorezm (which means lowland) from northern Iran and nearby mountains in the second millennium B.C. to farm in the regularly flooded fields. Later, Khorezm was included in one of the satrapies of the Akhaemenid Empire. The

contacts between the Khorezmians and Sogdians brought the people together many times and explain the commonality of traditions. Even after Khorezm became an independent state in 305 A.D. and had its own king, trade, political, and military relations between Khorezm and Samarkand continued.

When Bactria became a part of the Kushan Empire, the patterns of social organization changed considerably. The commune consisted of the aristocracy, merchants, free peasants, and craftspeople. Slaves and a dependent population existed in considerable numbers, but slavery was not the only and probably not the predominant form of labor. Little use was made of slaves in agriculture and handicraft work, because their labor was not profitable. The state had an effective social organization with ranks similar to those in the European feudal societies. The king ruled the Kushan Empire, and masters of the cities and local leaders of landed estates were his vassals. Small armies and personal guards of the king and local leaders maintained civil order.

Developments in agriculture and handicrafts and the consolidation of the supremacy of the Kushan Empire resulted in strengthening trade relations between different regions of Central Asia. Food and consumer goods such as cereals, fruits, textiles, pottery, and timber were traded regularly and extensively within the country. The main caravan route along the Syr Darya linked the northern regions of Fergana with regions near the Aral Sea. Many trading caravans stopped in Samarkand as it became a major trading center. Cereals, fruits, handicrafts, and weapons were transported to the nomads of the north in exchange for furs and skins, meat and milk products, livestock, and raw materials for weaving. Locally produced glass characterized by its colors, glossiness, and transparency was exchanged for Chinese silk, while substantial overland trade was conducted with India. Local merchants traveled by boat down the Amu Darya, over the Caspian Sea, and across Transcaucasia to the Black Sea. They also made their way to southern Siberia.

The Kushan Empire reached its peak between 105 and 250 A.D. During this period, large numbers of nomadic livestock breeders switched to a settled way of life. They resided in buildings constructed of large bricks and clay. The towns and fortified settlements of the Kushan period were built according to a clear and systematic layout. These settlements were the administrative and political centers of the various regions and provinces and contained palaces, temples, workshops, and dwellings. Public buildings were frequently of monumental size; palaces were built on high platforms and surrounded by strong fortifications. The massive walls of large chambers and high ceilings were decorated with murals and sculptures.

Because of extensive developments of the irrigation networks, all the main provinces of Central Asia were brought under cultivation at the beginning of the Common Era. More than a hundred archeological monuments of the

Kushan period show the establishment of crop-growing oases. At this time, large-scale irrigation systems were built in Tashkent and Samarkand oases and in the Zerafshan Valley. Some of the canals extended over a distance of more than 70 miles. In Tajikistan, remains have survived of the Kushan irrigation system in the form of embankments 50 feet wide and up to 8 feet high, extending over seven miles. Groundwater and water from springs were used for irrigation in addition to the thaw water from mountain streams. Groundwater was collected for irrigation in underground reservoirs consisting of horizontal water-bearing galleries and vertical ventilation shafts. An example of the construction and irrigation development during the Kushan period was the Dargom canal dam built near the Vargsar settlement in the middle of the first century A.D. The settlement was of strategic importance because it was the main water supply in the center of the Samarkand oasis. The conquest of the Vargsar settlement would result in a discontinuation of the water supply for Samarkand. Inhabitants of Vargsar were required to maintain the dam as a labor duty in exchange for being exempted from land taxes. The rulers of the Kushan Empire did all they could to defend the dam and always kept large numbers of troops there. Methods of cultivation improved during the Kushan period also. Wooden plows with an iron plowshare (which are still used in Central Asia today) were introduced in the first century A.D. Similarly, water-driven machines, including mills for grinding grain into flour, were used as well.

The circumstances under which the Kushan Empire collapsed are unclear. Widespread drought in the fourth and fifth centuries A.D. resulted in mass migrations of people from Sogdiana to the area south of Lake Balkhash. The evacuation of the territory during the drought left the previously irrigated farmlands unoccupied and enabled the people who remained there to acquire large land holdings. The invading Hephtalites (whose identity is still debatable) used the recession and desertion of the cities. Some historians refer to them as Huns who spoke a Turkic language. In 457, the Hephtalites conquered Bactria, and, by 484, almost all of Central Asia was controlled by the Hephtalites who defeated local states. The Hephtalites established a huge state in the Central Asian territories of eastern Turkistan, northern India, and eastern Iran. During Hephtalite rule, the economy and culture boomed and a stable government and strong military force were created, which prevented foreign aggressions and threatened Iran. Some Hephtalites were nomadic cattle breeders, others were involved in agriculture and gardening and produced rice, cereal, and cotton. During this period, land was primarily in the hands of the tribal elite and clergy. The ordinary population was not happy with the ongoing changes, and the first mass uprising called Mazdakism (after Mazdak, the revolt's leader and ideologist) occurred at the end of the fifth century.

TURKIC KHANATE

In 551, Bumyn from the Ashina tribe created a new state, the Turkic khanate. Originally, the word *Turk* did not have any ethnic meaning and meant hard or strong, but the word was used to identify members of the military aristocracy of this Mongoloid tribe of Ashina. Later, the larger union of tribes was called the Turks. Chinese dynastic chronicles provide original information about the Turkic tribes. Initially, the state of the Turks was located on the territory of northern Mongolia and southeastern Siberia; however, after several victories over the Chinese, this nomadic empire became hegemonic in Central Asia and extended its frontiers to the Aral Sea. In the middle of the sixth century A.D., several nomadic tribes who spoke the Turkic language combined into a unity under the leadership of their ruler named Istemi and moved into Central Asia. In 563 to 567, Istemi forces defeated the Hephtalites, who, at that time, suffered from Iran's growing independence. Iranians refused to pay taxes to Hephtalites and provided diplomatic and military support to the Turks, who turned the Hephtalite Empire into a vassal state. The decisive battle occurred near the city of Bokhara. All lands south of the Amu Darya went to Iran, and all the territory between the Caspian Sea and the western shore of the Amu Darya became the possession of the Turks. The Turks migrated into Central Asia in large numbers and demanded a regular tribute from local farmers. Because of the breakdown of the central government, some local leaders in the western part of Sogdiana gained independence. Persians, using the defeat of the Hephtalites, also moved their troops to Central Asia. However, instead of fighting, the Turks arranged a marriage between the Persian king and Istemi's daughter, which was followed by the establishment of a union between the Iranians and Turks.

The khanate was a hereditary empire, where the throne was given to the surviving adult relative of the emperor. All of the territory of the khanate was divided into districts run by the beks, who were members of the emperor's tribe appointed to perform governorship functions. The Turks did not interfere in Sogdiana's internal affairs and preserved its local government, its political, religious, social, and economic systems, and provided military and diplomatic coverage for them. Because of internal fighting, the empire was divided into eastern and western khanates in 603 A.D. In 618, the western Turks became stronger when Ton Yabg became their leader; he undertook an administrative reform, murdered all local dynasties, and installed Turks instead. Yabg intended to create a centralized state, but his idea was not implemented entirely, and after his death the khanate became unstable. Fights between aristocracies undermined the state and impacted all areas of life. Eventually, the state collapsed in 774. The Turkic invasion divided the people of Central Asia into two groups: one that spoke Turkish and one that spoke the Iranian language.

Today, the Turkish-speaking people of Central Asia are called Uzbeks, and the Iranian-speaking people are called Tajiks.

The Turkic invasion influenced the economic and cultural development of the region. Under the Turks, Sogdiana reached the peak of its development. Farmers cultivated wheat, rice, barley, and various fruits and vegetables. They grew mulberry trees for raising silk worms and produced their own silk. Local markets were held in the towns weekly. Cities, which hosted traders from many nations, were major commercial centers. Mining was of importance for the local economy, and the Sogdians mined gold, copper, iron, silver, lead, salt, and ore. Samarkand was the capital of the Turkic nation. Kings who resided in Samarkand strengthened the city and beautified it with palaces, temples, and other new buildings. Construction was improved with the replacement of square blocks by rectangular bricks. The prosperity was evident in all areas of life. A Chinese traveler wrote in the early seventh century that "all inhabitants of Samarkand [were] skilled merchants; when a boy [became five years old, he was] taught grammar; when he [began] to read, he [was] required to study commercial affairs." The Chinese traveler was also struck by the availability of water and called Sogdiana the most fertile country in the world, with the whole area looking like a garden.[10]

Cultural influences of Central Asian societies on neighboring countries were great. For example, the calendar accepted by the Sogdians demonstrates the high level of their culture. Each month consisted of 30 days, and 5 extra days were added at the end of the year to make 365 days a year. It is not known what they did for the leap year, but different names of months indicate that they may have conducted astronomical observations and defined the length of the year. The Sogdian alphabet was adopted by the Turks and Uighurs in China and was later passed on to the Mongolians. Buddhists and Manicheans in Turkistan also used the Sogdian language and alphabet for their writings. The first known Central Asian legal documents also were written during the time of the Turkic khanate. Events such as marriages and the buying or selling of property were recorded in the Sogdian language. An excavated marriage contract concluded in Sogdiana in the middle of seventh century contains eight provisions of local civil law describing mutual obligations of the parties and family customs, including polygamy, which was practiced by rich Sogdians.[11]

The region was still flourishing when the Arabs came to Central Asia one hundred years later.

NOTES

1. Ahmad Dani, *History of Civilizations of Central Asia* (Paris: UNESCO Publishing, 1992, v. 1), 124.

2. Raphael Pumpelly, *Explorations in Turkestan, Expedition of 1904: Prehistoric Civilizations of Anau* (Washington, DC: Carnegie Institution of Washington, 1908), 346.

3. The Geography of Strabo. Literally translated, with notes. The first six books by H. C. Hamilton, the remainder by W. Falconer (London and New York: G. Bell & Sons, 1903–1906), v. 2, 188; v. 3, 73, 89.

4. In 1771, the Avesta was translated into French and published for the first time by French scholar Anquetil-Duperron. Originally, the Avesta consisted of 21 books; however, only 4 survived and are known to historians today. The existing books include prayers, dedications to Gods, and collections of religious and legal rules. In 2001, the world celebrated the 2,700-year anniversary of the Avesta. The city of Khorezm in Uzbekistan was the site of all major events organized by UNESCO.

5. Because Samarkand was totally destroyed by Alexander the Great, no early written records were found there. The first known Samarkand writings are dated around the first century B.C.

6. One talant amounted to 70 pounds of silver.

7. Rene Grousset, *The Civilizations of the East* (London: H. Hamilton, 1934), 248.

8. See William Tarn, *The Greeks in Bactria and India* (Chicago: Ares, 1997), 286.

9. A revival of the Silk Road with regional development and a growing transportation network appears to be imminent. From time to time, the idea of recreating the Silk Road as a bridge between West and East is discussed by politicians and scholars. In 1987, UNESCO adopted a long-term program to show how the Silk Road facilitated trade and cultural exchanges among people regardless of wars and conflicts. In May 1993, the European Commission discussed the creation of a transportation corridor across Europe-Caucasus-Asia, which appears to be the first practical action toward restoration of the Silk Road. The Silk Road was the theme of an ethnographic and anthropological festival organized by the Smithsonian Institution in Washington, DC, in 2005.

10. Cited by Grousset (1934), 252.

11. David Law, *From Samaria to Samarkand: The Ten Lost Tribes of Israel* (New York and London: University Press of America, 1992), 63.

3

Early History: Islamization and the Birth of Central Asian Nations (Seventh through Fourteenth Centuries)

ARAB CONQUEST

The seventh century was the century of the Arab invasion in Central Asia. After the Arabs expanded to Syria and Palestine, they destroyed the Sasanid Empire in Iran. From there, their conquering armies moved to Central Asia and, in 651, attacked Merv. Armed with a new religious faith of Islam, the Arabs first raided Central Asia aiming to plunder and weaken prosperous Sogdiana in 673. During this attack, the Arabs took 30,000 prisoners and a large booty of valuable goods. Sogdiana was left almost helpless against the attacks of the advancing Arabs. Hopes that the Turks would defend Central Asia were not realistic, because the Turks were nomadic people who lacked military fortifications for fighting large invading armies.

Arabs' victories can be explained not only by their strength, but by the political and economic weakness of the countries they conquered. Because of the constant wars between the oases, Central Asia was not able to produce a forceful resistance to the Arabs. Kuteiba, who, in 704, was sent to the region to represent the caliph, helped one of the fighting rulers to defeat the enemy and then took the lands of those he had helped. The caliphate was successful because the Arabs could instigate fights between Turkic nomads and settlers in agricultural oases of Central Asia. Arabs' military superiority and their ability to use the resources of the conquered countries were of great importance.

Relations between the Arabs and the local people began with deception, when approximately fifty local lords from the Samarkand oasis were tricked into captivity by false promises of release when other prisoners would be delivered to Arabia. The Sogdians revolted and killed an Arab leader; the revenge, however, was taken soon. Unlike all previous invaders, the Muslims mercilessly killed all Sogdian resisters and, between 705 and 712, destroyed big cities and smaller oases, which were experiencing a period of great prosperity. The Arab invasion could enrich the Sogdian trade by expanding the trade routes, but the Arabic brutality against the traditions, culture, and religion of the local people and the transfer of the capital from Samarkand to Bokhara extinguished the promise of better economic relations.[1]

Initially, the Arab occupation of Central Asia was viewed by the caliphate exclusively as a resource for income; the entire population was levied with new taxes. The most draconic were the land and personal taxes imposed on those who did not convert to Islam. The Arabs plundered the locals, taking their houses for the occupying soldiers and Islamic clergy, and destroyed irrigation systems; prosperous lands turned to deserts under the Arab occupation. To attack cities, the Arabs used catapults and machines for breaking down the walls of the citadels. As a rule, upon entering the city, they drove all inhabitants against the opposite walls and demanded their submission to the army and their acceptance of the Muslim religion. Large numbers of people were killed, and cities were looted and destroyed. The peace treaty imposed on the Sogdians established an annual monetary tribute and an obligation to provide 300,000 healthy male slaves or soldiers for the Arab army. All localities were obligated to supply their own food and tools to build roads and city walls and repair irrigation canals. In 713, the Arabs outlawed the existing system of managing lands by village leaders and established tight control over farm land and subordinated local leaders to the Arab emir. The land became the property of the Arabs, and the farmers were relegated to the lowest class of tenants, having to pay rent as well as 10 percent of their harvest to the Arabs.

Later, the occupants understood the importance of religion in strengthening their power, and, in addition to military subjection, the Sogdians were forced to accept the Muslim way of life. The Arabs had a systematic program of destroying everything written or otherwise created by the Sogdians; cultural monuments were destroyed, and books were burned. Temples of Zoroastrians, Buddhists, and Christians were crushed, and mosques were built all over the acquired territory of Central Asia. All local people were required to come to the mosques and pray together with the Arabs. Many privileges were offered to those Sogdians who converted to Islam. For example, money was paid to those who attended mosques, and, initially, the converts were exempt from taxes and farm rent; however, because of an immediate substantial

decrease of tax collection (and thus the caliph's income), this system was deemed impractical.

The conversion of the Sogdian people to Islam was an integral part of the occupation policy. After imposing the Islamic faith over the Sogdians, attention was focused on the enforcement of religious obedience. Sogdian scholars were persecuted because the invaders believed that Sogdian writings were against their religion. The Arabs introduced their alphabet and declared Arabic the state language. According to the Muslim ban on portraying images of their gods, humans, or animals, Sogdian art was destroyed, including the murals in Sogdian palaces and temples. Only the earlier murals, which were already buried by this time, escaped the Arab mutilation. The Arab destruction was so thorough that it is now almost impossible to reconstruct the history of the Sogdians.[2] The heritage and culture of the Sogdian people that had been built for many centuries was lost completely. Tremendous looting of treasures accompanied by merciless mass murders of the local population eventually transformed the society into a product of Turkic culture and Muslim religion and resulted in Arabs achieving their main goal—converting people to the Islamic faith. The eighth century was one of gradual and steady coercive conversion of the local people to Islam.

ACCEPTANCE OF ISLAM

Within one century, Islam was firmly established in Central Asia, and it penetrated the customs and traditions of local people. This was not an easy process, though, because numerous local tribes and kingdoms were subject to a number of different and often incompatible beliefs, such as Buddhism, Zoroastrianism, nature worshipping, and Shamanism. Because Sunni Islam was more capable of accommodating and incorporating the pre-Islamic rituals and habits of the local, substantially nomadic population, this version of the religion attracted more adherents than the Shia version. Of all the different divisions inside Sunni Islam, the Central Asians adopted one of the most tolerant and flexible sects, Hanafi, which allowed them to develop Islamic thoughts creatively. The blend of Islam with Iranian culture, then dominant in the region, made Bokhara and Samarkand the birthplaces of the Islamic renaissance in the tenth and twelfth centuries. Later, the Turkic people, who now constitute the major component of the Central Asian demographic spectrum, accepted and developed this cultural tradition.

A specific feature of Central Asian Islam is that the most influential orders (fraternities or brotherhoods) of Sufism—a mystical movement that emphasizes the development of a personal spirituality and an internal comprehension of divinity—originated in this region. Sufi scholars and spiritual leaders played an important role in spreading Islam among the nomads of Central Asia.

Sufism's major features are the refusal of solemn and complicated rites of Orthodox Islam, the absence of clergy, belief in asceticism, internal contemplation, identification of nature with God, and nonparticipation in public social life.

In the ninth century, Central Asia became the center of khadis writing, a genre in Islamic religious writing of stories about Muhammad's life, his miracles, and his teachings. Most of the officially accepted khadis writers were well-known theologists who were born in Central Asia; the most famous were al-Bukhari and al-Termezi. Al-Bukhari studied, selected, compared and systematized, and discussed the authenticity of the khadises. His most important work was the collection of 725 khadises, many of which he knew by heart. Today, the Muslim world recognizes al-Bukhari's work as the second most important book after the Koran. Al-Termezi also collected khadises and provided interpretations of them. His book is considered one of the most authoritative sources in Islam.

The spread of Islam in Central Asia was not uniform and reflected the contrasts in the ethnic composition and life-style of the region's population. Islam first found strongholds among the urban population in places such as Bokhara, Samarkand, and Kokand. Simultaneously, numerous nomadic tribes migrating with their herds of livestock across the wide plains of Central Asia were more difficult to convert to Islam. What they eventually adopted as the Muslim religion was largely superficial, in part because many of these tribes were still undergoing the process of ethnic formation.

ANTI-ARAB RESISTANCE

During the seventh and eighth centuries, Arabic dynasties changed at the top of the caliphate. Political instability was accompanied with growing economic exploitation of the Central Asian people. Even when Sogdian leaders accepted the occupation, in many cities, people attempted to initiate uprisings, which were often supported by the Turks. However, the Sogdians were ill equipped to challenge the occupying army. Revolts in Samarkand and other parts of Sogdiana continued for several years after the Kuteiba's death in 715. The Turks supported this fight, and requests for help were sent to the Chinese with whom the Sogdians conducted trade for many years. Help did not come from China, and, in 721, Gurek, the master of Samarkand, again submitted to the Arabs and called for the Sogdians to follow him. However, most Sogdians considered Gurek to be a traitor, and the revolt continued under Devashtish, who declared himself to be the king of Samarkand and of Sogdiana. Devashtish held control over the city and some parts of Sogdiana for another two years and finally retreated to the mountains. After the defeat of Devashtish, the Arabs appointed Gurek again to be the king of Sogdiana under the occupational army.

Disagreements with the Arab rulers and revolts continued until 739. Gurek waged a general war and moved his troops to Persia. Even support of the Turkic khan did not help, and his army was defeated once again. After that defeat, the appointment of all local leaders and Samarkand rulers became an exclusive right of the regional governor in Balkh. The tax paid by Sogdian farmers increased from 10 percent to 20 percent, and local leaders received the right to stop the flow of irrigation water to farmers if the farmers refused to pay rents and taxes. Over time, the conservatism of Islamic rulers progressed and the new Abbasid dynasty, which was established in 748, imposed new religious restrictions, including the mandatory wearing of black clothes as a sign of observance of the Koran's teachings. In 750, a revolt against the Abbasids started in Bokhara, when the Abbasid army marched to Bokhara to restore its authority. The emir of Bokhara closed the city gates to deny entrance, and, in return, the Arabs burned down the city, killing most of the people.

Zoroastrians who remained in Sogdiana organized a broadly based force to oppose the Abbasids and to liberate Sogdiana from the Muslims. The group wore white clothes in contrast to the Abbasids' black clothes and became known as "the people in white clothing." They began with the assassination of the Persian governor when he visited Samarkand in 757 and, for almost 20 years, maintained an effective military force, staging many revolts and taking several cities. They showed strength in these battles before they were ultimately defeated in 780 and forced to accept Islam. Some followers of the people in white clothing continued their struggle until the twelfth century.

In April 776, under the leadership of Mukanna, a popular uprising started in the Zarafshan valley. The insurgents requested the elimination of economic inequality and Arabic oppression. Despite some military defeats from the Arabs, the insurgents achieved several victories and established control over Bokhara. The Sogdian aristocracy, which, at the beginning of the uprising, supported Mukanna, became afraid of the public revolt and turned to the caliph for protection. The caliphate's troops besieged Samarkand in 778, defeating Mukanna's followers, and took the fortress where Mukanna was hiding in 783. All of Mukanna's defenders were killed, and Mukanna himself, who did not want to give up, committed suicide. The constant fight with the locals weakened the caliphate, and, eventually, the caliphate rulers agreed to include the local nobility in the highest positions of the Central Asian government.

NEW DYNASTIES AND LOCAL AFFAIRS

Because of the vastness of the territory, the caliphate could not control the besieged people entirely. The central power was weakening, and there were chances of the territory breaking into several independent states. To strengthen their control over Central Asia, the Arabs raised land rents and taxes so that farmers were required to pay up to 40 percent of their earnings to local lords, who became tax and rent collectors for the Arabs in exchange for political independence. Fearing that the local nobility would demand full power, the Arabs killed prominent members of local clans from time to time and replaced them with representatives of other families regardless of how respectful and influential they were. Numerous short-term dynasties challenged each other between the ninth and twelfth centuries. One of the strongest local families that ruled in Central Asia was the Takhirid dynasty (821–873). Its founder, Takhir, befriended Caliph Mamun and, in return for his support of Mamun's internal fights, was appointed military commander of Baghdad (then the caliphate's capital city) and later governor of territories in modern-day Uzbekistan. A powerful and energetic person, Takhir ruled his province almost independently and was soon poisoned by the caliph's people. Despite Takhir's death, Takhirids continued to govern the province and became almost independent rulers having vassal relations with Baghdad. To strengthen the country and their rule, the Takhirids lowered taxes, built fortresses along the northern border to protect their lands from Turkic tribes, organized the construction of new canals, opened schools, and propagated Islam, which they saw as a pillar of their rule. It is generally recognized that the Takhirid rule began a period of a Central Asian revival after the Arab invasion and the forceful arabization of the local culture.

Defending the oases from nomadic attacks was always one of the main tasks of any power in Central Asia. For this purpose, special units of armed volunteers called *gazi* (fighters for the faith) were created. Large groups of *gazi* offered their services in border protection to local rulers; however, they often joined local uprisings against their employers. In 873, one such uprising led by the *gazi* brothers Yakub and Amir Leys overthrew the power of the Takhirids. According to some sources, Yakub was a copper craftsman, and the Arabic word for copper is *safar;* therefore, his dynasty was called the Safarids. Yakub and his brother recognized the power of the caliph and were appointed to govern the eastern provinces. Similar to previous rulers, they were almost independent from Baghdad. Representing the lower classes of society, the Safarids were not supported by the aristocracy and rich landowners. This lack of support led to their losing fights against the new Samanid dynasty (875–999).

Saman, the founder of the Samanid dynasty, was a native of Balkh. After being recognized by religious leaders, Saman converted to Islam. By appointing his grandchildren to rule major cities after Saman's death, Central Asia (except for Bokhara and Khorezm) was under the Samanids' control. Being formally subordinate to the caliph, Samanids were relatively free to rule Central Asia, and, at the end of their rule, Central Asia was freed from the Arab yoke. The local people were not strict followers of Islam, and the Samanids did not insist on the prevalence of a religious life over economic interests.

They diminished the influence of nomadic Turks, and once again made Samarkand the regional capital and international commercial center, which resulted in further government centralization and territorial expansion. Bokhara asked to be included in the Samanid Empire, and, after a series of attacks on the Turks, the frontier was moved far north. Lands with rich silver mines near present-day Jambul city in Kazakhstan became part of the Samanid Empire, the first centralized bureaucratic local and independent monarchy in Central Asia. The head of state was the emir, who had absolute power. The central government consisted of 10 departments (devans) responsible for overseeing particular areas—for example, mail, emir's guards, trade. This system was repeated on lower levels; district and city chiefs were appointed by the emir. The Samanids decreased rents and taxes levied on the peasants and helped to increase the production of agricultural goods and handcrafts. Under their rule, former trade along the Great Silk Road and the Great Spice Road resumed, and improvements to irrigation systems helped to increase agricultural production. New canals and dams were constructed, and the main canal, which brought water to Samarkand, was lined with lead. A lead aqueduct built during this period provided drinking water to Samarkand until the Mongol invasion in 1220.

The development of cities was one of the most significant Samanid achievements. Under their rule, Samarkand overcame the chaos that had followed the Arab invasion and that had resulted in the deportation of Buddhists and Zoroastrians, who constituted the majority of the city population. In the tenth and eleventh centuries, this oasis in the valley of the Zarafshan River became known as the Mirror of the World, the Garden of Soul, the Jewel of Islam, the Pearl of the East, or the Center of the Universe. Samarkand grew in the tripartite formation typical of Persian towns: a citadel with prisons; the shakhristan—a proper town containing government offices and a great Friday mosque protected by a moat with four main gates; and a rabid—suburbs for bazaars and warehouses. The streets were paved with stones, and benefactors supplied free iced water at some 2,000 locations. The surviving Zoroastrians were exempt from the tax to maintain the ingenious irrigation system of lead-covered pipes that fed every house and garden. The transition of power in the twelfth and thirteenth centuries resulted in the downfall of the city and a decline in the population from 400,000 to 100,000 after the Mongol invasion.

While Samarkand developed economically, Bokhara grew intellectually. With less religious interference, these oases prospered because foreigners of various nationalities came to these cosmopolitan cities to conduct business. Bokhara became the religious center of Central Asia and was called the Dome of Islam. Theological scholars from all over the caliphate met there and taught in Bokhara's religious schools. With an annual tribute, Bokhara kept Arab invaders at bay when Samarkand fell. In the late ninth century, when local Iranian governors broke with the caliphate, the city whose commercial and cultural vitality attracted the finest intellectuals of the time survived its golden age. Physician Ibn-Sina, philosopher Biruni, historian Narshaki, and poet Rudaki helped Bokhara become the center of a Persian renaissance and of Islamic science. Irrigation and urbanization increased the city population to 300,000, larger than it was in the Soviet era. In the ninth century, the city fell to nomadic Turkmen, and the period of decline began. Describing Bokhara, Richard Frye suggests that the cultural flowering that created new Persian literature was, in fact, also a successful attempt to transform Islam, to release it from its Arab background and make it a richer, more adaptable and universal culture.[3]

ARRIVAL OF TURKIC TRIBES

After the Turkic khanates disintegrated in the eighth and ninth centuries, they gave way to a number of short-term states, which were fighting and replacing each other during the tenth through twelfth centuries. These new state formations were associated with the westward movement of Turkic tribes from southern Siberia and eastern Turkistan to settlements on the eastern shores of the Caspian Sea and in the mountains of present-day Kyrgyzstan. The principle language was now Turkic, and Turks settled on farms and in cities. The Turkic states began as nomad tribes and principalities and changed into sedentary kingdoms and empires. The largest, though amorphous, tribal confederation was Oghuz, which came from northeast Mongolia and was the basis for building the Turkmen ethnos several centuries later. The Turkmens were not politically united and had no supreme leader until the eleventh century. The Kyrgyz, about whom reports first appear in Chinese chronicles of the Han period in the first centuries B.C. and A.D., were dwelling in the southern Siberian steppes and slowly moved to the area of their present location, where they were seen in the twelfth century. The twelfth-century report refers to a small isolated party and not the main body of the Kyrgyz majority, who stayed in Siberia until the seventeenth century, when pressure from the Russian Cossacks drove them south.

In the tenth century, various Turkish tribes from the Altai mountains formed a government known as Qarakhanids in eastern Turkistan. Several mountainous Turkic tribes united into a confederation that conducted incursions in Transoxiana, mostly to Fergana and Sogdiana. In 992, the Qarakhanids took Samarkand and Bokhara, bringing the whole territory of Central Asia under the control of Turkish-speaking people and making Samarkand their capital. Because Islam was accepted by the Qarakhanid Turks due to trade relations, the Samanids could not initiate a religious war against the Qarakhanids. In 999, the Turks ultimately defeated the Samanid Empire and established their rule in Central Asia for almost 100 years, their territory expanding from China to the Amy Darya. The Khans continued to keep their residence in Kashgar (in northeastern China). While in power, the Qarakhanids destroyed the previous government system and declared all lands to be the khan's property. The state was divided into many small units with unstable borders. Rulers of these small units were almost independent and were often allowed to coin their own money. In the eleventh century, the unity of the Qarakhanid dynasty was fractured by constant internal warfare, and the dynasty was forced to accept Seljuk's suzerainty.

The Seljuk Empire was named after Seljuk ibn Dudak, a tribal leader from the Oghuz who obtained prominence and founded a powerful state. Through intrigues, diplomacy, and military power, he and his descendants acquired vast lands in Central Asia and the Middle East. The Seljuks established control over the major cultural centers—Khorezm, Merv, Herat, Balkh, and other cities on the Silk Road. The Seljuk Turks allied with the Samanid rulers against the Qarakhanids around the year 1000. In 1044, the Seljuks took Khorezm and, in 1084, defeated Samarkand. They ruled until 1141, when they were defeated by another Turkic tribe, the Karakitai. With a decline in Seljuk power, in 1140, the Qarakhanids fell under the domination of the rival Turkic Karakitai confederation centered in northern China. In the early twelfth century, the independence of the dynasty was briefly reestablished when Chinese and Mongolian tribes were pushed out of the area by the Khorezm sultan, who remained independent mostly due to Khorezm's remote location. However, in 1211, the Qarakhanids were defeated by the sultan of Khorezm, and the dynasty was extinguished.

In the early twelfth century, Khorezm sultans, using an appropriate moment during the fight between the Seljuk Turks and Qarakhanids, seceded and declared their independence from the Turks. Originally, Khorezm was part of the Samanid Empire and was ruled by sultans from Urgench, their capital city. The rule of Sultan Tekesh (1172–1200) made Khorezm the most zpowerful regional state. In 1212, Samarkand was included in the state of Khorezm with more than 400 other cities, which paid tribute to the sultan of Khorezm and supported his army of 300,000. The sultan of Khorezm defended the area more than he exploited it; he undertook the rebuilding of the Samarkand city wall and continued his restoration program by building a citadel, government buildings, and ceramic water pipes through a tunnel in the citadel. As a new state, Khorezm did not have any allies among the Muslim rulers. As a newly converted Muslim, the sultan was not trusted by the Arabs and Persians, and relations between the sultan of Khorezm and the Arab caliph in Baghdad were so bad that, according to local legends, it was the caliph who supposedly petitioned Genghis Khan to attack Khorezm by sending Genghis Khan a secret message tattooed on a man's head who passed undetected through the territory of Khorezm. The power in the sultanate was divided between the sultan and his mother, who played a large part in the decision making. The Persians and Tajik were the sultan's subjects; soldiers stationed in villages were Turkic and had no interest in protecting the lands and those whom they despised.

JEWISH PRESENCE

Even though Islam was the official religion, other religions appeared in Central Asia, causing Samarkand and Bokhara to be divided into sections designated for various religious groups. Much of this diverse population consisted of Jews who traditionally were treated with respect as long as they remained loyal to the ruler—though they were not treated equally to followers of the predominant Muslim faith.

Until a mass emigration of Jews to Israel and the United States in the mid-1990s that almost terminated Jewish life in the region, the Jewish community in Central Asia had a long and rich history. The first Jewish communities were established before the Arab invasion and Islamization of this territory. The first Jewish settlements were established around the fifth century B.C. and did not lose their identity even during the last century.[4]

The Jewish arrival in Central Asia occurred between the fifth and sixth centuries B.C., when the Akhaemenid dynasty ruled all the lands from Egypt to China. Tolerant in religious matters, the Akhaemenids were well disposed toward the Jews. Being within the borders of a huge state and having no travel restrictions, some Jews penetrated Central Asia as far as Khorezm. Babylonian sources report that local Jews traveled to Merv to visit relatives in the fourth century B.C. Some researchers suggest that the first Jews appeared in Central Asia in the middle of the sixth century B.C. According to them, the Jews who were held captive by the Assyrians were liberated and taken to Central Asia by Cyrus the Great, who, in 535 B.C., built them a city in a secluded place between two mountain ranges, which the Jews called Samarkand. Because *kand* means city, their new home was named after their former capital, Samaria, or Samarkand.[5] Putting together fragmented archeological evidence, one can surmise that the main Jewish community in Central Asia during this period was in the city of Merv. The first archeological evidence of the Jewish presence along the Silk Road are attributed to the second and third centuries A.D. Hebrew scripts found in this region are dated between the fifth and sixth centuries A.D. Substantial Jewish migration to Central Asia from Iran occurred in the late fifth and early seventh centuries during the periods of the most severe Jewish persecution, and some historians argue that, at the end of the fifth century A.D., a small independent Jewish kingdom existed for seven years. From Merv, Jews expanded their presence to Bactria, Sogdiana, and Khorezm.

There is not much information about Jews in Samarkand and Bokhara in the early medieval period; however, there is a legend about the lead waterway in Samarkand being built by a Jew in the pre-Arab period.[6]

When the Arabs conquered Central Asian provinces, Jews and Christians, who were living there long before the conquest, were allowed to continue in their former faith as *dhimmis*—that is, as followers of recognized religions. All other religions were considered pagan, and a Muslim was obligated to fight against their followers in a holy war. Dhimmis, however, were obliged to pay *jizya*—the special tax for non-Islamic citizens of Islamic countries. Non-Muslim land owners were obligated to pay an extra land tax. These obligations were in existence for Jews until the early twentieth century, when Central Asia was entirely included in the Russian Empire. After the Arab invasion, Jews were under protection of authorities because they remained loyal and obedient taxpayers who fulfilled their social obligations. Later, Muslim treatment of the Jews varied depending on the policies of the caliphs and the attitudes of different local governors. In the eleventh century, Muslim rulers of Central Asia followed the rule "to keep agreements with *dhimmi* and let the Jews live peacefully." At the same time, synagogues and other non-Muslim houses of worship were destroyed or confiscated and were transformed into mosques. Many sacred Muslim buildings originated in the eleventh century and have a different appearance than traditional Islamic architecture: their floor plans coincide with the descriptions of major Jewish temples. This tendency co-incides with the eleventh-century ban on public buildings being taller than Muslim buildings.[7]

Chronicles of the twelfth century discuss the Jewish presence in Samarkand, but it is not clear whether Jews survived the Mongol invasion. Before the Mongol conquest, there was a sizable Jewish community (estimates vary from 5,000 to 50,000) in Samarkand, the largest city of Central Asia. There is an indication that Jews were expelled from Samarkand when it was under Islamic rule, because the city was regarded as sacred; however, it is not known when this expulsion occurred. Being members of protected communities, the *dhimmi* Jews lived in their own quarters and enjoyed some freedom of religion and appointed their own religious officials—subject to confirmation by the head of state and his officials. Jews were subjected to usual limitations, such as the wearing of distinguishing markings on their clothing and restrictions to bear arms and ride horses. Jews were largely occupied in trade and commerce as well as in medicine.[8]

Before the thirteenth century, there was a Jewish community in Bokhara. The History of Bokhara, written in 943 in Arabic by Abu Bakr al-Narshakhi, a native of the vicinity of Bokhara, reported that most of the population were *dhimmis* who paid the tax for non-Muslims. Bokhara was established as the largest and most important Jewish center in the region. The city's name was later associated with the entire Jewish population residing in Central Asia, which were called Bokhara Jews. This definition appeared first in the fourteenth century, when Tamerlane moved dyers and weavers from Bokahara to Samarkand. Because of the special legal status of the Bokharans after Russia established its colony in Central Asia, all Central Asian Jews who were not citizens of the Russian Empire at that time were considered Bokharans.

MONGOL INVASION

In the thirteenth century, Central Asia underwent a substantial transformation when Mongol hordes swept across Asia into the Muslim East, leaving a path of devastation in its wake. There is no evidence that Genghis Khan and his successors persecuted Jews in particular in their domain, but they did not give them any privileges either. Nor is there evidence that the Jews were involved in any significant religious struggle during the period of the Mongol invasion. The Mongols did not make any distinction between themselves and other conquered nations; they ordered the *jizya* to be paid by all settled people, Muslims and non-Muslims alike. This regulation did not make Jewish life easier, but at least it made the Jews equal to other Muslims in taxation.

A strong Mongol empire was created on the eastern border of the Khorezm sultanate in the early thirteenth century. As a result of Ming China's isolation behind the Great Wall, Genghis Khan rerouted the many channels of the Silk Road and combined them into one large stream directed northward to go through the Mongol steppes. The Mongols plundered the caravans to the extent that they used silk as wrapping and packing material. As a result of the decline of the original Silk Road, entire cities were marooned in the desert, and Central Asia was transformed from the shop window of Asia to an isolated and neglected wasteland.

Sultan of Khorezm and Genghis Khan kept trade relations between their states and exchanged delegates. Genghis Khan informed the sultan about his military victories in defeating the Turks and suggested a peace treaty, a diplomatic preparation for the future invasion. The *casus belli* was the murder of a caravan consisting of 450 Muslim traders sent by Genghis Khan in 1218. Many versions of this event exist. Some accuse Genghis Khan of plotting the murder and using greedy Khorezm officials, while others suggest that this was plotted by the sultan's mother with the purpose to overthrow her son and install her grandson Ozlag Shah on the throne. Genghis Khan was looking for an occasion to invade and found it; the invasion started in September 1219 and continued for three years. Genghis Khan's troops, armed with artillery, catapults, and battering rams, marched into Central Asia, destroying farms, cities, and people. In Samarkand, only 25 percent of the population survived the war. The looting and mass destruction devastated the area. Initially, the sultan declined the advice to concentrate all of his troops and fight a decisive battle against Genghis Khan and instead ordered his army to defend individual cities. Despite the fact that sultan's troops were two to three times larger than the Mongol army, they failed because the Khorezmians were dispersed.

The fall of Central Asia was deeper than that experienced by other conquered territories because of the region's higher cultural development. While in Europe, only priests were able to read, in every Central Asian village, several men were capable of reading the Koran and interpreting the Islamic law. The wars of Central Asia and Mongolia were not the usual types of wars known in Western civilizations, where armies generally engage in combat with enemies of similar technology and approximately equal force. The armies of Central Asian agricultural societies were different in composition from those of the nomadic people. Nomadic people were of a different cultural background that did not value farmlands and irrigation systems, and thus they destroyed them carelessly. The Mongols, whose level of development was lower than that of the Central Asians, defeated the rulers and people of Khorezm, which was a relatively new establishment with a heterogeneous population and continuing fights between different ethnic groups. The state remained weak and decentralized. Because most of the offices belonged to the local landowning nobility and could be inherited, the sultan had problems appointing appropriate officers. Constant wars required higher taxes, which were not favored by the population. Also, part of the Muslim population was unhappy with Baghdad's caliph, who was among the sultan's enemies and a victim of his attacks. These factors undermined the sultan's support base; when the Mongols appeared in his domain, few were willing to defend him or his country.

However, unlike the Arab invasion in 712, the Mongols did not impose their culture, religion, language, or government on the people of Central Asia. Instead, they punished those who were responsible for attacking their caravans. The survivors were able to rebuild their farms and cities after the Mongols' exit. In 1262, Marco Polo traveled through the area and described Bokhara as one of the best cities along his route, indicating that the former prosperity was reestablished after the Mongol devastation. Soon after the Mongol invasion, the initial destruction and shock of conquest were substituted by an unprecedented rise in cultural communication, expanded trade, and improved civilization.[9] While the territory was under the rule of the Genghis Khan's Mongol empire, roads were opened to commerce because all trade barriers were removed within the empire and a single legal order was established. The freedom of movement and forced resettlements were followed by a free exchange of ideas and knowledge. There were attempts to introduce a universal alphabet for writing in all languages. The custom of using carpets all over Central Asia also can be credited to the Mongols. For almost the next 100 years, local lords and merchants collected taxes and governed people, although the nominal rulers were Genghis Khan's relatives appointed by him.

Genghis Khan appeared in Central Asia and conquered Bokhara, the most important city in the sultanate of Khorezm, now in Uzbekistan, in 1220. Bokhara was chosen for the first Mongol attack because of its propaganda value. Not a major commercial or political center, Bokhara was the pillar of Muslim religion in the region because of its concentration of clergy and religious thinkers. Before attacking Bokhara, Genghis Khan took many smaller cities and villages, forcing the local population to flee to Bokhara for protection and creating a feeling of terror and havoc in the city. Initially, a garrison of about 20,000 defenders was placed in Bokhara, but the city defenders fled before the Mongol army arrived, leaving only about 500 soldiers in the city. Almost all of the soldiers retreating from Bokhara were caught and murdered by the Mongols, who remained close to the city. The civilian population of Bokhara surrendered, opening the city gates and welcoming Genghis Khan and his warriors.

Upon entering the city, Genghis Khan first ordered the local people to feed his warriors and horses. Feeding the Mongols was a sign of submission. The position of those who were hiding behind the thick walls of the citadel and planning the defense of the city was hopeless, not only because the attacking Mongols cut off the food and water supply of the defenders, but because the invaders tested their new warfare—catapults and trebuchets that for the first time in history hurled pots of burning liquids, explosives, and incendiary materials. The Mongols also used portable towers with retractable ladders from which they could shoot down the walls' defenders. Meanwhile, the miners dug underground passages under the wall. To mount psychological pressure on the defenders, the prisoners and ordinary city inhabitants were killed in front of the defenders. The attack on Bokhara was a success not only because of the quick surrender of the city but because of its psychological effects on the defenders of other Central Asian cities. When Samarkand received word of the Mongol warfare, it immediately surrendered. In the summer and fall of 1221, other major fortresses at Herat, Balkh, Termez, and Urgench were taken. During a subsequent campaign, the Mongols conquered all Central Asian cities. No citadel survived. Genghis Khan offered generous terms of surrender to communities in Central Asia along the path of his troops and was merciful to those who accepted the terms and joined the Mongols.

The Mongol invasion was the only case in history when agricultural countries of Asia were united under the power of one dynasty. The Mongols integrated the region by conquest, alliance, or ejection of their fellow tribesmen into a great military-political unity, absorbing, crushing, or submitting everyone. Genghis Khan used the political system of the conquered countries, which was fluid at the beginning of his reign, to his advantage. The impact of the Mongols on Central Asia was viewed as a disaster by the local people. The city of Tashkent, which was destroyed by Mongols, remained empty until the following century. The greatest destruction was inflicted on the Khorezmian irrigation system; the capital, Urgench was partially destroyed, and the course of the Amu-Darya was changed so that settlements on the left bank were flooded.

The destruction that was brought about at the beginning of the Mongol conquest spared nothing, including Muslim shrines and cultural centers. In regard to religion, Genghis Khan demonstrated absolute tolerance, not interfering in religious affairs; religious institutions were exempt from taxation, and conquered people were permitted to profess their religious views. However, these principles were completely disregarded by his successors. By becoming Muslim, Genghis's heirs vacillated between the Sunni and Shiite versions as it suited the political moment. When, during the last quarter of the fourteenth century, most of Mongol rulers in Central Asia became committed Shiites, a severe persecution of minority groups such as Jews and Buddhists was unleashed.

While Mongol troops were in Central Asia, they experienced the first wave of Islamic terrorism. A Muslim sect of Shiites named Nizari Ismailis, known to the West as the Assassins, established strongholds in the unconquered fortresses. Not limiting their attack to fights against the Mongols, the Assassins killed all who opposed them in any way, especially leaders and powerful people. The cult recruited young men who were willing to die in their attacks with the assurance that they would achieve instant entry into paradise as martyrs of Islam. The sect was based on the unconditional obedience of members and their submission to leaders whose orders were considered to have a divine nature. The Assassins were drugged to keep them obedient and fearless. The Ismailis became very powerful after the Mongol invasion in Khorezm and after the power vacuum that existed when Mongol troops withdrew from the Khorezm territory. Despite the initial loyalty oath to Genghis Khan, the Imams unsuccessfully attempted to murder the khan in 1256 and provoked an energetic Mongol campaign aimed at the extermination of the assassins.

POST-MONGOL NATION BUILDING

Warring among petty states, which came to an end as a result of the Mongolian conquest, reemerged as soon as the Mongol rule weakened. After Genghis Khan's death in 1227, the Mongol empire changed its form. The rules of inheritance within the family were applied to the rules of succession in the empire. According to the rule of equal patrimonial succession, both property and land were equally distributed among the sons. These parts of the empire, which acted like independents states, were called *hordes* or *uluses*. Mongol rulers and their Turkic troops who were brought to the region gradually assimilated with the original inhabitants of Central Asia. The nomadic tribes, which were included in the Mongol army, moved through the territory of present-day northern Kyrgyzstan, settling and hoping to stay there.[10] The Mongol language was replaced by Turkic, and Islam became a dominant religion once again.

The eldest son of Genghis Khan, Juchi, ruled in Central Asia and controlled his *ulus* in the territory of present-day Kazakhstan; the Mongol people were a minority in this domain. The second son of Genghis Khan, Chagatay, received territory to the east of Juchi's, around Samarkand, Bokhara, and areas in modern Chinese Turkestan. The people who resided in this *ulus* were sedentary and mingled with the Uzbek people, who, during this period, were formed as an ethnic unit on the basis of a single territory, economy, language, culture, and origin. The term Uzbek is attributed to these people since the fourteenth century, when they were under the rule of Khan Uzbek (1312–1340).

The Kazakhs established themselves in the eastern part of Chagatay *ulus* under chaotic conditions of the succession states and principalities of the late Genghis period. From the beginning of their history, the Kazakhs numbered over 1 million at the end of the fifteenth century, when the formative process took place. The Kazakhs were first united under Kasim Khan, whose descent can be traced to Genghis Khan. The Kazakhs soon broke into warring groups after the death of Kasim Khan and remained primarily nomadic pastoralists. They did not take up agriculture as part of their traditional economy until after Russian contact. Ethnic consolidation continued into the fifteenth century with an extensive consolidation of Turkmen tribes. Until the nineteenth century, the Turkmens did not have a single leader recognized by all the tribes; every tribe was ruled by its own khan. The Turkmens were organized into amorphous tribal confederations, speaking the Turkic language and continuously resisting attempts of the Khiva Khanate to establish control over them.

In 1360, the Khan of Mogolistan, a part of the former Chatagay *ulus*, invaded Central Asia and, facing no resistance, started to plunder ancient cities. Several military campaigns were trusted to a young warlord named Timur, who was presented with a province and an army of 10,000 persons. Being a governor of a rich province, Timur stopped supporting the khan and organized an army against him with another pretender to power in the region, Emir Hussein of Balkh. For 10 years, Timur and Hussein fought the Turkmens, who were employed by the Khan of Mogolistan. Uzbek historians consider this Timur's attempt to save the country from the Mongols. After the death of Hussein in April 1370, Timur married Hussein's widow (who was related to Genghis Khan) and was pronounced the single ruler of a reunited and centralized state within the approximate borders of the Chagatay *ulus* at the gathering of local nobility and military commanders. Because Timur did not belong to the Genghisid tribe, Timur never called himself a khan and had no legitimacy for the rule that was defined by virtue of being a descendant of Genghis Khan. It appears that Timur was satisfied with the title of emir, which means ruler in Arabic. Timur's genealogy, which establishes descent from Genghis Khan on Chagatay's side is probably the work of an official biographer and apologist. However, Timur's descendants, who were called Timurids, ruled by virtue of descent from Timur.

Timur's rule continued for 35 years, during which he demonstrated his talents in statehood, politics, military affairs, and general management, as well as his enormous ability for planning and implementing his decisions. In 1370, Timur made Samarkand his capital and restored the city walls that had been ruined by the Mongols almost 150 years before. Although Samarkand remained the capital city of the empire for 35 years, Timur spent only a year or two there. His court and harem traveled with him all over Asia, and the capital of his empire was constantly following his tent. In 1372, Timur launched a campaign against Khorezm, which was the last independent state in Central Asia. The rulers of Khorezm tried to use contradictions between Timur's state and the Golden Horde to their advantage, but they failed, and, in 1388, Timur seized Urgench, the capital of Khorezm and overthrew the local dynasty. He moved the inhabitants of Urgench to Samarkand and issued an order to raze the plundered and devastated city to the ground and sow the site with barley. In 1391, however, Timur ordered the restoration of Urgench; the city still exists today in Uzbekistan.

Timur was probably the first Central Asian leader who built the state on the basis of law and continuously implemented existing legislation. The state apparatus was compact and consisted of seven departments: the chancellery, military, finance, court affairs, justice, state security, and international relations. The executive power was represented by the council of eight *viziers* (ministers) appointed by Timur. The *viziers* oversaw changes in the population, trade development, implementation of laws, and informed the ruler on the collection of taxes and the administration's activities. Three *viziers* were responsible for monitoring the provinces and dependent states. The chief cleric and chief judges of the religious and civil courts were also members of the council. An official named *arzbegi* with responsibilities similar to those of ombudsmen in present-day society, was subordinated directly to the ruler. The *arzbegi* was responsible for accepting and resolving claims against officials submitted by citizens and military personnel. During the reign of Timur and the first Timurids, *arzbegi* did not distinguish between the citizens and accepted claims from everyone regardless of religion. Later, the right to submit a claim was preserved for Muslims only. A European-like state protocol was introduced in Timur's empire. Important decisions were made after they were discussed at advisory council meetings, which were comprised of top government officials, the elderly, and highly respected individuals.

Timur's empire was divided into financially independent provinces, which were further divided into districts. Province and district chiefs were usually relatives of the ruler or well-known military leaders. The main support for Timur's administration came from the warlike nomadic and semi-nomadic Mongol nobility of Central Asia. To broaden his social base, Timur befriended the local nobility and the Muslim clergy. Much attention was paid to the formation of the state apparatus, where only competent, honest, and enthusiastic people were allowed to perform state service. The state servants in Timur's empire were required to be knowledgeable about peoples' lives, tolerant, modest, and peaceful. Those who were known for their envy and submission of false claims about other citizens were banned from the service.

The system of taxation in Timur's empire was complex, which meant that land ownership relations and the state bureaucracy were highly developed. The system included several taxes, such as a tax on private land, a tax on gardens, the customs duty, and various other taxes. A general land tax was paid as well. A special tax called "gifts for officials who crossed the region territory" was introduced. The documents of Timur's era usually do not mention the religious affiliation of the people described, and the *jizya* is not mentioned among the taxes existing in Central Asia. This may lead to the conclusion that non-Muslims did not play a significant role in Timur's empire.

The Code of Timur, a major piece of fifteenth-century Central Asian legislation, was based on the analysis of various events and situations, and it prescribed rules for resolving the state's daily problems. The Code, a Muslim document by its nature, assigned each religious group a place in society. According to this legislation, the civil status of the nations ruled by Timur and their right to protection was identical. No religion was contrasted with another or singled out. Equal status of *dhimmis* was given to Christians, Jews, and Zoroastrians. The Code did not prevent non-Muslims from performing public functions; however, there is no record of a non-Muslim holding an administrative position in Timur's court.

After building a strong state within his empire, Timur was ready to fight outside of Central Asia. He expanded his domain by ruthless wars using a new army that combined the traditional military system of the Mongols with tactical and technical innovations, including the first cannons. In conquering the cities, Timur resorted to military force when negotiations of surrender failed, and he took extremely aggressive actions showing the city's inhabitants little or no mercy. Timur piled heads outside the cities and tortured the cities' defenders in public. (This was standard practice for fourteenth-century Asia.) Timur's military campaign did not affect a particular religion or ethnicity; the entire population of a besieged city, regardless of individual views, was victim of his conquests. Seeing anarchy in Iran, Timur moved his troops there in 1385, where, during the next 10 years, he defeated the Golden Horde and destroyed its capital on the Volga River. In the 1390s, Timur repeatedly raided the Transcaucasian countries from northern Iran. In early 1399, the war with Delhi ended with another triumph for Timur, who returned to Samarkand with an immense booty. While fighting in India, Timur lost many cities he had previously seized, including Baghdad, due to attacks by Ottoman Turks. In September 1399, Timur's armies started a western campaign, and in January 1401, after taking several Syrian cities, Timur besieged and set fire to Damascus. Timur did not stay long in the Holy Land and turned eastward to sack Baghdad. Afterward, Timur entered the territory of modern Turkey and demanded the sultan's submission. The decisive battle of Ankara occurred on July 20, 1402, during which Sultan Bayazid and his sons were taken prisoners. The taking of Smyrna (modern Ismir) in the same year continued Timur's conquests in Asia Minor. Timur's last military effort was a campaign against China. While marching to China in February 1405, Timur died at age 70.

Timur's reign from 1370 to 1405 initiated the most active period of Central Asian history. During this time, the Mongol yoke was thrown off, a central government and prosperous economy based on Sogdian traditions were established, and Central Asian people were united. The inclusion of vast geographic territories with different cultures in a unified state created the grounds for a quicker cultural development later, which was called the Temuridic renaissance. However, the accumulation of different states and provinces in Timur's empire created centrifugal tendencies, which caused the breakup of the empire into smaller fragments in the fifteenth century, when Timur's descendants began a new period in Central Asian history.

NOTES

1. The transfer of the capital to Bokhara entailed a change in the assortment of goods. Since the tenth century, most traded goods were cotton clothing and wool carpets instead of silk, and the focus of trade switched from China to Europe.

2. Lawrence Krader, *Peoples of Central Asia* (Bloomington: Indiana University Press, 1996), 132.

3. Richard Frye, *Bukhara: The Medieval Achievement* (Costa Mesa, CA: Mazda Publishers, 1996), 212.

4. Michael Shterenshis, *Tamerlane and the Jews* (London and New York: Routledge Curzon, 2002), 43.

5. Law (1992), 36; Richard Foltz, "Judaism and the Silk Route," *The History Teacher* 32, no. 1 (November 1998): 11.

6. Walter Fischel, "New Sources for the History of the Jewish Diaspora in Asia in the 16th Century," *The Jewish Quarterly Review* 40, no. 4 (April 1950), 380.

7. Shterenshis (2002), 54.

8. Law (1992), 39.

9. Jack Weatherford, *Genghis Khan and the Making of the Modern World* (New York: Crown Publishers, 2004), 23.

10. In the twelfth century, Kyrgyz tribes united in small khanates continued to migrate to southern Siberia. In 1207, they sent lavish gifts to Genghis Khan expressing their obedience to him. However, in 1218, they revolted against the Mongols, and Genghis Khan was obliged to send his son Juchi to pacify the Kyrgyz, who, after a month-long fight, lost their statehood and were included in the Mongol army. Many Kyrgyz were forcefully resettled in Central Asia.

4

The Medieval States of Central Asia (Fifteenth through Nineteenth Centuries)

THE COLLAPSE OF THE TIMURID EMPIRE

Immediately after Timur's death in 1405, a war of succession began throughout his empire, and most of Timur's 36 sons and grandsons participated in the war. The law of succession did not exist, and the struggle for the throne among the Timurid princes continued throughout the fifteenth century. The wars caused tremendous losses to agriculture and urban life and led to the depletion of treasuries spent on gaining support for the candidates among nobles and officials. Subsequently, this resulted in the impoverishment of the population due to overtaxation. The economic development of the country, which was divided into two large parts with centers in Herat and Samarkand, suffered.

Timur's grandson, Ulugbek, ruled Central Asia from Samarkand for 40 years between 1409 and 1449. Most of Ulugbek's wars were defensive, although Khorezm and Fergana were added to Samarkand's domain under his rule. Ulugbek was not a warrior, but rather a scientist who taught at the schools he had established. One of his greatest accomplishments was a three-story observatory built in Samarkand in 1428 to 1429, which enabled him to prepare his famous astronomical tables. Ulugbek's measurements of the year's length in seconds were more precise than anyone else's prior to the invention of the computer. Education and culture thrived in Ulugbek's Samarkand, and many famous scholars of the time were invited to work at the Academy of Science established by Ulugbek. Singers, dancers, poets, and musicians also made the city a cultural capital of the region.

This trend was interrupted by orthodox Muslims, who considered scientific and cultural advances to be contradictory to the teachings of Islam. Reactionary Islamists came to power together with Ulugbek's son, who murdered Ulugbek in 1449. Islamists reversed the scientific progress, destroying Ulugbek's observatory and forcing his students to flee Samarkand. Radical Islam caused a sharp decline in the cultural activity and economic development of the society. Ulugbek's successors could not defend the country from the radicals and the attacking nomadic Uzbek tribes. Three kings were murdered in two years, and in 1468 the Central Asians were occupied by nomadic Uzbeks. The Timurid Empire disintegrated by being divided into five independent principalities that lacked cohesion and political solidarity; their borders fluctuated depending on wars and intrigues.

Geopolitical factors also contributed to the failure of the state. Central Asia was a permanent target for incursions of neighboring tribes, such as Uzbeks, Kazakhs, Mogols, Turkmens, Mangits, and others who were attracted to the region's rich agricultural products, which were not available in their own countries. Nomadic invasions occurred frequently throughout the fifteenth century, destroying towns, irrigational systems, and crops. Stored wealth was plundered, and thousands of people were taken by invaders in slavery. The Timurids were not successful in retaliating and were unable to expel the nomads who attempted to settle within this empire. Fighting the Mongol threat, the Timurids invited the Uzbeks, a nomadic tribe living in camps in the northern part of Central Asia and in the mouth of the Volga River. The Uzbeks mainly subsided and based their commerce on cattle breeding. In the sixteenth century, the changing Uzbek rulers attempted to unite separate tribes and establish certain forms of centralized government. Because of their proximity to the Timurid Empire, the Uzbeks were drawn into its civil wars and intrigues. The Uzbeks occasionally raided, harassed, and plundered the settled population of Transoxiana. Often, the Uzbeks were joined by other indigenous people, who, since the late fifteenth century, underwent a long process of ethnic and political unification and gradually settled in the areas where they live today.[1]

STATE ORIGINS OF THE NATIVE PEOPLE

The Kazakhs were formed under the chaotic conditions of the succession of states and principalities of the late Genghisid period at the end of the fifteenth and beginning of the sixteenth centuries. The Kazakhs were nomadic pastoralists from the beginning of their history. Their pastures were originally along the Chu River; however, there is no evidence linking Kazakhs to this land prior to the fifteenth century. There is no precise explanation for the word *Kazakh*. It appears that, originally, the word did not have any political or ethnic meaning and could be used to describe any people who left their ruler or tribe and began to live life as adventurers who found food with their own knife, stole the enemy's herds, and wore the skins of killed animals. It was popular and advantageous in the sixteenth century to spend time *kazakhing*. Many local sultans and khans built their authority this way. According to this view, Kazakh is derived from a common noun meaning vagabond or wanderer.[2]

In the 1450s to 1460s, a large group of Kazakh tribes under the rule of Sultan Zhanibek settled in the river valleys of Chu and Talas in northern Kyrgyzstan. They mixed with the local population and participated in attacks on neighboring lands together. The first Kazakh state was created under the rule of Khan Zhanibek in the second half of fifteenth century. After that, the word Kazakh, in addition to its social meaning, received political characteristics as well, defining an independent khanate and then the name of the Kazakh people. Once formed into a demographic group, the Kazakhs have maintained their ethnic unity from the late sixteenth century. The Kazakh state was led by the Genghisid dynasty until the nineteenth century, when the Russians came.

In the fifteenth and sixteenth centuries, Islam was a formal but not widely accepted religion of Kazakh people who professed various pagan cults. The majority of Kazakhs did not know basic religious rules and requirements, and, even if they did, the nomads were unable to follow them. It was not feasible for wandering nomads to perform such Islamic rites as five prayers per day, fasting during the month of Ramadan, visiting holy places, and paying a special tax to support other Muslims in need. These historic roots affect modern religious developments, making Kazakhstan the least religious state in Central Asia today. However, the khans and sultans vigorously propagated Islam in search of support from influential Muslim clergies and Transoxiana's feudal rulers.

Some members of the Kazakh dynasty ruled in Khiva in the eighteenth century. The Kazakh monarchy was divided into 23 *uluses*. The population of the khanate was permanently growing and included about 1 million people in the sixteenth century.[3] During its entire history, the khanate was divided into three hordes, which were ranked by seniority just as the component clans, lineages, and families within the hordes were. The Great Horde was the senior horde, which nomadized between lakes Balkhash and Issyk Kul, close to the place of their earlier establishment. The Middle Horde was located in central Kazakhstan, north of Lake Balkhash. The place of abode for the Little Horde was to the west of the Middle Horde, along the northern and western shores of the Aral Sea. The political organization of the hordes was established in the sixteenth and early seventeenth centuries. In the seventeenth century, several smaller khanates were founded within these groups. The khanates did not have permanent borders, and their numbers fluctuated depending on military victories and failures of particular khans. Despite attempts by a number of khans to expand their power over other tribes, Kazakhstan did not exist as a fixed political or state unit.

In 1598 to 1599, after a series of military campaigns, Kazakh khans established control over Fergana and parts of Turkistan, including the Tashkent oasis. Fergana was retrieved in the early seventeenth century, and other lands acquired by the Kazakhs remained under their control. Treaties concluded between the Uzbeks and Kazakhs promised the Kazakhs that Uzbek khans would not interfere in the occupied lands' affairs. In 1594 to 1595, the Kazakhs attempted to establish relations with the Muscovite tsar. The Kazakh delegations visited Moscow and discussed a military union and possible accession with Russia. Diplomatic Kazakh-Russian relations resulted in the expansion of caravan trade.

Most of the Kazakhs recognized their accession with Russia in the middle of the eighteenth century; however, they continued to return to their traditional winter quarters on the Chinese territory (the Chinese frontier guards could not prevent the movement of Kazakh tribes). In 1767, Mancuro-Chinese authorities reached a compromise with the Kazakhs, allowing them to migrate to the Chinese pastures during the winter months in exchange for compensations paid to the Qin dynasty in the amount of 1 percent of the animals in the herd.

After being integrated into Russia, the local Kazakh population became subjects of the Russian government's authorities. Kazakh hordes were abolished, and their territory was divided into administrative units with mixed Russian and native administrations. The building of government institutions in Kazakh territories began with a new judicial system. According to the 1822 charters, a special Kazakh Code was introduced that restricted the jurisdiction of traditional *bek* courts and transferred all state crimes, high treason, and cases of murder, plunder, stealing, and some other dangerous crimes and significant civil cases to the jurisdiction of district administrations—the highest territorial power institutions. The district administrations consisted of the chief sultan elected by other sultans for a three-year term, two Russian lay assessors appointed by the central government, two assessors elected by the sultans, beks, and settlement elders. The bek court continued to exist but resolved only minor cases; rulings were based on the norms of customary law, and participation of two negotiators elected by the trying parties was required.

Further Russian advancement into Kazakh territories in the 1830s and the strengthening of Russian control over southern Turkistan made the issue of border delimitation even more important. The Beijing Treaty of 1860 confirmed the existing situation without taking the interests of the Kazakhs into

account. The newly defined border followed the existing geographical terrain and divided the established Kazakh communes. The Chugachak Protocol of 1864 recognized Kazakhs in the territory of each state at the moment of ratification, stating that these people should belong to the state, which controls the territory. This division forced many tribes to remain on Chinese territory, while other tribes, which were transferred under Russian control, lost their traditional camping areas.

The next phase of the Russo-Chinese border delimitation was the conclusion of treaties in 1879 and 1881. According to these treaties, the Ilii region was transferred under the Chinese jurisdiction, and people located there received the right to choose their place of abode and accept either Chinese or Russian citizenship. Approximately 70,000 of Kazakh, Uighur, and Dunghan resettlers moved to Russia under its protection. Officially registered in the districts that became part of the Xinjiang province were 137,623 Kazakhs.[4] On August 5, 1883, the Russian tsar decreed that all Kazakhs who wanted to keep their Russian citizenship had to leave their settlements and return to lands within the Russian borders, even if they were losing their pastures. The second mass resettlement occurred in the autumn of 1916, when 300,000 Kazakhs and Kyrgyz from the border area moved to Xinjiang. It is not clear how many remained in China nor how many returned to their traditional territory. In 1932 to 1934, many Soviet Kazakhs crossed the Chinese border seeking refuge from famine and excesses of the revolution and hoping to acquire Chinese citizenship and establish settlements.

The Kyrgyz formed a large tribal union in the northern parts of present-day Kyrgyzstan in the 1480s, through the cooperation with local Turkic tribes and the consolidation of Kyrgyz tribes. Khan Zhunus, a descendant of Genghis Khan, became the union's chief. He conducted several military attacks on Kashgar and organized the defense against attacks from the militant Uzbek Khan Sheibani. Since the eighteenth century, the Central Asian Kyrgyz tribes supported the Kyrgyz in eastern Turkistan in their fight against Chinese oppression. In the second half of the eighteenth century, the Kyrgyz became the target of Kazakh aggressions. The Kazakh khans attacked and destroyed Kyrgyz settlements with the purposes of increasing their authority and popularity among their subjects. The population of the Kyrgyz was approximately 800,000 people. In the nineteenth century, the majority of the Kyrgyz population was located on the Kokand Khanate territory. Although the power of the Kokand Khan extended to the territory of Kyrgyzstan, the khan could not interfere in the Kyrgyz affairs, which were under the control of local tribal chiefs. In 1852, after a revolt and fight against Tashkent and Kokand, the coalition of Kyrgyz tribes had chosen its own khan. The Kyrgyz led a passive political life in Kokand and remained neutral when the Russians fought with the khan of Kokand in order to accept the Kyrgyz tribes as Russian subjects.

Afraid of a potential war, many Kyrgyz moved into the mountains. In August 1860, Russian Cossacks took the fortress of Bishkek, the center of the Kyrgyz community. Attempts of the khan of Kokand to return the Kyrgyz under his influence were met with Kyrgyz resistance, which was strongly supported by the Russian military. In 1862, the Russians helped the Kokand Kyrgyz to establish their independence from the khan. In response, 200 Kyrgyz fighters helped the Russians to defeat the Kokand fortresses. After accepting that Russia was militarily superior to them in 1863, Kyrgyz leaders took an oath of loyalty to the Russian tsar. In 1865, the Kyrgyz were formally subordinate to Russia, recognizing its authority. Those Kyrgyz who resided outside of the khanate were admitted to Russia in 1855. The historic presence of the Kyrgyz people in the Fergana Valley, which is part of the Republic of Uzbekistan today, makes this territory the most ethnically mixed area in the region.

The Turkmens had a quasi-independent tributary relationship with the Mongol Empire and its succession state, the Ulus of Juchi. During the sixteenth century, the Turkmens on the eastern Caspian shore were under a branch of the Uzbek dynasty. Although subdued by Khorezm in 1524, the Turkmens did not become full Khorezmian subjects; they preserved their status of tributaries and made yearly payments in sheep. The Turkmen tribes that did become farmers paid their taxes in grain. Until the nineteenth century, Turkmens' involvement in Central Asian affairs remained minimal; however, connections between the Turkmens and Bokhara were reported since the late eighteenth century. In the nineteenth century, the Turkmens presented a great resistance to the Russian advance but were militarily reduced and finally conquered in the 1870s.

THE UZBEK STATE

The sixteenth century was the century of replacing the Timurids with the nomadic dynasty of Sheibanids. The Uzbek state was established and achieved a unique position in Central Asia under Sheibani Khan (1451–1510), who founded his own kingdom, which lasted for more than a century on the ruins of the Timurid Empire. For many years, Sheibani attempted to restore the power of his family in the Uzbek ulus, which was conquered by the Kazakhs. After several unsuccessful efforts, Sheibani switched his attention to the territory that belonged to the Timurids, which could be taken more easily because of the weaknesses of the Timurid state. In 1500, Sheibani attacked Bokhara and gave the city to his younger brother, while he moved to defeat Samarkand and other cities and fortresses between the Amu Darya and Syr Darya. Samarkand's inhabitants were robbed and plundered during the four months after the city was taken by Sheibani. The city revolted, and the noblemen plotted to change the power in favor of Babur, Timur's fifth-generation grandson, who ruled in the neighboring city of Andijon. The plot failed, Babur fled, and Sheibani made Samarkand the capital of his state—although the decline of the city could not be reverted.[5] After mixing tribes—which included Huns, Turks, and Mongols—with the Sogdians, Sheibani extended his authority over the entire region of Central Asia. In 1504, the Fergana valley was under Sheibani's control, and, in 1505, after a 10-month siege, Urgench opened its gates to the new khan. After Sultan Hussein of Herat, who was considered the formal head of the Timurid dynasty, died in 1507, Sheibani attacked Herat, demanding an enormous contribution from the city's inhabitants and then permitting his troops to take whatever they wanted during the next two days. The chaotic state of the Timurid state, diplomatic maneuvers, and military attacks helped Sheibani to establish himself as a regional ruler. Political changes did not affect ordinary individuals mostly because there was no change in religion, and religious fights did not erupt when Sheibani established his monarchy.

After conquering the Timurid Empire, the Uzbeks were absorbed by the local population speaking the same Turkic language. The name *Uzbek* was applied to everyone living in the territories subordinate to Sheibani Khan and began to define the people according to their area of residence within specific political or state borders. For many years, the word *Uzbek* was attributed to those tribes of the Uzbek ulus, which moved from the steppes into the Samarkand area during the Sheibanid period, but it did not apply to the locals who resided there before the Uzbek invasion. Even in the nineteenth century, the word *Uzbek* was rarely used in Central Asia, except when an Uzbek had to be compared with a member of another ethnic group—Sart or Tajik, for example.[6] After the formal division of Turkistan into national Soviet republics, the word *Uzbek* was used broadly to describe citizens of a particular Soviet state. It appears that the history of the modern Uzbek nation does not coincide with the history of its name.

According to Babur, a Timurid leader of Mogolistan, Sheibani was a barbarian warlord. Babur made fun of Sheibani by calling him a "destroyer of culture" and an "illiterate poet of a single talentless poem,"[7] However, it is known that Sheibani—who came from the Genghis dynasty, which ruled one of the nomadic khanates and existed in the steppes of modern Kazakhstan—as a boy was sent to Samarkand for hiding in order to survive murder attempts by competing Kazakh khans. He was home-schooled, studied the Koran, and became known as a poet whose literary name was Happy Statesman.

In 1510, luck turned away from Sheibani, and the triumphal march of his troops was stopped by Ismail Shah of Iran, Sheibani's enemy and neighbor. While Sheibani was in Merv with a small number of troops, Ismail surrounded the city. The attack could have continued for a long time, but the Iranians decided to trick the Uzbeks by imitating a retreat. When Sheibani attempted to follow them without waiting for reinforcement, Ismail's Shia army of 17,000 killed all of the Uzbek warriors, including the khan. After the battle, the Iranians found Sheibani's body, cut off his head, and brought it to Ismail Shah, who ordered the skin to be removed and filled with straw and sent to his other enemy, Sultan Bayazid II of Turkey. The skull was later gold-plated and used as a cup by Ismail. After a while, the Uzbeks found and brought back the mutilated body of Khan Sheibani to Samarkand to bury it in a *medrese* established by Sheibani.

The main reason that Sheibani could not resist Ismail Shah's attacks was the weakness of the state system he had created. Sheibani divided the conquered lands among members of his family and leading military commanders while he remained the military chief. This diminished the role of the central power and rendered him unable to form a united military force to repel the Iranian invasion. No one responded to Sheibani's request for help during difficult times because he had lost the power to force his subjects.

Ismail supported Babur and tried to install him on the throne in Samarkand. Although a legitimate heir, Babur was not accepted because of good relations with the Shia Iran, and he was forced into exile. The Sheibanids used popular resistance and returned to Samarkand in 1513. The dynasty strengthened under the rule of Sheibani's nephew Ubaidullah Khan (ruled 1533–1539), who proved to be one of the greatest Uzbek rulers of Central Asia in the sixteenth century. Ubaidullah expanded Uzbek rule over the entire Transoxiana and challenged the Persians militarily. Under him, Bokhara became the capital of the state, its influence increased, and, in the middle of sixteenth century, the city began to take its present form under a program of religious and secular construction.

The development of Islam was most profound during Ubaidullah's rule, when the rulers strongly depended on the support of the clergy, which proselytized Sufism—a branch of Islam that required full submission and subordination to the teacher. The clergy restricted cultural progress and did not support science, although there was gradual development in the art of calligraphy and miniature paintings, and medicine continued to develop. In the seventeenth century, a medical library, two medical schools, and a hospital existed in Bokhara. The Islamic clergy amassed great wealth and a strong economic position in the seventeenth century thanks to land and water holdings. Despite the important role of Muslim clergy in regional political processes, theocratic governance never had a place in Central Asia, no matter how powerful the role of Islam was in the region.

From the legal point of view, the khan was the head of the state and owned the treasury lands.[8] Those who worked these lands were considered renters and only had rights to the land during their life time. They could not bequeath it, transfer it, or assign it to someone else. The treasury lands gradually lost their specific nature and were later endowed to mosques and religious communities. Private property on land was an important part of land relationships. Several forms of private land ownership existed, depending on the type of taxes levied on them. Private landholdings could be passed to male descendants. Communal lands were regulated by special legal norms, and the irrigation works were handled in a manner corresponding to the land. A special tax was levied for the maintenance of the irrigation canals. There were three systems of irrigation: the state or large canals, middle sized or communal canals, and small or private canals. Only the large, state canals were taxed.

For better administrative management of the state, the khan appointed rulers of provinces called *emirs*, who effectively had all the lands divided among them, aside from the personal capital of the khan. In addition to landownership, the khan had personal properties in various provinces (emirates) of his domain to support him and his court. The state was supported by taxes levied in various emirates and delivered to it through the khan's ministers.[9] To increase the treasury's wealth, the khan usually requested monetary payments for his gifts in amounts determined by him. As a rule, the khan's appraisal was 10 times higher than the real price of the gift.

For the rest of the sixteenth century, the Sheibanid house was at the head of the former Timurid domain, although the real power was in the hands of the local emirs who almost independently ruled the territories they were charged to govern. The political system was characterized by a decentralization of power. The authority of the khan remained relative because numerous Genghis heirs led their tribes in the area. The khan's authority included the customary prerogatives to mint coinage, to have his name recited during Friday prayers, and to receive tribute from the subordinate territories. This decentralization led to the secession of rival city-states such as Khiva, Bokhara, Samarkand, Balkh, Termez, and Khorezm from the Sheibanid domains in the middle of the sixteenth century. The Timurids continued to rule in Mogolistan in the south. The decline of the Silk Road entailed barbarianism, economic stagnation, and religious fanaticism for the increasingly isolated countries along the Silk Road. There were brief recoveries, but they could not stop Bokhara's isolation and decline from an international to a regional player slightly involved in the future great political game of the leading empires. In the middle of the sixteenth century, territories under Bokharan control included three independent parts—Bokhara, Samarkand, and Tashkent—whose importance was steadily increasing. A large part of the Bokharan population consisted of Tajiks, who were concentrated in the western part of the Bokhara khanate and in the valleys of Fergana and Zarafshan. Unlike the other people of this area, the Bokhara khanate people lost their tribal division and were ethnically united.

The Sheibanid Empire disintegrated and ceased to exist in 1598, when, after a series of killings within the ruling family, the nation remained without a royal successor. Its abrupt end was not a downfall or a decline but rather a sudden thrusting of power from a vanquishing dynasty upon its female line of Ashtarkhanids, which received its name from the Russian city of Astrakhan. Juchi's ancestors ruled there over a local predominantly Muslim population for more than 100 years before Astrakhan was acquired by Russia, and the rulers fled to Sheibanids in search of asylum. The Ashtarkhanid dynasty consisted of eight khans and ruled between 1611 and 1747 from Samarkand and Bokhara. This dynasty's rule was characterized by internal wars and wars against the nomads. Kazakh tribes constantly attacked Central Asian states, and internal wars tore the land apart.

The wars did not produce a strong leader, and the khan was the formal head of state and an absolute ruler in Transoxiana. An advisory council consisting of the emirs, military commanders, and court officials gathered when an important decision was to be passed or in the case of an emergency such as a revolt or the death of a neighboring sultan. The khan's first assistant was called *kushbegi*. He was in charge of land tax collection, finances, and other administrative issues. The collection of other taxes was in the jurisdiction of lower-level officials. The courier who delivered the khan's letters, the person who waited on the khan's table,[10] and the chief of the khan's guard held important roles in the court. Guards patrolled the cities, and people who were caught walking at night were arrested as violators of public order and were submitted to the city chiefs for beating. Judges were appointed and dismissed by the khan, while the chief justice had the power to discipline lower judges. Judges monitored local officials, who controlled the usage of land that belonged to the mosques and reported on land use issues to the government. The nucleus of the army was the khan's escort, which consisted of Russian slaves. The local emirs had their own escorts and guards. The khan's army had no infantry until the nineteenth century, and mounted soldiers were the army's main element. Rifles and knives were the main weapons of warfare, and artillery was operated by the Russian slaves. Regular troops were financed by the state, and soldiers received their payments in the form of money and food; officers were paid with land instead of money. When the khan needed to eliminate someone, he declared the person out of law and permitted an open hunt on the person. A reward was usually given to the person who brought the head of the khan's enemy to the palace. Because of permanent in-fighting, the power of the khan weakened gradually and was often limited by the walls of his palace in Bokhara.

In 1705, a Bokhara delegation visited Russia and was received by Russian tsar Peter the Great, who supported trade between his empire and Asia. The tsar offered the khan Russian protection and citizenship, and was ready to dispatch a guard in exchange for the submission of the khan. However, the khan consulted emirs and the court, who did not support the alliance with Russia. Several attempts to establish relations with Bokhara were made later. Empress

Anna in 1731 and the governor of the Russian border province of Orenburg in 1739 sent delegates to Bokhara, but all these missions were unsuccessful because the Kazakhs of the Great Horde stopped, plundered, and killed these delegations.

Kazakh and Iranian attacks contributed to the failure of the state. Pushed by the expansion of the Jungar Empire in Inner Asia, Kazakh nomads migrated and invaded Transoxiana in the second quarter of the eighteenth century. No army was strong enough to defend the territory from this invasion. The invading nomads united with the disaffected Uzbek tribes to overthrow the Bokhara Khan. Mohammed Khakim-bei from the Uzbek Mangit tribe took the throne in Bokhara in 1747, after murdering the khan and his two children. Khakim-bei started the new Mangit dynasty, which established itself on the throne in Bokhara in 1785, when Shah Murad declared himself the emir.[11] The Mangit dynasty was the first non-Genghisid dynasty to rule in Transoxiana since the Timurids and became the last native monarchial lineage ruling there until 1920. The reign of most of the emirs was characterized by constant warfare with Uzbek tribes in Transoxiana and Turkmen tribes in the desert, which continued almost until the Russian conquest. Emir Nasrullah (ruled 1826–1860), who was called the Butcher Emir, broke the resistance of tribal chiefs.

THE THREE KHANATES

As soon as the Mangit dynasty was established in the middle of the eighteenth century, the territory of Central Asia was divided into three powerful khanates of Bokhara, Kokand, and Khiva. These three countries were named after the capital cities. All three khanates were closely related, and political events in one affected the interests of the other two. There was little difference in their political systems; the emir was at the top of the Bokhara emirate, and the khans ruled the khanates of Kokand and Khiva. Although formally the monarchs had unlimited authority, they depended on strong local rulers who strived for independence. In all states, the influence of tribal elites was fought not by the creation of centralized government institutions, but by the promotion of personally loyal individuals to higher positions.[12] The administrative organization of the khanates did not change since the sixteenth century. The establishment of standing armies appears to be the only institutional development of this period. States were divided according to the established irrigation systems, and complex bureaucratic administrations—which included taxation, police, and military officials—ruled the states. The clergy played an important role in governing state affairs and often exercised its control over the khan or emir. Orthodox Islam had become the official religion throughout all of Central Asia and among all of the Turkic-speaking people. The emir of Bokhara became the religious leader of all Muslims in the region. Bokhara was recognized as the religious and educational center of Central Asia. Three hundred mosques and 60 medreses of Bokhara accepted students from all over the region. Foreign trade was conducted with Iran, India, Afghanistan, and Russia.

The Emirate of Bokhara dominated the western part of Central Asia. Financial, administrative, judicial, and military reforms and tax cuts were implemented by Shah-Murad, the emir who reigned between 1785 and 1800. Instead of being called khan, he accepted the title of emir of Bokhara. Shah-Murad reorganized the system of regional governors, punishing and replacing those who were too harsh. The new court system allowed everyone, even slaves, to come to the court to resolve their claims; in the eastern part of the emirate, lands were surveyed and peasants were resettled there for further land development. For administrative purposes, the emir divided the emirate into several districts, which were, in turn, divided into sections for tax collection. Each district was ruled by a *bek* and each section by a *bekcha*. In addition to imposing and collecting taxes, the beks enforced the religious shariah law. According to these laws, land and natural resources became the property of the Islamic clergy. Crimes carried severe punishments, including the cutting off of hands or feet, large monetary fines, imprisonment in deplorable living conditions, or death by throwing the criminal down from the top of a minaret.

The strength achieved by the Bokhara emirate was lost in the early nineteenth century, when every few months a new in-fight began. Many of the wars were fought against city-state Merv by Shah-Murad's successors, Khidar (1800–1826) and Nasrullah (1826–1860), resulting in relocating the Turkmens in Merv to the Samarkand area. In the middle of the nineteenth century, the emirate was populated by more than 2.5 million people. The settled people consisted mainly of Turks, Tajiks, Arabs, Iranians, Afghans, Armenians, Chinese, Hindus, Jews,[13] and a European pharmacist named Reinhardt, the only Westerner ever granted Bokharan domicile. The nomadic and semi-nomadic population consisted of Uzbeks, Turkmens, Kazakhs, and Karakalpaks.

The Khiva Khanate was the first Central Asian independent state. In 1511, another branch of the Sheibanids created the Khiva Khanate, with the capital in the oasis of Khorezm in the lower Amu Darya near the Aral Sea. Khiva was the most intact and remote area along the Silk Road existing for as long as trade caravans stopped in the oasis. Its geographical location and relative political independence made the Khiva Khanate attractive to nomadic Uzbek tribes, who selected this area as the place for their permanent settlement. While Uzbek dynasties ruled from Khorezm, Khiva was changing hands between the Iranians and Uzbeks until early 1623, when Khan Ilbars, a descendent of Juchi Khan, declared Khiva's independence.

Since the end of the seventeenth century, there was no dynasty in Khorezm, and various leaders of Uzbek tribes took power at different times until the non-Genghisid Kungat dynasty was established, and the capital was transferred from Khorezm to Khiva. At the end of seventeenth century, for a short time, Khiva was included in the Bokhara Khanate. In attempts to get rid of Bokharan influences and suppress the unruly tribes of the region, the khan of Khiva approached Peter the Great. In exchange for Russian protection, the khan offered to become the tsar's vassal. Having little or no interest in Central Asia at the time, Peter did not respond to the offer. He later realized that the possession of Khiva, located midway between Russia and India, would provide a staging point in the region, shorter routes for trade caravans, and military guards for the tradesmen. An expedition was sent in 1717 to Khiva to belatedly accept the khan's offer and investigate rumors of Khorezmian gold and a waterway to India along the former Oxus riverbed. In return, the Khivan ruler was provided with a promise of a permanent Russian guard for his own protection, while his family would be guaranteed the hereditary possession of the throne. Alexander Bekovich, a converted to Christianity Muslim prince and an officer of the elite guards regiment, led the expedition of 4,000 men, including infantry, cavalry, artillery, and a number of Russian merchants with 500 horses and camels. When the party arrived, it was greeted by the khan, who personally explained to Bekovich that it would not be possible to accommodate so many people in the city and suggested splitting the party into groups so that they would be properly housed and entertained in villages around the capital city. Anxious not to offend the khan, Bekovich ordered to disperse the force, which was immediately slaughtered by the Khivans. Bekovich was arrested, stripped of his uniform, and hacked to death in the front of the khan. About 40 men survived the bloodbath, most of whom were sold into slavery by the captors. In celebration of his triumph over the Russians, the khan dispatched the head of Bekovich to his Central Asian neighbor, the emir of Bokhara, while keeping the rest of the body on display in Khiva. The trophy was hastily returned, though, probably because the emir feared the wrath of the Russians on his own head. However, Russian retribution did not follow because Khiva was not at the top of Tsar Peter's agenda. The second Russian expedition of 5,000 men and 10,000 camels, which attempted to reach Khiva in the winter of 1839–1840, was defeated in the desert by marauding Turkmen tribes.[14]

In the middle of the eighteenth century, the Persian shah conquered the region. Under the Persians, Khiva became a desert hideout for slave traders, thieves, and pirates. Constant wars against the Turkmen, Bokharans, Iranians, and Kazakhs brought about Khiva's decline. Previously strong military positions were lost due to the destruction of the khanate's irrigation system and the desertion from its farmlands. In the nineteenth century, Khiva established control over the Turkmen tribes in the Merv area and in the territories of the present-day Khorezm region, Karakalpak republic, and northern Turkmenistan. By 1855, Khiva fell into decline and was almost entirely deserted. The land was used by Turkmens to raise their cattle in the former oases, and less than 900,000 people resided here on the eve of the Russian colonization in 1864. At that time, confrontations between Khiva and Russia were significant, mostly because of Khiva's involvement in plundering Russian caravans, kidnapping Russian subjects, and slaughtering two expeditions.

The Kokand Khanate was established around 1710 as a separate part of the Bokhara emirate in the western part of the Fergana Valley. Originally, Kokand consisted of a number of independent provinces. The village of Kokand, which became the capital of the principality, was rebuilt into a fortress, and, in 1760, Kokand became an important center with a caravansary, four schools, and about 20,000 families residing in the city. The growing significance of the khanate coincided with growing territorial demands, which extended to the possession of the neighboring Kyrgyz tribes. The Kyrgyz were defeated in most of the battles, their cities taken, and tribes pushed away to the mountains. Some tribes voluntarily joined the khanate after they were offered tax exemptions, good pastures, and their leaders were awarded with honorable titles and positions at the khan's court. Those who did not want to become subjects of the Kokand khanate and had no power to resist the expansion moved to the north in the mountainous area. The newly acquired territories were added to the khanate as a separate province. The separation of Kokand was based on the influx of Muslim refugees with Sogdian roots who fled north from China's occupied mountains. The migration to Kokand impacted the growth of the city of Tashkent, which was located to the north of the khanate. This population shift started to move slowly the center of the Uzbek society from Samarkand to Tashkent.

Initially, Tashkent did not belong to the Kokand khanate; rather, it was an important trading center governed by independent rulers. In 1799, Kokand troops occupied the city and forced it to join the khanate. The word *Tashkent* means stone village in Uzbek language. Tashkent, this modern capital of Uzbekistan, a thriving metropolis with population of 2.3 million, is one of the oldest cities in Central Asia. The time of its establishment is unknown. Some archeologists suggest that a legendary square citadel named Kanka founded between the fifth and third centuries b.c. was located on the territory of modern Tashkent.[15] The Tashkent oasis lies on the Chirchik River, a tributary of Syr Darya and fed by mountain melt water within sight of the western Tian-Shan Mountains. At different times, the city was controlled by the Chinese, Sassanians, Hephthalites, Turks, Arabs, and Mongols. The fertile valley irrigated by 50 canals turned the oasis into an exporter of cattle, horses, gold, silver, and precious stones. The seventh-century remains of the ruler's fortress were found in the Russian quarter of Tashkent. City walls and other fortifications were erected under the Samanid rule in the ninth and tenth centuries. At that time, the city became a rest area for traders and caravans on their way from China over deserts and mountains before continuing to Samarkand and Bokhara. Visitors described the city as a place of vineyards, craftsmen, and bazaars. The Qarakhanid rule, from the late tenth century, maintained such prosperity and gave the place its current name. Tashkent was famous for its pottery, bowls, saddles, fabrics, and carpets. After devastations inflicted by Genghis Khan, the renaissance came during the rule of Timur and his successors in the fourteenth and fifteenth centuries. During the next three centuries, Uzbeks, Kazakhs, Persians, Mongols, and Kyrgyz all clashed for possession of the city. The Russians learned about Tashkent at the end of the sixteenth century, when a Tashkent ruler sent gifts to the tsar of Moscow. Until the nineteenth century, Tashkent traded hands and was ruled by Kalmyks, Turkmens, and the khans of Kokand and Bokhara.

Combining great ambition with ruthless efficiency, Alim Khan, who ruled Kokand in the early nineteenth century, hired a mercenary army of Tajik highlanders to curb hostile tribal chiefs and dissenting religious groups. Alim Khan secured the entire valley, took neighboring cities, including Tashkent, and made Kokand a prosperous trading and religious center, competing with those of Khiva and Bokhara. After admitting Tashkent and other important agricultural territories to Kokand, the khanate became a large Central Asian state with a population of 3 million. The khan's brother Omar took Turkestan in 1814 and built steppe fortresses against the Kazakh tribes. The subjugation of Kyrgyz territories was concluded in the first quarter of the nineteenth century. The fortress Bishkek—named after a famous fighter Bishkek Batyr who was buried here—and the future capital of the Kyrgyz Republic were established in 1825.

Kokand's independence continued until 1842, when Emir Nasrullah of Bokhara moved his troops to Kokand, killed the Kokand khan Mohammed Ali, and occupied the city. During the same year, Kyrgyz nomads occupied the farmlands of the Kokand khanate. This dual occupation continued for several years, with Bokharan troops staying in the cities and nomads occupying the farmlands, until the nomads were driven out by the Bokharan soldiers in 1852, and the entire area was consolidated under the rule of the Bokharan emir.

The rest of the century was spent in fruitless attempts to resolve differences between fighting neighboring khanates worsened by Bokharan and Russian incursions. The rivalry of the khanates and endless killings of khans by their brothers or cousins undermined the resistance to the common enemy, tsarist Russia. For the entire period of its existence between 1709 until Russian conquest in the 1860s, Kokand was ruled by the same dynasty. The last khan of Kokand, Khudoyar (ruled 1845–1875), was removed three times from the throne and reinstalled with the support by the emir of Bokhara. Since 1850, Kokandi troops were more active in fighting the Russian invaders than their Bokharan or Khivan counterparts, but prevailing enemy forces toppled their northern forts one by one. Appeals for British military assistance did not receive responses. After Bokhara became dependent on Russia, there was no force to support Kokand; the khanate was weakened by in-fighting and was eventually annexed by Russia in 1875.

CULTURE AND CUSTOMS

All Central Asian states had similar levels of technology and did not create significant challenges to each other's external security. Modern technology was not known in late medieval Central Asia. Mechanical labor was not used, and work was primitive. Much of the hard labor was done by slaves, many of whom were Russian subjects who had been taken by attacking nomadic tribes from the deserts and sold to Central Asian emirates. There was also little progress in military hardware. Even though copper cannons, cast-iron cannonballs, and lead rifles appeared in Bokhara in the early nineteenth century, wars were still conducted primarily with bows, arrows, and swords. During these years, the main activity of people in Central Asia was still farming. They also made handicrafts and sold pottery, iron goods, fabrics, and paper at their bazaars. The physical layout of the cities and life on the streets did not change for centuries. Most towns contained similar labyrinths of blind alleys, introspective courtyards, and narrow streets; they differed only in the number of mosques and caravansaries. The street traffic consisted of laden camels, donkey-led carts, nobility on horseback, and turbaned merchants.[16]

The semi-nomadic tribes such as Kazakhs, Kyrgyz, and Mangits continued to live in nomadic settlements until the early twentieth century in a pastoral manner. Explorers who visited the area reported unhygienic and semi-primitive living conditions and the prevalence of superstitions, sorcery, and shamanism. The nomadic way of life on the periphery contrasted sharply with many developed centers of civilization emerging in the hinterland. However, even in the largest cities, attempts to control regular epidemics by quarantining people with diseases were unsuccessful because of the continuing circulation of filth in the sanitation systems, the cutting off of the water supply for months during the summers, and the use of tainted water for drinking and washing.

Most of the Central Asian population was illiterate. A religious Muslim education for boys from rich families was the only known form of education. Local ethnic and religious communities ran their own schools, which provided basic elementary—mostly religious—education, similar to other premodern Muslim societies. Education was conducted in formal schools associated with mosques or in private houses of educated or wealthy residents; there were no formal requirements for teachers. Usually a school was attended by about a dozen children. Teachers did not receive a regular salary but were supported by gifts from parents in the form of weekly donations of food and money. Additionally, the teachers received gifts of clothes when a child finished a book. Education was aimed at the transmission of basic literacy and proper models of behavior. The educational process was characterized by a rigorous discipline based on severe corporal punishment and rote memorization of texts. The education of a Central Asian boy began when his father took him to a teacher and left him behind with the ritual phrase common throughout the Islamic world, "You can beat him as long as you don't kill him; the meat is yours but the bones are ours." The schools had no formal division of classes or examinations. After memorizing the alphabet, the students were introduced to selected verses of the Koran. All instruction was oral. Rarely, students stayed in school for the duration because families could not afford to remove their boys from productive agricultural labor for a long period. Schools for girls in many ways paralleled those for boys. A similar kind of instruction was provided by the imams' wives and daughters.[17]

The pupils acquired knowledge of the basic elements of culture through interaction with learned older men. Practical knowledge and skills were received in the context of work. Artisans were trained in craft guilds. The master usually took an apprentice at age 12 and taught him the secrets of the trade during the next several years. The master was also responsible for teaching the child rules of proper behavior and knowledge about Muslim law and mysticism if he was literate. Good behavior meant that the apprentice was not rude to his master, did not walk in front of him, sit down without his permission, nor address him by his name.

Education in religious schools was intended to produce a certain understanding of Islam. Students did not have access to the sources and never studied the Koran, the traditions of the Prophet, nor even the jurisprudence. Instructions were based on commentaries produced by scholars and approved by the rulers. The religious police regularly patrolled cities and randomly stopped people to quiz them on some aspect of Islamic law or the Koran. Any man deemed ignorant of his faith was carried off, beaten, and fined as a warning to others. Mullahs were also empowered to search any house for traces of alcohol without warning and to arrest and fine anyone caught asleep during prayers or smoking in public. The emir's spies were sent on missions to discover seditious activities. Punishments were often extreme. A convicted murderer could expect anything from decapitation to mutilation to being thrown from the top of a minaret in a cloth sack.

In 1820, a Russian trader reported "sexual enormities" of the local inhabitants, the details of which he was ashamed to divulge. The emir of Bokhara was said to have kept 40 dancing boys in his court, where "all the horrors of Sodom and Gomorrah were practiced."[18] According to religious requirements, all shops, without exception, were barred and closed before lunchtime prayers on Friday. Men heading to the mosque were decked in rustling silk and high-heeled boots with turbans set in the traditional 40 folds and heavy khalats, loose long-sleeved silk or cotton robes. Women, on the other hand, wore darker cloths and were rarely seen. Girls over the age of puberty were hidden behind black horsehair veils and long, loose paranja robes, so that they could not be recognized. Women walking in the streets were never to be addressed, and if any of the emir's harem were to pass by, men were admonished to look in the opposite direction to avoid being beaten by the emir's guard.

Teahouses and bazaars were places of socialization and also served as open stages for dancing boys, professional storytellers, and even dentists, whose patients would kneel with their heads between an assistant's knees as the dentist used his body weight to lever out offending teeth. Bloodletting—thought to rival a visit to a saint's tomb as the most effective remedy for sickness—was also practiced in teahouses.[19] Ram fighting and juggling complemented this type of entertainment. Tea and concoction of grape syrup poured over crushed ice were favorite drinks.

RUSSIAN PRECOLONIZATION ACTIVITIES

Russian and Central Asian traders exchanged goods beginning in the sixteenth century, after an English merchant Anthony Jenkinson arrived in Central Asia from Moscow in 1558. Furs, leather, wooden and metal utensils from Russia, Asiatic horses, silk and cotton clothes, herbs, musk, and spices were exchanged. The slave trade became part of the relations in the seventeenth century, when Bokharan envoys met with the first tsar of the Romanov dynasty in 1619, and three Russian delegations visited the area. For the entire period until 1868, merchants bartered raw materials for Russian manufactured goods, including cotton, which was an important part of this trade. The region also exported wool, silk, carpets, and a few agricultural products. Money, in the form of silver, gold, and copper coins, was used inside the khanates, but generally the economy was not cash based.

The Jewish population of Central Asia played the most important role in building commercial relations between the khanates and Russia. The role of Central Asian Jews at that time was already so significant that commentaries to the Russian rules on preventing Jews from entering trade unions and other professional organizations adopted in 1833 specified that the existing restrictions did not apply to Asians arriving in Russia—who, unlike the Russian Jews, were allowed to reside and work where Russian Jewish subjects could not.[20] That same year, Bokharan Jews were granted the same rights to trade in Russia as Muslim merchants from Bokhara and Khiva. The pattern of equal legal treatment for subjects of the emir of Bokhara was preserved during the entire colonization period and contradicted domestic Russian legislation, which remained extremely anti-Semitic. In 1842, the Council of Ministers of the Russian Empire passed a special resolution extending rights applicable to foreign Jews to the Jews of Central Asia.

Commercial relations with Central Asia were equally important for Russia as the military and political presence in the region. During this period, Russia attempted to establish itself as a power in this part of the world and facilitated close contacts with the people of Central Asia. After a tragic expedition to Khiva in 1717, Russia switched its attention to the lands populated by the Kazakhs of the Little Horde for more than one hundred years due to their geographical proximity to the Russian border. In 1730, Khan Abul Khair sent a mission to the Russians and moved his people closer to the border, which, at that time, was on a line from the South Ural mountains to the north of the Caspian Sea. In 1748, the Kazakhs formalized their relations with the Russians as tributaries. At the end of the eighteenth century, the Kazakhs asked the Russians to let them continue using pastures in the steppes that belonged to Russia; the permission was granted, and a group of Kazakhs settled on abandoned Russian territories. In the middle of the eighteenth century, the border with the Russian Empire was formalized and gradually pushed south- and eastward. The line established in 1745 included all of northern Kazakhstan, comprising almost all possessions of the Little Horde and the northern and eastern steppes of the Middle Horde. Following the Russian advance, towns were established for military, administrative, trade, and communication purposes. Most of these towns—such as Akmolinsk, Semipalatinsk, Ust-Kamenogorsk, Pavlodar, Petropavlovk—are in Kazakhstan today. Further advancements occurred between 1820 and 1850, when semi-desert lands of eastern Kazakhstan were acquired and four Kazakh hordes were suppressed.

The Russian invasion met local resistance, causing the Russians to fight a number of rebellions and resistance movements. The Russians were supported by the Kazakhs who were experiencing a decrease of the available pasturage area, because the best pastures close to the rivers were taken by the migrating Russians. A series of anti-Russian movements between 1783 and 1797, usually in the form of intermittent raids and expeditions into Russian territories, the burning down of Cossack settlements, the plundering of trade outposts, and the killings of military guards were instigated by the lesser local nobility, which achieved a relatively greater position in the society due to the weakening of Kazakh khans.[21] These attacks were more of a nuisance than a real danger to the Russians in the border areas. Occasionally, the rebellion leaders would be imprisoned by the Russians but then would be released upon the payment of ransoms by Kazakh khans. A relatively strong anti-Russian movement in the second quarter of the nineteenth century was led by Kenesary (1802–1847), a khan of the Middle Horde. He attempted to unite with the then-independent Tashkent against the Russians, but he was imprisoned by the Tashkent ruler and released only after the intervention of the khan of Khiva. Kenesary fought his war by destroying trade along all of the caravan routes in northern Kazakhstan and those leading to Central Asia. The success of his racketeering made him popular among the Kazakhs, and he was elected khan by the Little Horde. Later, Kenesary was supported by parts of the Great Horde as well. When the Russians intensified their military campaign against Kenesary, they pushed him out of the northern part of Kazakhstan. Kenesary discredited himself during an unsuccessful attack on Kokand, where he hoped to replenish his resources and tried to turn to the mountain pastures of the Kyrgyz. Instead, he was defeated, imprisoned, and killed in 1847. By the end of the 1860s, the Russians had acquired the steppe and semi-desert lands around the Caspian Sea, had reached the Aral Sea, and established themselves along the Chinese border in the lower Syr Darya and around Lake Issyk Kul.

In regard to the Turkistan area of Central Asia, Russia did not undertake any military or political activities in the eighteenth century. Advisors to Catherine the Great did not have a common opinion about whether colonial activities in Central Asia would be useful and necessary. Many believed that Russia did not have the means to support a speedy movement in the southeast. The desire of different tribes to acquire Russian citizenship was seen as an attempt to obtain benefits from the Russian crown without giving anything significant in return. In 1825, several constitutional projects were proposed in St. Petersburg; all of them viewed Russia as an undivided empire with orthodox Christianity as the official religion and Russian as the only language. According to these proposals, Central Asia was supposed to be included in the empire, and all disagreeing native people who resisted the rule of the Russian tsar were subject to a forceful resettlement in European Russia.

Russia reestablished its interest in advancing in the Turkistan area of Central Asia in the middle of the nineteenth century, mostly in response to British activities in India and Afghanistan. One by one, the ancient caravan towns and khanates of the former Silk Road fell to the Russians. The advance was conducted by Cossacks, who moved the Russian frontier closer to India. In 1819, a Russian delegation was sent to the khan of Khiva to deliver lavish gifts and a message of friendship and commerce. The Russian tsar offered the khan the opportunity to acquire luxury goods from Europe and the latest in Russian technology in exchange for 3,000 Russian slaves, men, women, and children who were kept there. These were the survivors of the 1717 expedition and those settlers and soldiers who were kidnapped or captured by Kyrgyz and Kazakh tribes along the Russian border. The issue of rescuing Russian slaves and prisoners was often used to justify Russian incursions. In 1838, a unit consisting of 5,200 infantry, cavalry, and artillery was formed to attack Khiva. The attack was averted by the British, who convinced the khan to release the Russian prisoners.

BRITISH INVOLVEMENT

Great Britain unsuccessfully attempted to establish a presence in Central Asia. In 1834, a British intelligence officer, explorer, and writer Arthur Conolly (1807–1842) published an account of his trip from Moscow to Herat through the Caucasus and Central Asia. In his accounts, Conolly expressed the idea to unite the three quarrelling khanates of Turkistan—Khiva, Bokhara, and Kokand—bring Christian civilization into a barbaric region, abolish slavery, and make the khanates a natural protection (with friendly Afghanistan) against the Russian threat from the north.[22] It appears that Conolly introduced the term *The Great Game* to describe the struggle between the British and Russian Empires for domination over Central Asia. Conolly's idea became popular in London society, and political efforts were undertaken for its implementation.

British activities intensified after the first Anglo-Afghan war of 1838–1842. Army officers and diplomats were operating in Central Asian states under the cover of the British East India Company; they were trying to forge alliances with local rulers against the Russians, whose advance into Central Asia was giving rise to fears about their future intentions, and reassure the rulers over British movements on their southern borders. In 1838, a group of Englishmen traveled all over the Khiva khanate. Upon their arrival in Khiva, the men were accused of espionage, and three of them were hanged. Charles Stoddart (1806–1842), a colonel of the British army, was captured by the emir of Bokhara, Nasrullah Khan, in December 1838, and was sent to Bokhara. The khan, who was fearful and suspicious of foreigners, held Stoddart in a 16-foot-deep vermin-infested pit beneath the mud-built citadel, where Stoddart was tortured and tormented for over three years. Stoddart's treatment depended on the rise and fall of the British Empire. When the British took Kabul in 1839, Stoddart was permitted to live in the house of the police chief. After threats to execute him on the spot, Stoddart became a Muslim and was rewarded with house arrest. In 1841, Arthur Conolly, then a captain of the Sixth Bengal Light Cavalry, undertook a single-person rescue mission to free Stoddart while traveling in Central Asia on government business and conducting a reconnaissance mission. Conolly was also arrested by the emir of Bokhara on charges of spying for the British Empire, and in June 1842, together with Charles Stoddart, he was publicly beheaded in the central market square of the city, where both prisoners were ordered to dig their own graves.[23]

In response, Great Britain concluded a peace treaty with the emir of Afghanistan, Dost Mukhammed, in 1855. Armed by the British, Dost Mukhammed annexed part of the Bokhara emirate, which became the Afghan provinces of Southern Turkistan populated by ethnic Tajiks and Uzbeks. British diplomatic pressure on Turkistan increased during the Crimean War (1853–1856). England's ally Turkey was used to create a regional military coalition aimed at fighting Russia. The plan and British military assistance were declined by local rulers mostly because of their isolation and ignorance of world affairs. The khans and emirs of Central Asia believed in their superiority over any enemy. Peter Hopkirk gives an example that emphasizes the isolation of the khans and their lack of understanding of the relative size of Britain, Russia, and their own small kingdoms. In the middle of the nineteenth century, the khan of Khiva asked a visiting British officer, "How many guns does Russia have?" The Englishman replied that he did not know for sure, but it would be a very large number indeed. "I have twenty," replied the khan proudly.[24]

Isolation secured Central Asia from a colonial invasion, and modern powers did not threaten Central Asian rulers until the middle of the nineteenth century, when the growing competition between Great Britain and the Russian Empire for regional domination and control over Afghanistan provoked Russia's economic and military intrusion.

NOTES

1. Beatrice Manz, *The Rise and Rule of Tamerlane* (Cambridge and New York: Cambridge University Press, 1999), 196.
2. Krader (1996), 64.
3. Francis Skrine and Edward Ross, *The Heart of Asia: A History of Russian Turkestan and the Central Asian Khanates from the Earliest Times* (London and New York: Routledge Courzon, 2004), 284.
4. Gregoire Frumkin, *Archeology in Soviet Central Asia* (Leiden, The Netherlands: Brill, 1970), 87.
5. From the sixteenth century, Bokhara grew at Samarkand's expense. Consequences of the end of the Silk Road trade, earthquake damage, looting, and in-fighting left Samarkand virtually empty until the Bokharan emir repopulated it in 1770 by repairing the houses, the citadel, and the city wall.
6. Krader (1996), 118.
7. Soucek (2000), 152.
8. Treasury lands were part of the national property formally belonging to the khan. These lands could not be divided or sold.
9. Private property on the land was clearly defined only among the agricultural people. The Turkmens, Kyrgyz, and Kazakhs, still partly nomadic, identified all their lands as communal. Individual private ownership was not practiced among them.
10. The khan's waiter was also the chief irrigation officer.
11. According to Svat Soucek, *A History of Inner Asia* (Cambridge and New York: Cambridge University Press, 2000), 142, the change of the ruler's title from khan to emir meant a shift from a tribal Turko-Mongol to an Islamic legitimization, having its roots in the prestigious Arabic title of the *caliph amir,*

which meant "commander of the believers." Other scholars suggest that the Mangit rulers called themselves emirs because that was their original identity. Emirs were tribal and military leaders of non-Genghisid ancestry.

12. Soucek (2000), 154.

13. All three khanates remained relatively tolerant of the Jews, whose assimilation was generally limited to a language change and garment adjustments. Because there was no influx of population due to trade or conquest until the Russian colonization, the Jewish society remained closed until the late nineteenth century, when the Ashkenazi Jews from the Russian Empire came to Turkestan. During the entire period, Jews were involved in trade, medicine, and translation. They worked as dyers, cobblers, and in other crafts. The restrictions applied to positions in the areas of administrative, fiscal, judicial, and military service.

14. For more details, see Peter Hopkirk, *The Great Game: The Struggle for Empire in Central Asia* (New York: Kodansha International, 1995).

15. Wolfgang Scharlipp, *Die Fruehen Tuerken in Zentralasien* (Darmstadt, Germany: Wissenschaftliche Buchgesellschaft, 1999), 74.

16. Frye (1996), 116.

17. Adeeb Khalid, *The Politics of Muslim Cultural Reform* (Berkeley: University of California Press, 1998), 27.

18. Alexander Lehmann, *Reise nach Buchara und Samarkand in den Jahren 1841 und 1842* (Osnabrueck, Germany: Biblio Verlag, 1969), 164.

19. Khalid (1998), 53.

20. Shterenshis (2002), 119.

21. Krader (1996), 100.

22. Arthur Conolly, *Journey to the North of India; Overland from England through Russia, Persia, and Afghanistan* (London: R. Bentley, 1834).

23. Hopkirk (1992), 182.

24. Hopkirk (1992), 215.

5

Russian Colonization (1865–1917)

In the second half of the nineteenth century, when other countries already had colonies overseas, Russia advanced into Central Asia. A complicated interconnection of strategic political objectives and economic interests of the Russian Empire in Asia were reasons for the colonization campaign. Before the 1860s, Russian leaders did not consider Central Asia to be of strategic value, because the frontiers and access to Asian markets were already secured after the Kazakh steppe was subdued. Since the early nineteenth century, Russians began to establish fortresses in the northern part of Central Asia and build trade relations with Bokhara. Russia was obtaining cotton—which accounted for two-thirds of all Central Asian exports to Russia—and other raw materials, while selling metallurgical products to Central Asian states. In 1859 to 1861, several government conferences on issues of Central Asian politics were held in St. Petersburg, and the Asian Department was created at the Russian Foreign Ministry in 1861. Its head, a 28-year-old diplomat of the rank of major general, Nikolai Ignatyev, thought that by conquering England in Asia, Russia would be able to resolve its problems with Europe, and he pushed for an immediate offensive in Central Asia. Originally, it had been hoped that cordial relations and commercial cooperation might be established with the individual khanates by means of alliances, thereby avoiding bloodshed, expense, and any risk of provoking British reaction, but military commanders insisted that this was naive. Ignatyev said that rulers of Central Asia were untrustworthy and incapable of keeping any agreement; he thought that conquest was the only way of keeping the British out. This view gained the support of the war minister, Count Milyutin.

POLITICS OF CONQUEST

The conquest was prepared by the advancement of small Russian forces, which seized Turkistani oases at almost no cost of lives and money. The entire lower Syr Darya fell into Russian hands, and the frontier was moved to the edges of Turkistan after the Kokand fortress of Aq-Mosque (now Kzyl-Orda) was taken in 1853. In 1854, the southern coast of Balkhash Lake was under Russian control, and the city of Verny (now Almaty) was founded. Ill-trained and poorly armed troops of Central Asian khanates and emirates could not resist the Russian army, which had modern warfare and recent experience of fighting Muslim tribes in the Caucasus Mountains.[1]

The military part of the colonization was relatively brief, lasting only 20 years and ending in 1884 with several decisive battles between 1865 and 1868. After the siege of Tashkent in 1865 and the taking of Samarkand in 1868, the khan of Bokhara submitted to Russian protection, the khanate of Khiva was conquered in 1873, and the Kokand khanate was accessed in 1876. The Russian conquest of Central Asia was completed by 1884 with the acquisition of Merv, a fertile oasis and a pre-Islamic historic town located close to Afghanistan's border and British India.

The need to defend Russian caravans and local tribes residing on the Russian territory from the "barbarians'" attacks was used as a justification for the invasion. Strong diplomatic British support to Poland, which revolted against Russia in 1863, scared the Russian emperor and urged him to finalize his expansion plans into Asia. In November 1864, Alexander II signed all of the necessary directives defining two major goals of Russia's Central Asian policy—to prevent Great Britain from including Central Asia into the sphere of its interests and to satisfy the interests of the growing Russian economy and trade. These goals were to be achieved by building Russian strongholds in Asia. The military was named as the main force in conducting territorial acquisitions in Turkistan. Avoiding direct hostilities, the Russians started with local operations at the Kokand borders, and moved south along the Syr Darya toward the Kyrgyz Mountains. The khan of Kokand begged for military assistance from the British; however, this was politely declined because of the doctrine of masterly inactivity, which guided British policy in Central Asia. Encouraged by the British failure to respond to the khan of Kokand's plea for help, the Russians advanced further. Russian foreign minister, Prince Alexander Gorchakov, explained Russian views in his 1864 memorandum:

> The position of Russia in Central Asia is that of all civilized states which are brought into contact with half-savage nomad populations possessing no fixed social organization. In such cases it always happens that the more civilized state is forced, in the interests of the security of its frontiers and its commercial relations, to exercise a certain ascendancy over those whose turbulent and unsettled character make them undesirable neighbors.[2]

Most British leaders understood Russia's need to advance in this region. In 1864, Lord George Clarendon stated,

> Russia's policy in Central Asia is framed in the same way as ours in India; she is compelled to move gradually from the North to the South just as we were obliged to do in our march from the South to the North. She is doing services to civilization, and we do not care much even if she takes Bokhara.[3]

Prince Gorchakov responded, stating that Russia had its own interests, its activities in Turkistan did not differ from English actions in India or Afghanistan, and the small military units simply defend the empire's border and will not go further than Chimkent.

THE SIEGE OF TASHKENT

In early 1865, Tsar Alexander II decided to establish the Turkistan Province on the occupied territory between the estuary of the Syr Darya, the Aral Sea, and Issyk Kul Lake and made it subordinate to the governor general of Orenburg (a Russian province bordering Central Asia). The task of the occupation regime was to collect taxes and support troops, which were preparing for the second colonial war. General Mikhail Chernyaev was appointed as the province's military governor. While the Turkistan province was governed from the Russian city of Orenburg, it was obvious that Tashkent was the only place that could become the center for the Russian administration in Central Asia. Tashkent was the richest city of Central Asia and had 100,000 inhabitants. Tashkent prospered because of its abundance of natural resources, the entrepreneurship of its merchants, and its proximity to Russia, with which it had long traded. In five months after the Turkistan province's establishment, General Chernyaev, the commander of the Kokand frontier region—under his own initiative and contradicting the opinion of the tsar and the government, who were worried about the future British reaction—undertook the Tashkent offensive.

Claiming the need to defend Tashkent from a seizure by the Bokharans, who were fighting the khan of Kokand, Chernyaev assembled a force of 1,300 men sufficient to take Tashkent with 30,000 defenders. At this time, the city was surrounded by a 16-mile-long defense wall with 12 gates and 50 cannons. Chernyaev hoped that, in case of success, his disobedience would be overlooked; he ignored orders to not attack Tashkent and started the offensive on June 15, 1865. The defenders were spread along the wall and were unable to concentrate. The Russians were better trained, armed, and led and knew that, once they were in the city, they would find sympathizers among the population. The smaller force made a feint attack designed to draw off a large number of defenders, while the main force advanced toward one of the city gates—where, according to reconnaissance information, the wall was at its lowest. At 2:30 A.M., Russian soldiers unloaded the scaling ladders from their camels and bore them to the walls beside the gates, which were to be attacked. By accident, they encountered prisoners, who showed them a secret passage under the wall. The defenders were taken by surprise, and the Russians opened the gate and entered the city within minutes and without losses. The superior firepower of Chernyaev eliminated the resistance, and, by afternoon, the Russians were in possession of the city.

Understanding the risk of having the city reduced to rubble, the city elders submitted on the next day and gave Chernyaev the honorific title of Lion of Tashkent. General Chernyaev accepted the surrender terms on behalf of Tsar Alexander II, although he had no authority to do so, and appointed himself military governor of Tashkent. Chernyaev paid a visit to Tashkent's principal Muslim leader at his home, bowing respectfully as he entered, and pledged himself to allow the city elders to run the city's affairs as before and not to interfere in their religious life. Aware of harsh taxes imposed by the khan of Kokand, he freed everyone from paying taxes for a year—an immensely popular move—and rode alone through the streets and bazaars talking to ordinary people and accepting bowls of tea from strangers.[4] The emir of Bokhara attempted to resist the Russians, detaining the Russian mission in Bokhara and demanding that the Russians leave Tashkent. The emir's people harassed Russian troops but were unable to stand up to a regular European army.

When the tsar learned about Chernyaev's action, he called it "a glorious affair" and awarded Chernyaev and his men. Russian foreign minister Alexander Gorchakov named the taking of Tashkent a "civilized mission" and insisted that "Asiatic people respect nothing but visible and palpable force."[5] St. Petersburg newspapers declared the occupation of Tashkent to be no more than temporary, insisting that it had been done strictly to protect Tashkent from Bokharan annexation, and, once the danger was over, independence and the khan's rule would be restored. The British government protested

Ministry. Khiva presented the most problems to Russia. Its involvement in trade with Russia was minimal, and the khan's subjects never stopped their traditional practices of plundering caravans engaged in trade with Russia and encouraging Russia's Kazakh subjects to revolt against Russia.[11] After sending several expeditions to punish robbers who had been attacking Russian trade caravans, von Kaufman demanded Khan Sayid Muhammad Rahim Bandur II (ruled 1864–1910) of Khiva to punish the robbers, restore stolen property, guarantee free entry for Russian merchants, and liberate all Russian and Bokharan captives. To convince the khan of Khiva, von Kaufman reminded him of the fate of Bokhara and Kokand, where similar acts had taken place. The situation worsened because Turkmen tribes continued to disrupt trade in the city of Krasnovodsk on the eastern shore of the Caspian Sea and gave refuge to Russian Kazakh fugitives. The British administration in India recognized the fairness of Russian demands and refused to mediate between Khiva and Russia. In May 1873, a full-scale offensive against Khiva began. Facing the advance of Russian troops, the khan attempted to avert the catastrophe by liberating 21 Russian prisoners kept in Khiva, but von Kaufman said that he would negotiate after capturing the capital. Two days later, the khan who fled to the Turkmens sent his cousin to von Kaufman to accept unconditional surrender, but von Kaufman requested meeting with the khan in person and entered the Khivan capital with 12,300 troops. The news of Khiva's capture was the first message sent to St. Petersburg from Tashkent through the newly built telegraph line. After receiving Russian assurances of personal security and return to the throne, the khan came back to Khiva and surrendered. As a trophy, the royal archive was sent to St. Petersburg, and the khan's throne was shipped to Moscow.

The khan was restored to rule under Russian protection from Turkmen tribes and other enemies by Governor von Kaufman. During the following three months of Russian occupation, von Kaufman organized the khanate's administration because the khan was no longer an independent ruler. Anti-Russian government officials were dismissed and exiled to Russia, and a council consisting of three Russian officers, a merchant from Tashkent, and three Khivan dignitaries became the highest state authority. Von Kaufman personally appointed four Russian members of the council and approved the remaining three Khivan members. Sessions of the council were held not in the capital but outside of the city in the vicinity of the Russian camp. The council abolished slavery and introduced strict measures against disobedience. Former slaves, who were mostly Persians, received full legal status and were allowed to live anywhere in the khanate or to leave it. The Khivan occupation coincided with military operations against the Turkmen tribes in the southwest of the khanate. The Yomuts, the largest tribe, which included almost half of the entire Turkmen population of Khiva, was slaughtered together with their livestock; their settlements and crops were devastated by Russian troops.

TREATIES WITH THE KHANS

The Russo-Khivan treaty, which weakened the khanate even further by making it a Russian protectorate, was concluded on August 12, 1873. The Russian authorities had no problem negotiating with Khan Sayid Muhammad Rahim Bandur II of Khiva, who owed his throne to the Russian governor. The khan even declared himself the obedient servant of the Russian emperor. The treaty restricted the khan's right to conduct foreign and military policy without the consent of the governor general. A permanent Russian garrison was placed in the capital city, and borders between Russia and Khiva were delineated. A part of the Khivan territory was transferred to the emir of Bokhara as a sign of appreciation for his loyalty during the Khivan campaign. The treaty gave Russians extensive commercial privileges, including the right to own real estate in Khiva, priority over Khivan creditors, and transfer of all civil and criminal cases in which a Russian was involved to the jurisdiction of Russian authorities. Russia got control over navigation on the Amu Darya, established trading posts along its banks, and the Khivan government became responsible for the safety of Russian subjects. Unlike in other parts of Central Asia, Khiva did not experience an influx in the Russian population, partially because Khiva was on the edge of Turkistan and was of little military importance since it did not have neighboring states that might threaten Russia.

The majority of the Turkmen tribes, however, did not recognize the treaty and continued to fight against Russia. Being accustomed to the climate and terrain, the Turkmens made unexpected attacks and disappeared in the desert. The essence of Russian military actions took the form of extermination operations. In 1878 to 1879, Russian troops took fortresses in the Caspian area, and, in 1881, Ashgabat (capital of present-day Turkmenistan) was taken. The brutality of the Russian attackers exceeded expectations. All city defenders, including those who laid down their arms, were killed, and those who tried to run away were caught and murdered. After the defeat of Ashgabat's defenders, the Turkmen resistance declined, and inhabitants of the Turkmen oases accepted Russian citizenship.

The conclusion of the Russo-Khivan treaty and the establishment of a special regime for Russian trade in Khiva required relations with other parts of Central Asia to be brought in accordance. For this purpose, the 1868 treaty with Bokhara was replaced by another on August 28, 1873, which remained in force until 1917. In general, this treaty followed the agreement with Khiva, reaffirming the borders, permitting Russian subjects to engage in Bokharan industry and possess real estate, opening the Amu Darya to Russian ships, and limiting the access of Bokharan caravansaries to the territory of Turkistan (but not throughout the entire Russian Empire as formerly). Unlike the treaty with Khiva, Bokhara was not declared a dependency formally and continued to exist legally as a fully sovereign state. Despite this fact, Russia treated Bokhara as its protectorate, and Britain recognized Bokhara's inclusion in Russia's sphere of interests. The emir abolished the right on independent relations with foreign states, and his agreements with the neighbors required a prior Russian approval. On several occasions, Russian troops were deployed in Bokhara to suppress disorders. Emir Muzaffar of Bokhara was the most powerful monarch remaining Central Asia; he prevented a complete takeover of Bokhara by Russia because of good relations with Russian elites in St. Petersburg and in Tashkent, who frequently received personal gifts and public donations from the emir.

Bokhara's independence gradually diminished. In 1885, Bokhara became part of Russia's customs boundary, and a Russian political agency modeled after the British experience of dealing with the princely states of India was established next to Bokhara city. The political agent was appointed by the governor general, and his duty was to promote Russian influences in the emirate. The agency was not created in Khiva, and all relations were conducted through the chief of the agency's Amu Darya department, who served as a part-time Russian diplomatic representative in Khiva. The Transcaspian railway that was built in the 1880s to connect major Central Asian cities with the Russian ports on the Caspian Sea also cut through Bokhara. A new treaty granted Russian sovereignty on the railroad and at all stations along it. Although Russia was present in the region with 40,000 troops, it could not immediately terminate the khanates of Khiva and Bokhara because they were not acquired until the middle of 1920s, when British influence in the area became minimal.

In eight years after the fall of Tashkent, all three khans became Russia's vassals, and a large part of their territory became a Russian province. Popular resistance continued after the occupation because of Russian violence, exploitation, and discrimination of the native people. In 1868, Emir's son Abdulmalik led the Tashkent uprising, and a wave of public unrest shocked the Fergana Valley and the Kokand khanate in 1873. Many Kyrgyz took part in the unrests, mostly because of their internal fighting among the tribes and growing discrimination by the khan. The rebellions in Kokand forced its Khan Khudoyar to seek refuge in the Russian mission. The Russians helped him to escape the khanate and find asylum in Tashkent, then the center of Russian regional administration. Disorders continued until Russia fully annexed this territory and established the Russian military administration. Polot Khan, the Kyrgyz leader of the uprising, was hung on the bazaar in the settlement where he was caught. The unrest stopped completely as soon as 400 other activists were arrested, brought to Kokand, and hung there. Southern mountainous territories populated by the Kyrgyz were taken with force and cruelty, causing many Kyrgyz to migrate to China and Afghanistan. "Law and order in Asia are directly related to the number of beaten up people and cut off heads," said Russian General Mikhail Skobelev,[12] who pacified the Kyrgyz and suppressed the Andijon uprising of 1876. As a result, on February 2, 1876, Tsar Alexander II signed the decree on the termination of the Kokand khanate, and the Fergana province was created instead. Because of his experience in suppressing local people, Skobelev was appointed Fergana's governor.

FIGHT OVER AFGHANISTAN

After conquering all three khanates, Russia advanced to the Afghan border. Despite the fact that, after establishing itself in Central Asia, Russia did not want to risk a new war against Great Britain, London was alarmed, and Queen Victoria was proclaimed Empress of India, manifesting the British intention to remain a major player in the area. Negotiations between Russia and Great Britain were conducted during the winter of 1872–1873, resulting in the conclusion of a treaty on the division of the sphere of influence. The treaty established the border between Bokhara and Afghanistan along the Amu Darya. All of the territory to the south of the Amu Darya was recognized as the English sphere of influence, and territories to the north went to Russia. The agreement with England untied Russia's hands and allowed it to subdue the Khiva khanate.

After pacifying the Kyrgyz tribes and taking all of Turkmenistan in 1877, Russia intended to invade India and sent a mission to Kabul to prepare for an 1878 invasion in Afghanistan. Great Britain was not sure that its possessions in India would be secured and, in 1883, commanded an Afghan military expedition, which fought in southern Turkistan for two years before these troops were defeated and disarmed. The border between Afghanistan and Russian Central Asia was finalized in 1887.

For the next 10 years, Russia fought diplomatic wars to gain recognition of its acquisitions. In 1895, the Agreement on Pamir was signed between Russia and Great Britain. In 1907, the Anglo-Russian Convention was concluded, which obligated both countries to respect each other's zones of interest and created the Afghan corridor, an elongated strip of territory between Pamir and Kashmir in the Wakhan Valley as a buffer between Russia and then British India. For the British, the convention failed to fulfill the aim of halting Russian expansion in areas strategically important to the defense of India and hindered the British quest for security on the eve of World War I.[13]

POPULAR RESISTANCE

After the conquest, popular movements lost their initiative and became local responses to real or fancied injustices inflicted by Russian authorities regardless of the scale of the uprising and the number of atrocities. Only Turkmens continued to fight the Khiva khanate and the Russians for a reason of vital importance—land and water. Protests against Russian dominations were in the form of sporadic rural riots as a response to the ongoing industrialization and impoverishment. Often, the natives protested by refusing to pay taxes, ignoring local elections, attacking government officials, and burning government buildings. About 200 antigovernment protest actions were registered in Fergana in 1880 to 1890.

The first serious outbreak of mass disorders, based on cultural anguish, occurred in 1892, during the cholera epidemics in Tashkent. Being unaware of sanitation rules, the locals opposed Russian orders to stop the burials of victims of epidemics in city cemeteries. Burials of those who died from the infection were allowed in special places far away from the city with minimal rites. Local residents viewed this requirement as discriminatory and antireligious, believing rumors that Russian physicians distributed the infection to poison the natives. The mob beat the Russian city commandant and killed 80 inhabitants. To prevent further anti-Russian pogroms, the governor sent troops; 10 instigators were killed and 28 other participants were sentenced to imprisonment. Following these events, the Statute on Enhanced Protection of Public Order was adopted, which extended the rights of local administrations, including the right to use military force to suppress antigovernment uprisings. One Russian general described the essence of this statute as: "The harder you hit them, the longer they remain quiet."[14]

Russian rule met almost no resistance, except in the Fergana Valley, where insurgents led by members of the Muslim mystical brotherhoods, the Sufi orders, attacked the native population and caused little trouble to the Russians. The administration did not pay attention to these disturbances.[15] The first large anti-Russian revolt occurred in 1898, when approximately 2,000 followers of Madali Ishan, a local religious leader, armed with knives attacked Russian barracks in Andijon while the soldiers slept and cut the throats of 22 people and injured 20 others. After 15 minutes, the attackers were dispersed by the Russians and fled, leaving behind their own dead and wounded. The Andijon uprising was badly planned and organized and failed to materialize in other cities. Although localized, the participants of the revolt divided into separate groups of up to 400 people in each and continued to attack Russian military garrisons during the next two weeks. The administration, which considered the native population generally friendly to its rule, was surprised by the attack and arrested 550 people, of whom 18 were hanged and 360 were exiled to Siberia. The village where the cleric used to preach was replaced by a Russian settlement. The attack reaffirmed Russian fears about the brutality of Islam. In a memorandum to the tsar, Turkistan's governor general Sergei Dukhovskoi wrote: "Islam…excludes all possibilities of a complete moral assimilation of our present Muslim subjects with us. A pure Muslim, strongly believing in the letter of the Koran, cannot be a sincere and trusted friend of a Christian."[16]

Most of the authors name three major reasons for the uprising: strong conservative religious feelings against the infidel rule; the disruption of the local economy caused by the increase in cotton cultivation, which made the local population vulnerable to fluctuations in world prices and dependent on credits; and the indigenous political struggle, because Russia's takeover weakened the power of tribal leadership.[17] The motivation of the participants was not strong, and they made no specific complaints about Russian rule.

The next wave of popular unrest, known as the rebellion of 1916, began in Kazakhstan because of land seizures, tax increases, and horse requisitioning for the Russian army fighting at the fronts of World War I. Although the colonization slowed during the war, the situation of the dispossessed nomads was so desperate on the eve of the war that even the limited colonization of 1915–1916 exceeded the tolerance of the region. "The Kyrgyz no longer have anything but the summits of the mountains, where there is no pastures any more," stated one petition to the governor general.[18] After the Russian government decided to draft Central Asian Muslims, traditionally free from mobilizations, into labor units to serve in the European Russia, the uprising extended to the Fergana Valley and cities of Andijon and Khojent, where 50,000 people took part in the revolt. Local officials and some Russians were killed, and communications facilities were destroyed. A military expedition smashed the rebels, but other disorders erupted throughout Turkistan. In Kyrgyzstan, where Russian army units were absent, local Russian colonists formed armed groups and preventively massacred the native population. The Kyrgyz struck back, and for almost a month, the region was an arena of bloody fighting in which 2,000 Russian settlers were murdered by the natives and even greater numbers of locals were killed. All natives who participated in the revolt were resettled from their lands into the mountains of eastern Kyrgyzstan; their villages were torched, and lands were given to the newcomers from Russia. Approximately 250,000 Kazakhs, Uzbeks, and Kyrgyz fled to Chinese Turkistan, Afghanistan, or died of famine. The government ignored expressions of public anger, which were directed primarily against the results of the Russian colonization policies[19] and, instead of confronting these tensions, suppressed them.

POLICIES OF COLONIZATION

The history of colonial expansion in Turkistan is a nonstop attempt of the tsarist regime to exploit the area's resources. Russian social policy was aimed at the formation of pro-Russian elites in Central Asia and the preservation of the status quo of the local population. Russian methods were selective and depended on particular circumstances. For purposes of nonintervention in local people's affairs, the Russian administration did not allow Russians to purchase land and prohibited Russian settlements outside of towns. To corrupt local leaders, some ruling families received noble titles and admission to the Russian armed forces; warlords who fought against Russia were usually pensioned and settled with dignity in European Russia. Changes in property relations introduced by the 1886 statute undermined the economic power of tribal chiefs. Later, the elections for administrative positions created a new class of local administrators. Wealthy merchants interested in the development of economic ties between Russia and Central Asia served as intermediaries between the colonial regime and the local society; they were trained in Russian language, technology, management, and how to navigate the tsarist bureaucracy.

The program of Russification was undertaken. The Directorate of Learning Institutions in Turkistan was established in 1870 to manage schools aimed at teaching the people the Russian language, handcrafts, and agriculture without interfering in traditional educational affairs. Children were taught arithmetic, history, and geography. The Russians also brought medical knowledge and built hospitals, medical offices, and pharmacies and gave medical treatment to local people.[20] The Russian presence changed the urban landscape of Central Asian towns. Russian quarters were kept separate from (but adjacent to) the original parts of the cities, and they were built according to a plan with straight wide streets contrasting to the labyrinthine neighborhoods of the traditional towns. In some nomadic territories, these were the first examples of urban life. All present-day major Central Asian cities—Almaty, Bishkek, and Ashgabat—were established as Russian settlements. Samarkand was converted into a new European-style city with radial streets; parks were established, and a bank, post office, theater, and other buildings were built as well. The Russians encouraged artistic shows and performances, contrary to the views of the religious fanatics.

Educated Russians viewed their presence in Asia as part of the greater European imperial expansion of the nineteenth century and hoped to replace the arbitrary despotism of local rulers with a good government, pacification of the countryside, and an increase in trade and prosperity. The growth of trade was seen as the key to the future prosperity. For this purpose, lower levels of taxation were introduced in Turkistan, and biannual trade fairs were organized in Tashkent.

Economic development and Russian colonization brought other ethnic groups to Central Asia. Ukrainians, Byelorussians, Poles, Germans, Armenians, and Jews together with the Russians took part in exploring Central Asia. In the early twentieth century, the largest ethnicities in Turkistan were the Kazakhs and Kyrgyz (43%), Uzbeks (35%), Russians (10%), Tajiks (7%), and Turkmen (5%). On the territory of Kazakhstan, the Russians made up 30 percent of the population. The Russian government attempted to transform

Central Asian colonies into regular Russian provinces and into inalienable parts of Russia. In 1912, non-native people comprised 9.2 percent of the entire Turkistan population because Russia's military advance to Central Asia was followed by a large resettlement of Russian subjects, mainly into Kazakhstan; in 1917, there were 2 million Russian resettlers there.[21]

Turkistan gradually moved from a ground of diplomatic and military competition with Britain to a resource of raw materials, a market for manufacturers, and a land reserve for resettling peasants. Colonial politics made Central Asia the source of income for the Russian Empire. Between 1851 and 1861, Central Asian trade with Russia tripled, and Russian exports to the region increased sixfold. In the 1870s, Turkistan had more than covered its expenses. It had contributed to the expenditures of the troops stationed there and even provided funds to Russia's administrations in the western Siberian provinces.

Turkistan's economic contribution to the Russian economy increased rapidly with its integration into the Empire, after which the region was called "a jewel in the crown of the Russian Tsar."[22] Economic developments not only enriched the Russians, but local merchants and officials as well. The emir of Bokhara profited from commerce and gifts given to him by Russian agents. The telegraph arrived in Tashkent in 1873, and the first bank opened in 1875. Railway transportation connected the region with major trade centers of the continent, and, by the end of the nineteenth century, the railroad linked all major oases, cities, river valleys, and Caspian Sea ports with industrial centers in Russia. The railroad became a tool for integrating, defending, and pacifying the region. In 1893, commodities were not moved by rail; by 1897, the immediate traffic equaled 250,000 tons; in 1909, the total movement of goods exceeded 1,250,000 tons.

The tsarist government supported the production of cotton, which became the main agricultural product through improvements in irrigation, transportation, and credits to small farmers to achieve independence for the Russian textile industry from cotton imports from the United States and India. The amount of land under cotton cultivation between 1886 and 1914 increased 46 times. In 1900, Central Asia supplied 24 percent of Russia's cotton needs. In 1913, the share of Central Asian cotton in the Russian industry was about 50 percent. Simultaneously, the cotton industry was developing. There was one cotton refinery in 1873, and 350 cotton enterprises were in operation in 1916. Raw silk remained second among Turkistan's exports. Most of the locals worked in food and cotton industries 17 to 18 hours a day without labor protection; because of political and educational reasons, the railroad did not employ them.

World War I undermined the region's economy. The government established fixed prices on cotton from Central Asia because of decreases in the import of cotton. During the first years of the war, prices on cotton increased

50 percent. At the same time, bread prices increased 400 percent. The purchase of bread from Russian provinces became more complicated and stopped entirely in 1916, causing many people to suffer from famine.

Economic changes were not supplemented by political reforms. The Russian administration, local rulers, and the conservative clergy favored the suppression of independent thought and vigorously implemented political restrictions imposed in the Empire. In Bokhara, reformers were forced into exile or had to operate from secret societies, which contributed to the rise of the revolutionary movement. Prominent leaders of Soviet Turkistan emerged from the Bokharan underground, including future Uzbek communist leader Faizulla Khojaev.

THE RUSSIAN MUSLIM POLICY

Russian colonial expansion was not a crusade to disseminate orthodox Christianity. It was driven instead by practical imperialist goals—the capture of new territories and the achievement of military superiority necessary to make Russia a superpower. Turkistan never experienced the politics of a religious conversion. The Russian Orthodox Church did not conduct missionary activities in the region, but rather served the Slavic settlers inside the Russian outposts; likewise, Russian tsars did not attempt to interfere in the religious affairs of Muslims. The mosques were mostly untouched, except in cases when resistance to Russian expansionism originated directly from Islamic clergies. Islamic cultural and educational institutions were largely left intact under the Russian colonial administration.

After the colonization began, Russian tsars were faced with the problem of legitimizing their power to the new Muslim subjects. Repressions alone were not sufficient, and the Russian state cooperated actively with some Muslim leaders in support of commonly agreed upon goals, such as social peace. Soon after capturing Tashkent, General Mikhail Chernyaev entered into an elaborate agreement with local religious scholars, guaranteeing to uphold their authority and that of other Muslim institutions, such as mosques and charities. In return, the elders had to deliver the loyalty of local people. The relations between tsarist and Islamist authorities were complex. The Russian regime did not merely tolerate the clerical elite but helped it to fight heresy and uphold the Shariah law. Given that Sunni Islam lacked a formal clerical structure, the Russians sometimes had to coax one into existence by boosting the authority of their favorites, and the representatives of the Russian state often adjudicated the grievances of the Muslim subjects in Islamic terms.

The local judicial system based on Islamic law was modified by the Russian authorities. Traditionally, Islamic judges were appointed by local rulers. In 1866, there was a brief attempt to replace single judges with panels of judges appointed by the Russian governor; however, the plan was abandoned. The Provisional Statute of 1867 applied similar rules for the population of settled and nomadic areas and provided that Turkistanis could elect their officials and elders, who would in turn appoint the judges. While no attempt was made to alter the Islamic law, the jurisdiction of religious judges was limited to minor cases (with punishments of no more than 18 months of imprisonment) and family law; and their decisions were subject to review by local Russian courts. Cases that involved Russians were heard only in Russian courts.

Some argue that the politics of nonintervention in local religious affairs chosen by the Russians was rather the politics of ignoring Muslim institutions and limiting their influence on political structures.[23] No religious dignitaries were appointed to positions of authority. Administrative positions that had to be filled with religious leaders were abolished, and individuals who graduated from Islamic religious schools were not employed by government institutions because knowledge of the Russian language and civil education were required.

Russia's view of Islam as a conspiratorial religion extremely hostile to Russia, Europe, and the entire West was based on the experience of French and British rule of Muslims.[24] Russian authorities were very cautious in regard to local life and tried to leave everything not of a political nature untouched. This position was traditional for Russia, where tolerant views toward Islam were declared by Catherine the Great in 1773. While orthodox Christianity remained the official state religion, all other beliefs were tolerated as long as they did not contradict state interests. Loyalty to the state system and the ruling family was the only requirement for all subjects, including Muslims.

At the end of the nineteenth century, there were approximately 14 million Muslims in the Russian Empire, and the tsarist policy was aimed at integrating the Muslim population while decreasing the Muslim clergy's influence on political processes. Both education and health care were selected as the main areas where the state could have demonstrated its interest in supporting Muslim subjects, because, as Russian prime minister Pyotr Stolypin stated in 1909, "Islam is the strongest threat to the security of the state; however, the Muslim issue is not dangerous in itself."[25] This policy had two major components—the separation of Russian secular public schools in the Turkistan colony from religious classes, giving local people the alternative to choose their means of education and complicating the foreign contacts of the Muslim clergy to prevent the distribution of Panislamism and Panturkism ideas.

BOKHARAN JEWS

For about 2,000 years, Jews resided in Central Asia, surviving previous invasions and meeting Russian colonization, which was crucial for defining their legal status in a miserable, semi-isolated state. There is no precise information on how many Jews resided there before the Russian conquest. Because most of the Jews were located in and around Bokhara city, on the territory of present-day Uzbekistan and Tajikistan, the entire Jewish population of Central Asia was called Bokharan Jews. The Jews spoke Bukhrit, a combination of Hebrew and Farsi, and professed Sephardic Judaism. Because of constant close contacts with other locals, food, clothing, home decorations, customs, rites, and music of Bokharan Jews contained many elements typical of the Tajik and Uzbek population; this tradition continues today in the few remaining Central Asian Jewish communities.

At the time of the Russian colonization, Central Asian Jews were a national and religious minority on the periphery of social, political, and economic life. Apparently, Emir Nasrullah of Bokhara had some benevolent feelings toward Jews because they supported him financially and helped him to win the throne; however, the discrimination of Jews continued and the 21 prohibitions for Jews were strictly enforced, including requirements such as living only in designated areas and restrictions on purchases of new houses. Even within the ghetto, Jews were not allowed to buy houses from Muslims. All houses occupied by Jews could not be higher than houses of their Muslim neighbors and had to have an identifying sign. Similar restrictions applied to shops owned by Jews, and Jewish merchants were prohibited from being seen by their customers. The construction of new synagogues was not allowed either; however, this ban did not apply to the renovation of existing temples. Jews could not leave their quarters and enter the city after sunset, and they were not allowed to ride horses within city walls. Sometimes this ban extended to even riding donkeys. While walking on the streets, Jews had to belt themselves with a rope, and it was prohibited to wear coats over the ropes. Among other attire restrictions, Jews were supposed to wear special hats of a determined form, color, and fabric; black clothes were not allowed. All Jews were subject to a special tax, and their statements and testimonies were not accepted by the court if a Muslim was mentioned, even if such statements were in favor of a Muslim. When Russian troops conquered Tashkent, there were 27 Jewish families (about 100 people),[26] all of whom were very poor, and, because of the ban on real estate purchases, their only communal property was a small cemetery. The sale of silk fabrics was the only source of income for all Jews. There was no Jewish clergy in Tashkent, and teachers at the only Jewish elementary school with education in the Tajik language were invited from Bokhara.

The expansion of Russian territories to the borders of Bokhara improved the status of Bokharan Jews. Although discriminated against at home, Bokharan Jews received the same rights as other emirate subjects under treaties concluded between Bokhara and Russia in 1868 and 1873. They were free to move within the Russian empire and join Russian professional and trade organizations, which remained closed for Russian Jews. Under Russian rule, the Bokharan Jews proved their abilities as traders and monopolized the cotton trade with Russia. Unlike the Bokharan Jews, who were only discriminated against within the emirate, Jews of Russian Turkistan were recognized as Russian subjects and were treated in the same discriminatory way as all other Jews of the Russian Empire. All Jews who moved to Central Asia following the Russian advance were automatically restricted in their rights. The colonial administration made Russian anti-Jewish laws applicable to Central Asian Jews. Residence restrictions, bans on professions, and trade exclusions similar to those that applied to Russian Jews were imposed on Jewish residents of newly acquired territories as long as they did not live on these territories before the Russian conquest. Jews became subject to forced resettlements, were prohibited to live closer than 65 miles from the state borders, and were not allowed to reside and have property in Russian villages of Turkistan. The only way for Jews to conduct business in Turkistan was to have a Russian intermediary or companion. Regular night inspections were conducted in Russian settlements, and Jews who were found during such passport checks were subject to imprisonment. Separate city blocks for Jews were established under the Russian administration. Inhabitants of these ghettos were employed mostly as tailors, barbers, jewelers, bakers, laundry washers, coachmen, and shoemakers. Women who could dance and sing performed in weddings, including those of Muslims. Before the arrival of the Russians, Jews were involved in winemaking, but the new Russian administration confiscated all Jewish wineries.

Russian Jews began to arrive in Central Asia since the middle of the 1860s, mostly as soldiers, who served in units involved with campaigns on these territories. Craftsmanship was their major occupation. Because Turkistan was outside of the Jewish Pale of Settlement, only former military personnel, university graduates, craftspeople, and traders whose income was in the nation's top 5 percent were allowed to live there. The exact number of Jews who moved to Turkistan from Russia is unknown because, according to census rules, Russian and Bokharan Jews were counted together based on religion. At the beginning of the twentieth century, the Russian administration reported the presence of about 5,000 Russian Jews who made up approximately 2 percent of the entire European population of the colony. About half of them resided in Samarkand, about 1,500 in the Fergana Valley, and 350 to 400 in Tashkent and Almaty.[27] The newly arrived Russian Jews were active in local newspapers, book sales, and publishing, owning 7 out of 10 printing shops in Tashkent.[28] The only field of art in which Jews were allowed to engage was architecture. Jews were restricted from participating in other arts, especially music. Jewish musicians, except for military musicians, were prohibited from residing in the Russian colony of Turkistan.[29] Neither colonization nor the influx in the

Jewish population from Russia and from neighboring countries of Afghanistan, India, and Persia who were attracted by business opportunities broke the isolation of Central Asian Jews or contributed to their emancipation.

Between 1865 and 1917, 11 men served as governors of Turkistan. During this period, the region's significance for Russia changed from a military camp to an area that brought Russia strategic and economic benefits far exceeding administrative and conquest costs. While under Russian rule, Central Asia experienced extensive economic and cultural development; however, some political stability and positive changes brought by modern civilization did not affect most Central Asians, who suffered from loss of land to settlers, speedy industrialization, transformation of the cotton industry into a detrimental monoculture, dependence on food imports and finished products from Russia, and the collapse of their traditional way of life. Dissatisfaction was growing, and people were ready for social and political changes.

NOTES

1. English and Russian visitors noted a great variety of uniforms and arms among the Bokharan troops. Foreigners observed that Bokharan troops knew neither how to shoot nor how to march in step; discipline and martial qualities were absent, and equipment was even worse. Only one in five infantry soldiers had a rifle, usually an ancient flintlock or musket dating from the beginning of the nineteenth century.

2. Cited by David MacKenzie, "Turkestan's Significance to Russia (1850–1917)," *Russian Review* 33, no. 2 (April 1974): 168.

3. Ibid.

4. Hopkirk (1992), 238.

5. Hopkirk (1992), 241.

6. Ibid.

7. Cited by Francine Hirsh, *Empire of Nations, Ethnographic Knowledge and the Making of the Soviet Union* (London and Ithaca, NY: Cornell University Press, 2005), 44.

8. Edward Allworth, *Central Asia: 120 Years of Russian Rule* (Durham, NC, and London: Duke University Press, 1989), 68.

9. American diplomat Schuyler visited Tashkent in 1873, and observed a clique-ridden military society: "the officers had little resource but gambling and drinking, and in many instances young men had utterly ruined themselves, some even had to be sent out of the country—and a man had to be really bad to be exiled from Tashkent." Ibid., 69.

10. Michael Rywkin, *Moscow's Muslim Challenge: Soviet Central Asia* (Armonk, NY: M. E. Sharpe, 1990), 56.

11. Allworth, *Central Asia: 120 Years of Russian Rule* (1989), 181.

12. Rywkin (1990), 65.

13. Ira Klein, "The Anglo-Russian Convention and the Problem of Central Asia, 1907–1914," *Journal of British Studies*11, no. 1 (November 1971): 126.

14. Cited by Rywkin (1990), 69.

15. Beatrice Manz, "Central Asian Uprising in the Nineteenth Century: Ferghana Under the Russians," *Russian Review* 46, no. 3 (July 1987): 271.

16. Cited by Khalid (1998), 60.

17. Elisabeth Bacon, *Central Asians under Russian Rule: A Study in Culture Change* (Ithaca, NY: Cornell University Press, 1980), 173.

18. Allworth (1989), 207.

19. Jeremy Smith, *The Bolsheviks, and the National Question, 1917–1923* (New York: St. Martin's Press, 1999), 80.

20. Seymour Becker, *Russia's Protectorates in Central Asia: Bukhara and Khiva, 1865–1924* (London and New York: Routledge Courzon, 2004), 214.

21. Becker (2004), 192.

22. Rywkin (1990), 72.

23. Khalid (1998), 115.

24. Becker (2004), 63.

25. Cited by Stephen Williams, *Liberal Reform in an Illiberal Regime: The Creation of Private Property in Russia, 1906–1915* (Stanford, CA: Hoover Institution Press, 2006), 98.

26. Shterenshis (2002), 153.

27. Michael Aronson, "The Attitudes of Russian Officials in the 1880s toward Jewish Assimilation and Emigration," *Slavic Review* 34, no. 1 (March 1975): 14.

28. Khalid (1998), 148.

29. Michael Sacks, Privilege and Prejudice: The Occupation of Jews in Russia in 1989, *Slavic Review* 57, no. 2 (Summer 1998): 261.

6

The Revolutionary Era (1917–1924)

In February 1917, Russian Tsar Nicholas II abdicated and a democratic provisional government was created in St. Petersburg. In Central Asia, these events were met favorably, and raised hopes of independence. The provisional government was supposed to run the country before the popularly elected all-Russian Constitutional Assembly chose the form of the future nation's political system and permanent government. However, the provisional government was uncertain regarding the nationalities problem and decided to leave the resolution of this issue up to the Constitutional Assembly. At the same time, the provisional government continued to fulfill Russia's previous commitments to continue World War I.

PROVISIONAL GOVERNMENT POLICIES

In Turkistan, Russian officials and settlers were unanimous in their desire to save Russia's authority, and Governor General Kuropatkin attempted to preserve the tsarist power. But on April 7, 1917, he was placed under house arrest, and the provisional government replaced the authority of the former governor of the Turkistan province with a Provisional Executive Committee composed of five Russians and four local Muslims, mostly members of the centrist Constitutional Democratic Party, while the Kazakh territory in the steppe region remained under central administration. The Soviets—the parallel power structures comprised of various left-wing parties that expressed the interests of radical workers and received support from Russian troops stationed there—were formed in Tashkent and other Turkistan cities in March 1917 and became an important political force in autumn of that year. The Soviets refused to recognize the power of the provisional government, accused the committee of continuing the policy of the old regime, usurped the power, and dismissed the committee. The native population mostly did not participate in these events.

Immediately after the tsar's abdication, many local Muslim organizations were founded, and it was believed that these organizations would fight Russia's domination. Although some of them had political aspirations, most of these organizations were concerned with cultural and educational issues. For example, the Splendor of Islam Society aimed to "acquaint the people with the present situation and to send people to the villages to spread ideas of citizenship and knowledge in order to prepare our brothers for the Constituent Assembly and to reform our schools."[1] Among the political organizations formed in 1917 was the Social Turan Party, which united middle-class, teachers, interpreters, traders, and students. Because the party's goal was to create a unified Turkic state, the Social Turan Party was prohibited as a reactionary even before it was officially formed. The reformist cultural Jadid movement represented by clerisy and religious educators had a conflict with the traditional Islamic clergy and scholars regarding women's rights in the new era. The provisional government granted electoral rights to all citizens of Russia over the age of 20, regardless of sex. The Jadids welcomed these new rights and initiated the registration of women voters. They saw the right to vote as a boost to women but also believed that a women's vote was important to the success of Muslim candidates in an election based on proportional representation. However, the clergy ruled that women's right to vote contravened Islamic laws and was therefore impermissible. Eventually, some Muslim women did vote, but the issue proved highly divisive. The Jadids later transformed themselves into Muslim communists and asserted the claim to speak in the name of the Muslims of Turkistan.[2]

Turkistan elites sought to use the freedoms allowed by the revolution to ensure full participation for Turkistan in the political life of the Russian republic. In April 1917, the first regional Muslim congress convened in Tashkent to discuss the future of Central Asia and the new Russian state. Without making any significant decisions, the congress demanded the cessation of Russian colonization in Central Asia and the return of confiscated lands to the local population, but Russian authorities did not comply. The congress elected the Turkistan Central Council of Muslims, another regional governing body, which became known as the National Center with an ethnic Kazakh and westernized Turkistan nationalist Mustafa Chokaev (1890–1941) as its chairman. The National Center tried to win acceptance for the Central Asian cause among local Russian authorities and communicated with the Muslims in other parts of Russia, although without much success.

The Russians did not intend to share their power with the locals. Their view of the situation was described by one of the members of the local Executive Committee, in response to the Muslims' demands for independence: "The revolution has been waged by Russians, that is why the power is in our hands in Central Asia."[3] As everywhere in Russia, Central Asian political forces were strongly divided between conservatives and reformists. The Russians attempted to build an alliance with the local politicians, and, during the elections of the Tashkent city council in the summer of 1917, provisional government authorities united with the native conservatives. Together they won 60 percent of the votes, while Muslim reformists received only 10 percent. The former Russian governor responsible for the 1916 repressions in Fergana became the mayor of Tashkent. During the elections, some riots occurred, and several candidates were killed in Kokand and other places. The second Muslim congress was held in Tashkent in September 1917. Local leaders wanted to create an autonomous republic of Turkistan, which would be federated with Russia but organized according to its own standards and Shariah laws. Discussing economic issues, the conference opposed the intensive cultivation of cotton and called for the local production of grain so that Central Asia could supply its own food. At the end of 1917, the economic situation in the region became disastrous; due to a gradual decline in local grain production, food supplies from Russia (on which Turkistan had depended since the beginning of the twentieth century) were stopped during the revolution period. It is estimated that between 1917 and 1920, almost one-fourth of the native rural population died because of chaos, war, epidemics, and starvation.

Revolutionary changes took other forms outside the Turkistan province. The Turkmens did not have their own political organization and were passive during the revolutionary period. Their political expression had taken the form of war, in which they participated with the Uzbeks and Tajiks until it was suppressed in the late 1920s. In Kazakhstan, the previous organization was not changed in 1917. Although the tsarist officials gradually disappeared during 1917, the local administrations continued to work. The land question was much more important than political issues for the Kazakhs. The Kazakhs wanted to stop colonization and stabilize the indigenous people on arable lands. In the fall of 1917, more than 30,000 Kyrgyz returned home from work in the Russian territory where they were mobilized. Kazakhs and Kyrgyz who fled to China in search of asylum after the 1916 revolt returned to their homes in 1917, after receiving news about democratic changes in Russia; however, their former properties were occupied by Russian settlers. The Turkistan committee of the provisional government issued a special resolution prohibiting the return of such refugees. A serious fight developed between the return-ing natives and the Russians who defended their newly acquired proper-ties. The Russian landowners did not allow the Kyrgyz to pass through their lands, and cases of ambushing and murdering of the returning people were reported. Local Russian garrisons favored the settlers in their attempts to preserve peace.

In March 1917, the Kazakh liberation movement—named *Alash*, the ancient war cry of the Kazakhs—was formed by a radical and nationalistically oriented group of Kazakhs in southern Central Asia who called for complete indepen-dence of Kazakhstan. In December 1917, during the Kazakh congress, which proclaimed the autonomy of the Kazakh people, the movement transformed into a political party. The Alash activists clashed with the more cautious Ka-zakh leaders who supported the provisional government and opted for lim-ited autonomy with the local administration. The conservatives decided to introduce the Kazakh language in schools, courts, and administrations. They saw Kazakh's future as a federation with Russia and did not entertain the possibility of establishing an independent government—which, according to them, would require more unification than existed among the semi-nomadic tribes and clans. After the autonomy of the Kazakh people was declared in December, the Alash movement pronounced the establishment of the Alash Horde state. The steppe region populated by the Kazakhs was divided into two administrative zones; each zone had to organize itself and turn to its nearby allies for support. The desire to stop the spread of Bolshevism unified the Kazakh activists, who wanted to make an alliance with the anti-Bolshevik government of Siberia but were not supported by the Russian White (anti-Soviet) army. The Russian anti-Soviet military commanders denied assistance to the Kazakhs and ordered to suppress them, fearing anarchy in the plains.[4] The movement had no active base abroad, and its armed force never gained more than a local significance. The Bolsheviks crushed the movement, and some of its leaders were killed, while others made peace with Moscow.

1917 IN BOKHARA AND KHIVA

The rulers of Bokhara and Khorezm tried to get rid of the Russian domina-tion while dealing with internal power struggles. In Bokhara,[5] the emir was maneuvering around the provisional government, the Jadid Young Bokharan Party, his own regional governors, and the Bolsheviks in an effort to retain his power. In March 1917, the Russian resident in Bokhara,[6] Alex Miller, ques-tioned the necessity of conducting gradual liberal reforms, which would not have violated the autonomy of the country that for about half of the century had been under the Russian protectorate. He intended that such reforms would not contradict the Shariah laws because neither active Russian involvement nor the accession of Bokhara would have called for an immediate response from Afghanistan, which positioned itself as a defender of Islam in the region. Miller hoped that progressive Jadids, who fought for the liberalization of the emir's despotic rule, would support Russian efforts.

On March 20, Miller submitted to Russian leaders in Petrograd a draft of the Bokhara Reform Manifesto that had been prepared by the residency and accepted by the emir and his court members. This draft included such measures as the creation of a fair court system, control over the bureaucracy with fixed salaries for the emir's servants, the founding of a state treasury and national budget, the organization of a national publishing house, and permission for people to elect a council of respected individuals who would manage the capital city improvements. The confirmation process within the Russian government was very slow and was affected by fears of unrests in Bokhara, initiated by the conservative clergy and by the demands of the Young Bokharans, who accused Miller and his staff of preserving the old regime and keeping close ties with the emir. The emir and Miller were afraid that the local radicals would overthrow the emir and initiate reforms, because they began to seek support from the Samarkand Muslim community for this purpose. To prevent further escalations, on April 7, the highest officials, clergy, representatives from the tradesmen, craftsmen, Bokharan Jews and Shiites, and five members of the Samarkand Executive Committee (municipal authority) were invited to the emir's palace, where the chief justice declared the emir's intention to begin the "possibly broad improvement of all areas of state affairs and the elimination of abuses of power through participation of elected representatives."[7]

A peaceful demonstration in support of the reform was stopped by a large counterdemonstration of religious fanatics. The creation of a municipal self-governing body, the Executive Committee, provoked further anti-emir and anti-Russian sentiments. On April 8, 1917, local Muslim leaders brought 8,000 people to the streets of Bokhara to protest reforms drafted by the representative of the provisional government. The local people organized a series of pogroms in the Russian quarters of Bokhara and attacked soldiers and horses of the Russian garrison. Young Bokharans who were not satisfied with the proposed reforms and attempts of the Russian provisional government to preserve the emir attempted to organize a military revolt in hopes of achieving power through Russia's military assistance. The garrison did not support the Young Bokharans and was afraid that Russian involvement in the revolt would provoke further anti-Russian actions among the local people. The Jadids had to flee from Bokhara to Tashkent to avoid riots and further persecutions,[8] although some court and tax improvements were introduced, and a representative assembly was established.

The Bolsheviks did not tolerate the status quo of Bokhara and continued to undermine it. In early 1918, the chairman of the Turkistan government arrived in Bokhara and demanded the transfer of power from the emir to the Young Bokharans, who, together with the local communists, pretended that they were able to lead the emirate and conduct socialist reforms. Military forces were stationed around Bokhara to support the position of the Turkistan government. After the troops penetrated and looted the city on March 2, 1918, the population decided to support the otherwise unpopular emir, and the invaders were routed. Before the emir's troops intervened, several hundred innocent Russian inhabitants of Bokhara were slaughtered by the Muslim mob, and the Young Bokharans fled for their lives. Later, the Tashkent Soviet recognized Bokhara's independence and signed an agreement with the emir, who remained on the throne until 1920. In return, the emir agreed to deliver "White Russian" agents to the Soviets and to exchange prisoners without compensation.[9] The economic situation in Bokhara during the years of independence was grave because almost all external trade contacts were cut, and internal resources were insufficient to support the population; most of the nation's herd was destroyed, and lands were not irrigated.

In Khorezm, 44-year-old Khan Isfendiyar had been on throne since 1910. During his reign, settled Uzbeks and nomadic Turkmen fought over taxes and water rights, creating a long period of instability. As a result, a Russian garrison entered Khiva to protect the khan. In 1917, the Khivan Soviet formed by the Russian workers cooperated with the Jadid reformers and pushed the khan to establish a representative assembly, where the Turkmen held several seats. In June 1917, Khan Isfendiyar reasserted his authority, abolished the assembly, and imprisoned the Jadids.

BOLSHEVIKS' ARRIVAL

In Russia, the provisional government did not resolve the most important problems. Workers did not receive the rights that they fought for, the war continued, and social politics worsened workers' well-being. Similarly, issues that were important to the Central Asians were not resolved. The population was disappointed that the recognition of the right to self-determination for everyone was postponed, and people began to support the Bolsheviks, who promised full autonomy to everyone from the former empire. Prior to the October revolution of 1917, the Bolsheviks exploited the nationalist aspirations of the people of the Russian Empire. Lenin openly upheld every nation's right to self-determination and stated that every nation could secede from an oppressing one and establish a new independent state. Many nationalist leaders of Central Asia were attracted by Lenin's thinking and supported the Bolsheviks during the revolution, but it was difficult to foresee that the Bolsheviks did not want to break up the Russian Empire. In fact, many new states that were established in Central Asia ceased to exist as independent political entities within several years. After the Bolsheviks came to power during a military revolt in St. Petersburg on October 25, 1917, during which they ordered the transfer of all power to the Soviets, they followed the tsarist style of governing the country and integrated the imperialist aims of the Communist Party with its previous program of supporting the self-determination of oppressed nationalities.

In Central Asia, the news about the regime change sparked war among the pro-tsarist Russian troops and administrations, native nationalists, and pro-Bolshevik Russians. On November 1, 1917, Russian settlers claimed control over the Fergana Valley, and on November 27, 1917, the Fourth Turkestan Muslim Congress passed a resolution proclaiming Turkestan's territorial autonomy within the Russian Federation, establishing the *Turkeston Mukhtoriyati,* an autonomous government of Turkestan within the boundaries of the former khanate of Kokand, alternative to the Tashkent Soviet. Mustafa Chokaev became chairman of the new government based on the ideas of Turkistan autonomy proposed earlier by prominent Muslim jurists Munavar Kori, Mahmudhoja Behbudi, and Mirza Kushbegiev. For the first time, the idea of a democratic parliamentary republic was announced and implemented in Central Asia.

The autonomy was interpreted very broadly and provided for Turkistan independence in all internal affairs, such as finance, application of Shariah law, culture, justice, and education. Defense, monetary policy, customs, and foreign relations remained in the jurisdiction of central Russian authorities. The program provided for a regional legislature and executive authorities with local self-governing bodies in lower-level administrative units. Equal and secret voting rights were granted to all members of the society older than 20 years regardless of gender, property, or religion. The state did not recognize Islam as the official religion, but it also did not say that Turkistan would be a secular state. The influence of Islam and Muslim law on the state program was strong. An independent judiciary was supposed to be one of the pillars of the new state. Drafted bills projected an obligatory participation of an attorney in a trial and a system of punishments defined by the legislature. It was also intended to provide free education, equal and accessible to all, and mandated the study of local and Russian languages as well as science.

Before the convocation of the Constitutional Assembly, which could pass founding documents for the new state, all power was concentrated with the Turkistan Provisional Council and the Turkistan People's Assembly. The 12-member government consisting of the Provisional Council members was supposed to be the executive authority. The Provisional Council consisted of 32 people, all delegates elected to represent Turkistan in the all-Russian Constitutional Assembly. The 54-member People's Assembly, which was viewed as a representative body, included delegates from the localities and public organizations with one-third of the seats in the assembly reserved for the representatives of the non-native, European part of the population (about 7 percent of the total population). The new statehood was built on principles of proportional representation of all ethnic and national groups and the combination of democratic and national values.

Being fully legitimate, Turkeston Mukhtoriyati was the implementer of the right to self-determination declared by the Bolsheviks when they came to power. However, the Bolshevik leadership was not interested in building an economically prosperous democratic society in Central Asia. Implementing Marxist and Leninist ideas, the Bolsheviks did not consider national interests of the previously oppressed people and existing social realities. The existence of the Kokand autonomy became a problem for the Tashkent Soviet, which was afraid of any political competition and declared the state formation in Kokand illegal. Branded counter-revolutionary by the Bolsheviks, this democratic self-governance was overthrown by a military unit of the Tashkent Soviet. Breaching the walls of Kokand on February 18, 1918, the Red (Bolshevik) Army began a three-day rampage of rape, plunder, and arson, leaving 14,000 slaughtered and the old city ablaze. Mustafa Chokaev escaped to Bokhara and then to Paris, as his army chief Igrash Bey channeled Fergana's outrage into a holy war. His guerilla groups (named *Basmachis*) harassed the Red Army throughout the next decade of the Soviet rule from their mountain strongholds.

During 1918, the power gradually passed to the local Soviets, and the Tashkent Soviet established itself as the most powerful institution on the territory of the former Russian Turkistan province, strong enough not to make serious attempts to win Muslim allegiance. During the winter famine of 1917–1918, the Russian troops requisitioned food in villages implementing Moscow policies. All cotton was confiscated under the penalty of death. Muslim peasants suspected of sympathy to nationalist guerillas were shot. The Russian revolutionary slogan of freedom became known among the Muslims as puny freedom and was synonymous with lawlessness and looting.[10] The result was predictable—everyone was ready for revolt, which occurred in June 1918, echoing an anti-Bolshevik uprising in Moscow. The local tribesmen and the White Russian officers arrested and shot the provincial Bolshevik government. Supported by the British, they ejected Soviet troops and established an anti-Soviet administration consisting of Russians, Turkmen, and Armenians, which existed for just a few days. Understanding the necessity to gain popular support, the Communist Party, which was very small and listed no more than 250 members in Tashkent, merged with the nationalists. This merge improved the numerical strength of the Communists but weakened them ideologically. The communists made several insignificant gestures toward the

Muslim population, recognizing the Uzbek language as equal to Russian and expressing confidence in the Uzbek proletariat.

SOVIET TURKISTAN

In October 1918, the former province was transformed to the Turkistan Autonomous Soviet Socialist Republic (ASSR), which joined the Russia—known at that time as Russian Soviet Federation Socialist Republic (RSFSR)—to become a constituent component of the Russian Federation as an autonomous soviet socialist republic. During initial stages of the Soviet development, the Bolsheviks were unable to define what status would be given to a particular ethnic group, and the creation of Turkistan ASSR appears to be a compromise and an expression of a general intention to give autonomy to the Muslim people of Central Asia. After the Bolsheviks were able to establish better control over the territory and create a national cadre of supporters and promoters of the Bolshevik policies, they could move forward and divide Turkistan into nation-based republics with a more privileged status for specific people and particular territories assigned to them.[11]

The decision to create the Turkistan ASSR was supported by the Soviets in Samarkand, Dzizhak, Khojent, Andijon, and other localities. A plenipotentiary representation of Turkestan at central Russian authorities was established in Moscow, and, in October, the Constitution of the Autonomous Turkestan was passed. The government of the Turkistan Republic consisted of 10 people's commissariats, 5 of which (food, finance, economy, workers' and peasants inspection, posts and telegraphs) were directly subordinate to the corresponding commissariats of the RSFSR. The other 6 commissariats (interior, justice, education, health, social welfare, and agriculture) and the Extraordinary Commission (a prototype of the future KGB) operated independently but were responsible to the Russian Central Executive Committee (the highest government authority in the RSFSR and in the Soviet Union until 1936). The appointment of all people's commissars was subject to the approval of the corresponding commissariats of the RSFSR. Military matters, foreign affairs, and trade remained the sole responsibility of the RSFSR. The Turkistan Soviet government was dominated by Russian elements and had a strong colonial character. In November 1917, Muslims were excluded from government positions by the Tashkent congress of local Soviets—a practice cancelled by the next congress in May 1918, although natives rarely attained high positions.[12]

Revolutionary changes in Central Asia began with land and court reforms aimed at the redistribution of property rights over lands and waters of the Fergana Valley in May 1918, when the Bolshevik government in Moscow passed a decree on irrigation works in Turkistan. The decree gave start to land confiscations and redistributions from natives and Muslim endowment lands. Decrees of November 1917 (which abolished private property) and of January 1918 (on the separation between church and state) legally justified the confiscations. These reforms were implemented by groups of three established in all settlements, which included representatives from the Bolshevik Party, local Soviets, and locally stationed military units or the police. The groups' main goal was to register all of the peasants' lands and property for further confiscations and tax assessments.

The followers of the tsarist and provisional government resisted the establishment of Soviet power and fought a civil war between 1918 and 1920. During the civil war, power in the localities changed constantly, and each change of the authorities was followed by the hanging of activists of the overthrown regime. For two years, while Turkistan was cut off from the rest of the country by the events of the civil war, the socialist revolution remained in the region mainly as the settlers' affair. Menaced by the tsarist army officers, threatened by Muslim nationalists, and too weak to control the former Russian protectorates of Khiva and Bokhara, the authorities in Tashkent only had stranded Russian army units, railroad workers, and a few leftist settlers to rely on. The settlers' support was bought by protecting their privileges.

During the war period, contacts between Moscow and Tashkent were sporadic. The Bolsheviks could not secure state control in the region, and the tsarist court system continued to exist. A part of the courts followed Shariah law, and rulings were issued in the Muslims' native languages. Other courts followed Soviet law and used the Russian language for the Europeans. A special commission was established to mediate conflicts between religious and secular law codes. For several years, many so-called people's courts continued to judge solely on the basis of Shariah law, and certain provinces did not have a Soviet court; short training courses for secular judges were established. Experiencing an acute personnel shortage, the Bolshevik government provided money and promoted secular education, increasing the number of primary schools almost four-fold between 1917 and 1920.

In the fall of 1919, when contact with central Russia was restored, the special Turkistan Commission under the leadership of Mikhail Frunze, commander of the Eastern Front was dispatched to Turkistan with the accompanying army units. Despite the fact that the main goals of the commission were, according to Lenin's statement, to correct errors in administering the nationality policy and to stop the continuation of the colonization policy by Russian functionaries, Frunze led the suppression of the counter-revolutionary forces in Turkistan and enhanced Soviet power. Moscow institutions established total control over Central Asian affairs, limiting the autonomy of the region. In 1919, the Army Special Sections took over the local secret police, and the Ministry of Foreign Affairs of Turkistan—a symbol of far-reaching regional autonomy—was abolished, and its functions were transferred to the department of external relations within the Commission for Turkistan Affairs that arrived from Moscow. To stop Moscow's growing influence on local affairs in Turkistan, Russian settlers in and around Tashkent (including communists) began to advocate for local autonomy and to court local Muslims.

In the course of the civil war, Kazakhstan was governed by the Revolutionary Committee, which was appointed in Moscow in 1919. The committee became a nucleus of the future government and included some Alash Horde leaders. In August 1920, all organizations inherited from Alash Horde were liquidated, and the Kara-Kyrgyz (Kazakh) ASSR, part of the RSFSR, was established.[13] The government included as many Kazakhs as Russians and Europeans. The opposition between the Bolsheviks and the Kazakh leaders arose in September 1920, when the Bolsheviks drafted laws regarding the composition of the constituent assembly. Following the Russian rules, the Bolsheviks wanted to terminate the voting rights of those who belonged to the so-called former privileged class—the clerics, landowners, traders, and activists of the imperial government. The exclusion from the list of voters was followed by the termination of many other social and political rights, such as the right to reside in particular areas; professional restrictions; and prohibitions for these individuals, their children, and other family members to study at colleges and universities. Because there was no other political force in Kazakhstan except Alash Horde, and because of the deficiency of personnel and educated Kazakhs, the Bolsheviks were forced to tolerate and agree with the Kazakhs' requests. However, later, all of Alash Horde's activists were named nationalists and were accused of conducting policies that led to widespread famine and of making ideological mistakes that led to nationalism. As a rule, such accusations were followed by criminal trials and executions.[14] In June 1921, Siberian lands were added to the autonomous republic, and, in April 1921, a temporary Commission for the Affairs of Turkistan was sent from Moscow to carry out the policy of Soviet power in the national question. In 1922, when the USSR was created, the two previously established autonomous republics in Central Asia—the Kyrgyz (Kazakh) ASSR and the Turkistan ASSR—were included in the RSFSR as its constituent components. The Kyrgyz (Kazakh) ASSR was divided into two parts: the territories populated by the Kyrgyz were included in the RSFSR as the Kara-Kyrgyz Autonomous Province, and the part of the Kyrgyz ASSR inhabited primarily by the Kazakhs was renamed the Kazakh ASSR and remained part of the RSFSR until 1936. The Syr Darya province of the Turkistan ASSR, with a predominantly Kazakh population, joined the Kazakh ASSR.

The Kyrgyz who resided in the Turkistan ASSR were dispersed in several provinces, where they became a minority. In March 1922, the creation of the Mountainous Kyrgyz Province within the Turkistan ASSR was declared, the first attempt to form a Kyrgyz state. Stalin viewed this effort as a local initiative and prohibited the implementation of this decision. The province was declared illegal, and its leaders were prosecuted as bourgeois nationalists and counter-revolutionaries. The Declaration on the Creation of the Kyrgyz Autonomous Province was adopted on January 15, 1925, the day Kyrgyz statehood was established. The first secretary of the Kyrgyz provincial party committee (local leader), who was appointed by Moscow, attempted to establish his own power, and fought against the locals for this purpose, accusing them of taking bribes and corruption and making personnel changes according to his own preferences. Thirty native members of the Communist Party wrote a letter to the Central Committee criticizing the non-Asian party leadership. This act was considered an attempt to destroy the party unity and discipline. The authors lost their party membership, were fired from the offices they occupied, and expelled from the province. The separation of the Kyrgyz province from Turkistan was the first step in the process of dividing the population of Central Asia into distinct national groups.

SOVIETIZATION OF BOKHARA AND KHIVA

Of special importance for the Bolsheviks was the elimination of the Khiva khanate and the Bokharan emirate, because both were counter-revolutionary centers providing support to the Basmachis and negotiating arms deals with foreign countries. In attempts to change the old system of government in Bokhara and Khorezm, the Bolsheviks engaged the Bokharan and Khorezmian Jadids and their political parties of Young Bokharans and Young Khivanis in the liquidation of monarchies, insisting on nondemocratic, Bolshevik forms of development. Under Lenin's propaganda, the hopes of Muslim intellectuals to achieve independence seamed to be real, and Young Bokhrans and Young Khivanis who were fighting the reactionary regimes in their countries joined the revolution. Lenin's concept of national autonomy was based on a real autonomy with strong participation by the native population within the limits of the basic unity of the country and the centralized, Moscow-controlled authority of the party. This position made cooperation with Moscow attractive and inspiring for local leaders.

In 1918, in Khiva, the khan was assassinated by the Turkmen leader, Junaid, who installed Muhammad Abdullah as khan. In 1919, the small Young Khivanis Party and local militia supported the Bolshevik revolt and invaded Khiva,[15] overturning the khan and organizing the revolutionary committee on February 1, 1920.[16] For two months, this committee, chaired by Mullah Jumaniyaz Sultanmuradov, passed legislative acts and implemented them. In April 1920, the First Assembly of Peoples Representatives in Khorezm declared the creation of the Khorezmian Peoples Soviet Republic, still independent but loyal to Russia. A new 15-member government, which included leading Jadids and heads of Turkmen tribes, was formed; the first prime minister was Povlon-niyez Yusupov (1861–1936).

The leaders of the new Khorezm Republic continued the old anti-Turkmen policy and suspected treason from the three Turkmen tribal chiefs who became members of the Khorezm government. On September 15, 1920, the Turkmen chiefs were arrested and executed. The next day, their 96 followers were also executed. About 300 prisoners were tied in groups of four and walked to Tashkent for investigations. Those who could not walk fast enough and slowed down the movement of the group were killed during the march. When the surviving Turkmen prisoners were transferred by the Russians under Uzbek protection, the Uzbek guards cut off the heads of the wounded Turkmen and proudly displayed them. Junaid Khan united 4,000 armed Turkmen riders to fight the Bolsheviks and the Khorezm government. The Khorezmian Uzbek government requested that the Tashkent Soviet send a Russian punitive expedition to burn down settlements, which belonged to the armed tribes under Junaid Khan. The chauvinistic policy of the Uzbek government in Khorezm and mass executions of Turkmen leaders with the support of the Russian representative ended all illusions of the first days of the republic and showed the impossibility of a union between the Uzbeks and the Turkmens. Iran attempted to organize an international campaign to protect the Turkmens whose property was taken, and wives with children were sold, but this effort was unsuccessful.

On September 13, 1920, a union treaty and a trade agreement between the Russian Federation and Khorezm were concluded in Moscow. According to the treaty, Russia recognized the independence and sovereignty of Khorezm and established that banks, factories, trade offices, and other enterprises and institutions formed by the Russian capitalists on the territory of the Khiva khanate before the 1917 Russian revolution would be nationalized. The border between Russia and Khorezm was defined as the state border, and the Khorezmian army was formed under the RSFSR supervision, according to the treaty. After signing the union treaty with the Russian Federation, the Uzbek government demanded full independence in its nationalistic policy and, following the provision of the treaty regarding military cooperation with Russian troops, demanded that the Russians disarm the Turkmen, which seemed impossible.

Russia did not take the treaty's provisions seriously and, using a large military contingent located in Khorezm, constantly intervened into the republic's internal affairs. On March 6, 1921, a military coup d'etat was initiated—a fraudulent trick of the Russian activists and Khorezm Red Army soldiers, who were dissatisfied with the food supply. Following the coup, the Yusupov government was overthrown, and Yusupov was arrested while trying to leave the country. Other members of the Khorezmian government, afraid of being caught by the Red Army, joined Junaid Khan's guerilla formations. The revolutionary committee—consisting of representatives of the communists, Russian troops, and the poorest inhabitants of Khiva—accepted the all-powerful functions. In May 1921, the Bolsheviks called a new Congress of People's Representatives and organized new elections for power authorities, similar to those in Russia. Later, during the next four years of the Khorezmian Republic's existence, Moscow's Bolsheviks changed leaders of these pro-Soviet institutions 10 times, arresting, expulsing, and executing members of previous governments.

Beginning in 1922, democratic reforms were stopped and the building of a socialist society was declared as the major goal. Political changes and consequences of state revolts were reflected in the Khorezmian constitutions. Every year between 1920 and 1923, a new constitution for Khorezm was adopted. The first constitution of 1920 declared democratic freedoms and political rights for the entire population. Under the request from the Communist Party, the constitution was amended in 1921, with provisions limiting the electoral rights of the people and making their voting dependent on the lack of property possessions.[17] In October 1923, the Khorezmian Republic was transformed into the Khorezm Soviet Socialist Republic, and a new socialist constitution was adopted. The constitution prohibited the owning of private lands and eliminated communal lands. Soviet courts and law enforcement bodies were to be established instead of local judicial institutions as well. In 1923, the local currency was substituted with Russian money, and the following year it became a part of the united Russian financial system; the national army was dissolved as well. On November 2, 1924, the fifth all-Khorezm Congress of Peoples Representatives decided to terminate the Khorezm Soviet Socialist Republic (SSR). Twenty-three administrative districts of the Khorezm Republic with predominantly Uzbek populations joined the Uzbek SSR as the Khorezm province. Other former Khorezm areas were included in the Turkmen SSR and the Karakalpak Autonomous Region.

After subduing Khorezm, the Russians switched their attention to Bokhara, where the emir negotiated with the British, who had occupied Ashgabat, and the emir of Afghanistan. The neutralization of Afghan involvement in Central Asian affairs was a strategic political objective for Russia, which had difficult relations with Ammanulla Khan, who ruled Afghanistan in 1919–1929—although, officially, the relations were friendly. The politics of Ammanulla Khan was a display of strong support to Central Asia and a manifestation of Islamic compassion, on one hand. On the other hand, this policy was characterized by unfriendly actions toward Russia, pan-Islamism, and attempts to annex foreign territory. After the victory in the third war against Britain, the ambitious Afghani leader wanted to become even more popular as a unifier of the Islamic word after the fall of the Ottoman Empire. He was under the strong influence of the reform movement of the Young Afghanis and tried to show himself as a defender of Islam in the region. Also, the Afghan people and Central Asians, although divided by a state border, were relatives and had common Muslim sacred places in Bokhara and Samarkand, including burial sites of famous Islamic clerics on the territory of modern Tajikistan and Uzbekistan; most of the Afghan Sunni clergy studied in Bokhara. To fight England in Asia and gain access to the Indian Ocean, the Bolsheviks prepared to spread their revolutionary activities into Afghanistan. In the case of military success, the Afghan Revolutionary Party was prepared in Tashkent, tasked with the duty to eliminate the existing system and establish the People's Soviet Republic.

As soon as the Anglo-Afghan Treaty of August 8, 1919, was passed, it left Afghanistan officially free and independent in its internal and external affairs. A high-level delegation was sent to Bokhara to discuss the perspectives of an anti-Bolshevik Afghani-Bokharan alliance. Negotiations did not produce any practical results; however, to support the Bokharans, the Afghan military instructors with 12 cannons arrived in Bokhara. Historians explain cold relations between Bokhara and Kabul as due to political differences between the emirs. The young reformist Afghan emir had nothing in common with the old-fashioned conservative pro-English Bokharan dictator. It appears that Ammanulla Khan was more interested in the Basmachi movement in the Fergana Valley and wanted to penetrate and destroy its connections with the Russian White Army and the British consul in Kashgar, Percy Etherton. The Afghanis promised the Peasant Army of Fergana 5,000 rifles and up to 10,000 soldiers to fight the Bolsheviks. In exchange, the Basmachi leader Madamin-bek was supposed to request protection from Afghanistan. The Fergana insurgents were not sure of the real intention of the Afghani government, which had just finished fighting the war against Britain, and remained loyal to Moscow. Under initiatives of the White Army officers, who were afraid of the growing Islamic nationalism, the Ferganis decided to ask for military assistance but postpone declaring Fergana as Afghanistan's protectorate. In February 1920, the Fergana delegation arrived in Kabul. While negotiations slowly continued in Kabul, the pro-Bolshevik Muslim Military Brigade was transferred to Turkistan under Lenin's orders. Czech and Austrian prisoners of World War I were also located in the area, and, together with the Red Army regiments, they increased the Bolshevik presence and conducted punitive operations against guerillas. After a number of military defeats, Madamin-bek and other Basmachi leaders refused to continue their fight, and Kabul sacrificed Turkistan in favor of better relations with Moscow.

After an agreement with Afghanistan had been reached, the next step for the Russians was to include Bokhara in the sphere of their influence. They wanted to create a government that would look as if it had native support and cooperated with the former Jadid leader Faizulla Khodjaev, who used the Bolsheviks to gain power. A short period of Bokhara's relative independence was stopped on September 2, 1920, by the Turkistan front troops under Mikhail Frunze. The siege of Bokhara was conducted in the form of assisting the revolting people with the use of the native military units, which were trained and armed by the Red Army. The anti-emir forces could not take the city and conducted air bombardments, which ruined and destroyed many historic buildings in the city center. The emir escaped to Afghanistan,[18] but his sons were sent to Moscow as hostages with the emir's throne as a trophy, where it still remains. After the troops entered the city, a wave of violence began. Treasures from the emir's palace were stolen, and mosques were turned into barracks and stables. Some military leaders were investigated, but no one was convicted because Moscow decided that, politically, this would be more harmful than useful.

Faizulla Khojaev became a chairman of the newly elected government, the People's Council of Nazirs (ministers), and, on October 8, 1920, in the former emir's summer palace, the Bokharan People's Soviet Republic (BPSR) was proclaimed. The new Communist government immediately nationalized all water supplies, unoccupied lands, and large private real estates for redistribution among the poor peasants. The Tajiks living in areas surrounding Bokhara were incorporated into the state; the Uzbek language was declared the state language, displacing the Persian of the emir and the Tajiks who made up 20 percent of the population. The new constitution of the People's Republic of Bokhara declared the nation's sovereignty and established a government responsible to the people. Also, the constitution defended the right of private property and established Islamic law as the leading legal system. Freedom of religion and freedom of expression and assembly were guaranteed. On the local level, the Soviet authority was combined with the traditional authority of the elders. Men and women older than 18 years of age were granted electoral rights dependent on one's social status, income level, and previous associations with the emir's government. Because most of the population was illiterate, poverty-stricken, and attached to Islam, the government experienced a shortage of skilled personnel. The restoration of some religious principles and the old regime's officials' return to power were necessary to avoid a clash with the people and the failure of government institutions.

The RSFSR was the first foreign state that declared the full recognition of the Bokharan Republic. Later, in Tashkent, military and political agreements were concluded between the BPSR and the RSFSR, and, on March 4, 1921, the union treaty entered into force. Following major provisions of the treaties concluded between Russia and Khorezm, these documents restricted independent political activities of the Bokharan leaders and transferred some of their authority to Moscow. The treaty legitimized the presence of Russian troops on Bokharan territory. For many years, Russia had to keep in Bokhara a strong military unit of up to 30,000 soldiers, who suffered from guerilla attacks and malaria. These troops, which moved about at will and imposed requisitions on the population responsible for the troops' maintenance, seriously undermined Bokhara's independence.

Economic agreements of 1924 were aimed at subjecting the Bokharan economy to Russian planners. According to the new rules, all Bokharan exports could be sold only through Russian foreign trade organizations. Bokhara's foreign policy was determined in Moscow as well, and the borders of this republic were guarded by the Red Army. Although the Bokharan government existed only because of Russian support, it was not an entirely puppet government. Russian representative in Bokhara, Valerian Kuybyshev, reported that many decisions were passed without his involvement and that he could not control the government of an independent country. The Young Bokharans gradually changed their policies and opposed the Bolsheviks. In 1921, the Bokharan chief of state, Usman Khodjaev, requested Afghan assistance against Russian violations of Bokharan sovereignty. The change of the state language from Persian to Turkic was a sign of moving toward the creation of a greater Turkic state. With the Basmachi danger, the Bolshevik regime was forced to tolerate the Young Bokharans' demands to integrate original specifics into the social revolution. Unlike in Khorezm, there were no revolts nor coups in Bokhara, and Faizulla Khojaev led the country during these years.

In the spring of 1922, Ammanulla Khan of Afghanistan decided to become involved in Central Asian politics again, and he supported the failed anti-Bolshevik revolt in Bokhara. The insurgents received weapons for this revolt from Afghanistan in exchange for cattle and money collected in Bokhara as a tax for fighting the infidels imposed by the fundamentalists. Afghanistan's troops were concentrated near the border but did not dare to enter the battle after the Russians massacred about 10,000 Tajik fighters and an unknown number of civilians. Although the formal Afghan troops did not participate openly in the conflict, two groups of supporters of 300 persons each were sent to Bokhara. According to some reports, Bachai Sakko, the future emir of Afghanistan, was one of the fighters. The Red Army's victories in Bokhara in the spring of 1922 and British indecisiveness in assisting Central Asians forced Ammanulla Khan to return all of his subjects to Afghanistan within a 20-day period and to remove troops from the border. The failure of the Bokhara emirate and the subsequent losses of the Basmachis entailed a mass emigration from the Bokharan border area; about 250,000 Bokharans immigrated to Afghanistan in the first half of the 1920s. The refugees were provided with moral and material support; however, the Kabul regime denied Bokharans political assistance in their fight against the Soviets. Meanwhile, the Soviets did everything possible to secure their southern borders, including conducting direct invasions into Afghan territory. Several raids were conducted to eliminate leaders of the Bokharan diaspora in Afghanistan.

Being an independent state, Bokhara had its own constitution, coat of arms, flag, anthem, national currency, and army. The constitution was adopted in 1921 and provided for equal political rights of all individuals. The constitution provided for the Tajik and Turkmen autonomous provinces within the Bokharan Republic and guaranteed minority rights in areas of education and culture. Despite the fact that the Bokharan national currency was stable and stronger than the monetary systems of other countries in the region, the local money was substituted with Russian currency in 1923, allowing for the Bokharan involvement in a single economic space of the former Russian Empire. Attempts to form a national army were not supported by the population, and a military draft was totally ignored. Because of that, in addition to a permanently located Russian garrison, several regiments were transferred from the Turkistan ASSR to Bokhara. Bokhara tried to conduct an independent foreign policy and provided financial assistance to the Turkish government of Kamal Ataturk; concluded trade agreements with Germany, where large groups of students were sent to study; and created a favorable investment climate for businesses from Japan, China, and Iran. Afghanistan was the second country that recognized the Bokharan independence. In 1922, the Bokharan ambassador to Kabul signed a secret treaty with the emir of Afghanistan regarding the expulsion of the Red Army units from Bokhara, provoking a significant international outcry when it became known. Upon Russia's request, the Bokharan Embassy in Kabul was closed on June 18, 1923. Since then, all interests of Bokhara in Afghanistan were represented by the ambassador of the Soviet Union. Bokhara's independent democratic policy could not satisfy Moscow; party officials trained in Moscow and Tashkent were put in Bokharan government bodies, and, under strong pressure from Moscow, the constitution was amended in 1923. According to the amendments, all salespeople, entrepreneurs, and people who possessed more than the administratively defined amount of property lost their voting and other social and political rights. On September 20, 1924, the name of the republic was changed to the Bokharan Soviet Socialist Republic; at the end of 1924, the republic was terminated, and its territory was divided between the Uzbek and Turkmen Soviet Socialist Republics. For the Tajiks, an ASSR was created as a part of the Uzbek SSR.

THE BASMACHI MOVEMENT

Throughout the revolutionary period, the Bolsheviks were fighting the insurrection against Soviet rule all over Turkistan. What began as a movement of peasant origin because of destitution and dispossession of the local inhabitants changed from being anti-Bolshevik to anti-Russian. The insurgency, known as the Basmachi movement, was a combination of Muslim traditionalism and common banditry.[19] Initially, the Basmachis were active in the states independent of but allied with Soviet Russia. Throughout the 1920s, the Basmachis operated mostly in the eastern parts of Soviet Central Asia and in northern Afghanistan, using the mountains for protection.

Although the first gangs were formed by Junaid Khan in Turkmenistan, historians believe that the movement was formed by the deposed emir of Bokhara, Sayid Mir Alim, who fled to Dushanbe in 1920 and formed the Basmachi movement there. Following the advance of the Russian army under Mikhail Frunze, the emir fled to Afghanistan in March 1921, where he joined Ibrahim Bek; in December of that year, he attacked Dushanbe and recaptured the city with 15,000 men. The Basmachis were especially strong when Enver Pasha, commander of the Ottomans during World War I, moved to the area and became the professional leader of the movement. Enver Pasha posed as a commander and chief of all Muslim troops and turned the fight into a struggle of all Muslims, seeing the insurrectional movement as an instrument of achieving his goal of building a Muslim Central Asian state. At the height of the movement, the Red Army sent about 20,000 soldiers to contain the guerillas. Even though Enver was captured and executed in 1922, the Soviets had to spend considerable resources until the ultimate suppression of opposition. The Russians blamed aid from the Afghan emir and British arms in continuing fierce resistance to the Red Army. The Basmachis lost their dominance in local affairs after the Afghani emir stopped supporting the insurgents and removed Afghan troops from the Soviet border.

The Basmachis fought a number of campaigns between 1922 and 1931, before they were defeated by the Soviet army. For example, in 1922, the Basmachis created a government crisis in Bokhara when the state's police chief joined the resistance and took the entire force with him. The unity of the ruling party was broken, and the Bokharan government faced the question of whether to support the insurrection or remain faithful to the revolution. In mid-January 1924, Junaid Khan attacked Khorezm, starting uprisings throughout the country. It took seven months for the Red Army to expel the rebel force. In July, Junaid Khan managed to escape to Persia and then to Afghanistan. The Soviets sent as many military and secret police resources into Khorezm as they could spare, but guerilla raids and other anti-Soviet activities continued for the remaining months of the Khorezm republic despite harsh repressions. It appears that the Basmachi movement was never completely destroyed. These Islamic fighters against bolshevism relocated to neighboring Afghanistan and continued their resistance from there. Their descendants contributed to defeating the Soviet army during its Afghanistan intervention in 1979 to 1987 and are currently supporting the Islamic movements of Central Asia in their fight against remnants of the communist elite and secular leadership.

SOVIET NATION BUILDING

After defeating foreign intervention in 1921 to 1923 and failing to spark social revolutions in Europe, the Soviet Communists switched their attention to socialist developments in the East. The power and unity of a centralized Soviet government was seen by the Moscow Bolsheviks as a necessity, and the Red Army was considered as a proper tool to bring indigenous governments on the territory of the former empire in conformity with the Soviet doctrine.[20] The Bolsheviks wanted to consolidate all of Turkistan under Soviet control by ordering an economic union of the three republics. For this purpose, two parallel institutions were created to rule the region. The Central Asian Bureau, which worked as an intermediary between the central committee and the regional parties, supervised the political parties of Bokhara, Turkistan, and Khorezm and communicated conditions in the field to Moscow. The powerful Central Asian Economic Council was the Central Bureau's companion agency. The council distributed cash, credit, and access to industries for new republics and spent most of 1922–1923 unifying the economies of the People's Republics of Khorezm and Bokhara with that of Soviet Turkistan—although, formally, these republics remained outside of the Soviet state.

At the end of 1923, the economies of the three Central Asian republics were merged, and the Soviet authorities prepared for the complete dissolution of the three Turkistani republics and the incorporation of new Soviet Socialist Republics of Uzbekistan and Turkmenistan into the Soviet Union. The efforts to install identical Soviet legal systems, schools, land relations, and government structures in Khorezm and Bokhara were all intended to smooth the way for a complete incorporation. For this purpose, the Bolsheviks placed trusted local people in high-level offices. Following major communist principles, the authorities established a state monopoly on the cotton trade, closed farmers markets and bazaars, prohibited individual trade, and introduced numerous labor duties.

The idea to divide Turkistan into a number of autonomous republics according to language and ethnicity was based on the assumption that the separation would help to prevent nationalist conflicts in the future and eliminate the inequality in the development of the native people. The drawing of borders was done largely by Central Asian communists and reflected their senses of divergent national identities. Stalin and the Commissariat of Nationalities[21] favored the idea of a national territorial autonomy granted to clearly defined national groups rather than to the broad mixed territories.

The Soviet administrative structure created in 1924 was aimed at providing each major ethnic group in the region with a separate administration.

On October 14, 1924, the All-Russian Central Executive Committee (then the highest state authority) passed a resolution on the creation of national states for the people of Central Asia. Initially, only two major union republics were created. Uzbekistan received the central part of the former Bokhara emirate, the southern part of the old Khiva, and the regions of Samarkand, Fergana, Amu Darya, and Syr Darya, formerly included in the Russian Turkistan. The territory of Turkmenistan included Turkmen regions of western Bokhara, Khorezm, and the former Transcaspian region. All other parts of Central Asia were established as constituent components of the Soviet republics with different degrees of autonomy. Lands traditionally occupied by the Kazakhs and Kyrgyz were defined as an autonomous republic within Russia, and the Tajiks received mountainous regions of former Bokhara with an Iranian-speaking population. The name of Turkistan was a symbol of unification—one of the reasons that this word disappeared from the map.[22]

During the Soviet era, researchers thought that the creation of five separate republics in Central Asia reflected a divide-and-rule policy in response to the danger of pan-Islamism and pan-Turkism. Recently, historians recognized that the delimitation was based largely on dogmatic visions of Lenin and Stain, who believed that all people had to go through a national stage of development before they could reach the socialist stage.[23] Among other reasons for creating these ethnically based political units, the specialists name the necessity to administer the fractious and economically backward region, and they cite economic resources and their management as a factor in the delimitation.[24] In February 1925, the first all-Uzbek congress of Soviets in Bokhara passed the Declaration on Creating the Uzbek Soviet Socialist Republic and formed its highest authorities. Faizulla Khodjaev became the chairman of the republic's government, and a peasant from the Fergana Valley was elected to chair the Central Executive Committee (formal head of state). Samarkand was chosen to be the capital city, and the newly created Uzbek republic immediately submitted its application to join the Soviet Union, which was granted soon thereafter. On March 25, 1925, the Tajik ASSR was created within the Uzbek SSR. The formation of Tajik and Uzbek republics was done on the basis of ethnic, economic, and administrative considerations—although the primary difference between the Tajiks and Uzbeks was linguistic, because there were no clear territorial lines where the different languages were spoken.

The newly created Central Asian states received a certain degree of cultural and linguistic autonomy but were deprived of political and economic independence. The main goal of the state-building process in the region was to replace a unified Central Asia with smaller national republics. After turbulent years of revolutions, in 1925, Central Asia found itself again under the control of the Russian Empire—although this time the empire was ideologically driven and its name was the Soviet Union.

NOTES

1. Allworth (1989), 220.

2. Khalid (1998), 286.

3. Allworth (1989), 221.

4. Krader (1996), 109.

5. The Bokhara khanate was located on the territory of present-day Uzbekistan, Tajikistan, and a large part of Turkmenistan. It bordered Afghanistan in the south, Russian Turkistan in the north and east, and the Transcaspian province of the Russian Empire in the west. The population of Bokhara was 2.2 million people, 35,000 of whom were Russian subjects.

6. Plenipotentiary government representative, a position equal to the rank of an ambassador.

7. Allworth (1989), 228.

8. The Jadids returned to Bokhara in 1920, with the help of the Red Army.

9. Rywkin (1990), 20.

10. Rywkin (1990), 22.

11. Jeremy Smith, *The Fall of Soviet Communism 1985–1991* (Houndmills, Basingstoke, England and Hampshire, NY: Palgrave Macmillan, 2005), 84.

12. Rywkin (1990), 19.

13. The designation Kyrgyz was applied to the entire Kazakh-Kyrgyz area of the present day.

14. Allworth (1989), 233.

15. Khiva had a population of 550,000 people and bordered the Bokhara Republic and Turkistan ASSR.

16. Three months later, the khan was arrested for counter-revolutionary activities and was expelled from the country.

17. Attempts to declare gender equality and deprive the clergy of voting rights provoked a mass uprising during which about 300 locals were killed by Russian troops.

18. After a brief attempt to mount a resistance from Tajikistan, the emir of Bokhara, Sayid Alim Khan, found refuge under British protection in Afghanistan, where he lived for the rest of his life. The emir, the last reigning descendant of Genghis Khan, died in Kabul, Afghanistan, in 1944, virtually unnoticed.

19. Some historians believe that the potential military threat that basmachi represented to the Soviet power was recognized but overestimated because, according to its organization and goals, the movement was based on local solidarities without embracing the idea of a national struggle. See Khalid (1998), 286.

20. Allworth (1989), 250.

21. A cabinet-level government agency responsible for developing and conducting the Bolshevik policy in regard to religious and ethnic minorities. Joseph Stalin was the first head of the Commissariat for Nationalities when it was created immediately after the Bolshevik Revolution in October 1917. This position was Stalin's first government-level appointment.

22. Allworth (1989), 259.

23. Shoshana Keller, *To Moscow, Not Mecca: The Soviet Campaign against Islam in Central Asia, 1917–1941* (Westport, CT, and London: Praeger, 2001), 62.

24. Arne Haugen, *The Establishment of National Republics in Soviet Central Asia* (Houndmills, Basingstoke, England and Hampshire, NY: Palgrave Macmillan, 2003), 154.

7

The Soviet Rule (1925–1991)

The Soviet government viewed the creation of modern Central Asian states as the notion of a national identity based on ethnicity and language. Cultures and histories were developed by the Soviets for each of the republics, giving each nation its share of the events that had happened in the region during the previous centuries.

Some people believed that the Soviet promise to provide local people with opportunities for the development of their statehood and independence was genuine. Immediately after the Tajik ASSR was created, 8,000 Tajiks who lived in the mountainous Badakhshan province of Afghanistan protested against discrimination, the introduction of mandatory education for girls, and some other reforms, and they asked for refuge in Soviet Tajikistan. After some consultations in Moscow, the issue was transferred to Tashkent, where local administrators viewed any form of mass protest and improvements in cross-border relations between Central Asian people of the same ethnicity with suspicion. Not willing to harm relations with Ammanulla Khan of Afghanistan, the authorities ordered the expulsion of the refugees back to Afghanistan, where they were met with firing squads. This episode of disregarding the interests of the constituent people by Communist authorities began the Soviet period of Central Asian history.

CENTRAL ASIAN REPUBLICS IN THE SOVIET UNION

The Soviet Union was a federation of 15 national union republics. Legally, all union republics had equal status with the same degree of self-government and dependence on the federal power, having uniform systems of governing bodies and political institutions and being subordinate to those of the Soviet Union. The formal governing body in each republic was its own popularly elected legislature, the Supreme Soviet, which met twice a year for three-day sessions to enact bills prepared between sessions by staffers. Because the Soviet doctrine did not accept the concept of the separation of powers, the Supreme Soviet elected its chairman, who was the formal head of the republic. It also appointed a prime minister and other members of the cabinet, who, according to their positions, were awarded with parliamentary seats. The government together with the staff of the Supreme Soviet influenced the formation and work of the provincial Soviets and their executive committees, a kind of provincial government. The heads of these committees were the provincial Soviets' chairpersons simultaneously. However, the real decision-making authority in the republic was the Central Committee of the republic's Communist Party. The USSR constitution provided for the Communist Party's leading and directing role. Following this constitutional principle, the secretaries of the Central Committee provided guidelines to all agencies and institutions of the republic, monitored their daily activities, defined who would be elected to the Soviet positions, made all key appointments in state institutions, and organized the work of lower-level (provincial and district) party committees, which were in charge of governing their respective territories.

A union republic enjoyed special rights, even if these rights were granted only theoretically. Being part of the union, each republic had individual representation in federal authorities. All chairmen of the republics' Supreme Soviets were simultaneously deputies of the chairman of the USSR Supreme Soviets. First secretaries of the Communist Party Central Committees in the republics had a seat in highest political organs, and one of the federal legislature's chambers—the Council of Nationalities—represented national units by a fixed number of delegates per unit: union republics had 25 seats each, autonomous republics had 11 seats, and autonomous provinces had 5.

Formally, each republic of the Soviet Union was a sovereign state with its own constitution and symbols of sovereignty such as a flag, coat of arms, and national anthem. The USSR constitution and the constitutions of each republic—which were largely identical and were passed in 1937 and 1978, following changes in the federal Constitution—retained the right of free secession from the union by the republics. Usually, constitutions of the republics elaborated major principles declared by the USSR constitution and customized them according to local conditions. Central USSR authorities controlled the conformity of the republics' laws with the USSR legislation, whose superior role over the laws of the republics was secured by the constitution.

The Soviet constitution provided for three types of jurisdiction: all-union, mixed union-republican, and exclusive republican, where local authorities could exercise some degree of autonomy. From time to time, the federal government transferred particular areas of industry and culture from one jurisdiction to another. For example, defense, national security, and foreign relations were always the exclusive jurisdiction of federal authorities.[1] Agriculture, health, education, public order, social security, and justice were under the joint jurisdiction of the USSR and republics. Republics were largely responsible for control over local industries, communal economies, services, and road construction.

Constitutions of all five Central Asian republics proclaimed basic human rights—specifically those of women—and they contained statements about struggles with old customs, which excluded women from participating in social, economic, and political events. Unlike all other constitutions, the constitution of Turkmenistan specified that contract marriages, bride purchases, restricted choice of husbands, and the resistance to drawing women into study or work were punishable by laws. Constitutional provisions were implemented and national laws were adopted by the republics' Supreme Soviets. Varying in only minor details, they were based on the same principles provided by federal legislation. National codes in the area of criminal, civil, and procedural law were issued in the late 1950s and early 1960s for the first time; before that, the RSFSR codes were applicable in the Central Asian states.

Uzbekistan was the first of all union republics to adopt a new judiciary law, criminal code, and criminal procedure code. The main feature of the criminal code of Uzbekistan, passed on May 29, 1959, was the decriminalization of minor offenses—such as minor theft of public property by employees—and the transfer of such cases into the jurisdiction of courts of peers, which could discipline and reprimand the defendant. Decriminalization of minor offenses was a response to Stalin's past policy of severe prosecution of all violations. On the other hand, new offenses, such as violations of an individual's freedom and interference with the privacy of home and postal communications, have been included in the code. Similar provisions were added to the codes of other Central Asian republics.[2] These provisions were never upheld, because it was impossible to bring suits against the government—the only possible violator of privacy rights during the Soviet era—and they can be viewed as propaganda. Among other regional specifics included in the code were violations of the equal status of women, forcing a woman to enter a marriage, interference with the obligatory education of all children (presumably taking girls out of school), and damaging cotton plants. This last provision was intended to increase the general sanctions against malicious damage of this especially important crop and criminalize harm done even by mere negligence in that particular section of agriculture.

Despite the fact that all republics were legally equal, federal treatment depended on the loyalty of the republic and its geopolitical and industrial status. This status defined the amount of federal investments allocated to each republic, access to international contacts, and the rank of the republic's leaders in the highest Soviet authorities.[3] Sometimes, different geographical and cultural regions within the same republic received different treatments depending on party strength, which historically varied from one nationality to another. While the republics were part of the Soviet Union, Russian was the common language for interethnic communications and one of two official languages of each republic. Russian was taught to children starting with the first grade; professional education was conducted in Russian language as well. All official documents issued by the republican authorities were published in two languages—Russian and the native language of the respective republic. Local authorities avoided Russian and used the native language as a rule. At the end of the Soviet rule, almost half of the Kazakhs and Uzbeks reported fluency in Russian. In Kyrgyzstan, Tajikistan, and Turkmenistan, which were less industrially developed, one-third of the population spoke Russian in their daily life.

All important personnel decisions were made in Moscow according to the principle of dual leadership. Under this principle, a leader of the republic was a native person but always had a reliable Russian assistant to supervise and provide reports to Moscow, where most of the key positions were occupied by ethnic Russians and other Slavic people. A similar scheme was exercised at all other levels of government. In 1962, Soviet leader Nikita Khrushchev introduced the short-lived Central Asian Bureau of the Communist Party Central Committee. The bureau worked as a political and economic coordinator of four Central Asian republics and one province of northern Kazakhstan. The agency restricted the authority of the republican institutions and served as an intermediary between Moscow and the republics. Soon after Khrushchev's dismissal, the bureau was closed in order to establish direct relations between the federal center and the republics. Moscow authorities did not interfere deeply in internal affairs of the union republics as long as local leaders met planned requirements for taxation and production supply and behaved according to the rules accepted by the party. The local communist elite knew how to deal with Moscow and assured central authorities that everything in the republics was under control. This situation continued until the end of the 1980s. With some insignificant variations (depending on the political priorities of Moscow's leaders during the Soviet period), all five republics were subjected to the relatively same industrial, agricultural, and social policies.

INDUSTRIALIZATION

Over the course of Soviet rule, Central Asia experienced huge successes in industrial development . In the late 1920s and early 1930s, the Soviet Union doubled its gross domestic product (GDP); however, in Central Asia, during the same period, the GDP increased five-fold, and before World War II, the overall industrial output was six times greater than it had been in 1913.[4] In large and heavy industry, the growth was even larger, and the 1913 level was increased 95 times. These impressive figures were based on the fact that industry was almost nonexistent in the region before, and primary developments occurred in the areas of food processing, fuel and power supply industries, and the production of local crafts. The main feature of the economic development was total nationalization of the economy and establishment of a state monopoly in all areas of technological development, including small local individual enterprises, which were united into state-controlled cooperatives.

The economic development of Central Asia coincided with massive ideological campaigns aimed at creating enthusiastic feelings among the local proletariat. Mandatory lunch time and after-work classes on Marxism and the Communist Party's history were supplemented by severe administrative measures aimed at strengthening workers' discipline. As soon as the Soviet power was established, all religious holidays were cancelled and it was prohibited to take off from work any day except Wednesday, because the Bolshevik revolution of October 25, 1917, had occurred on a Wednesday. In 1925, the government of the Uzbek SSR ordered to move the weekly day off to Friday because the majority of the population was Muslim. The Bolsheviks did not tolerate this proreligious retreat for long, and, in 1927, labor laws in Central Asia were brought in conformity with the rest of the Soviet Union.

The Central Asian economy was the most specialized in the Soviet Union and relied almost exclusively on cotton. This specialization developed as a result of the region's climatic conditions and its land and water resources, which favor cotton cultivation. Since the first days of the Soviet rule, federal authorities were focused on building a specialized infrastructure to serve the cotton industry: irrigation networks, branches of machine building, chemical industries to produce mineral fertilizers, cotton processing plants to clean the cotton and produce cottonseed oil, textile mills, and some garment factories. The absence of a long-term strategy made the industrialization of Soviet Central Asia uneven. Despite the fact that about 3,000 new enterprises opened in Central Asia in the 1920s and 1930s during the entire Soviet period, the region had the lowest ratio between population and industrial output in the USSR. Soviet economists explained the slower development of Central Asia and the disproportion between the resource extraction and technological industries as being the legacy of economic backwardness from prerevolutionary times. The building of an economy began in the late 1920s with the region's basic industry—the processing of agricultural products. It was easier for the state to revitalize previously existing meat packing plants and wool washing facilities, which could serve as examples of expedient developments along the empire's periphery; however, this development turned out to be very limited and specialized. An uneven concentration of newly created enterprises in the existing big cities preserved the underdevelopment of the remote and rural areas.

Turkmenistan, which remained largely underdeveloped during the Soviet period, provides a typical example of Central Asian republic's economic development. With the exception of gas and oil, the minimal economic activity that existed was largely maintained by Soviet central subsidies. The industry unrelated to gas and oil complexes was generally not commercially viable. The country's specialization in cotton production was based on massive irrigation subsidies.

Until 1930, food processing was the main branch of Central Asian industry. In Kazakhstan, for example, it comprised 57 percent of the total production, while the share of mining was only 6 percent. An effective restoration of nonferrous metal production and coal industries required large amounts of capital, complicated equipment, and good transportation networks—factors that were absent in the region. In the years before World War II, the pace of industrialization slowed because federal resources were redirected toward defense industries. Most of the military-related construction occurred in the European part of Russia. The European zone was responsible for 80 percent of Soviet national industrial production and energy consumption, although this area was poorly supplied with resources. Conversely, Soviet Asia had a bulk of resources but only a small share of industrial production. There was no substantial development of communications lines as well. The old Tashkent-Orenburg railroad remained the main transportation artery supplemented by the Turkistan-Siberian railroad completed in 1930. This railroad was built to deliver grain to southern Central Asia more rapidly and free more lands for cotton growing. The line did not live up to its expectations, mainly because the Siberian economy failed to meet Central Asia's needs for grain. Eventually, this line became the main evacuation route after Germany invaded the Soviet Union and was later used for shipping timber to Central Asia.

There is an opinion that following the divide-and-rule policy, Moscow was not interested in establishing industrial branches in Central Asia with a complete production cycle—from extraction of the raw materials to the manufacture of finished products.[5] This policy was reverted during World War II, when Central Asia became the evacuation destination for major Soviet industrial enterprises that moved inside the country to be saved from invading German troops.

In preparation for World War II, the leadership of each Central Asian republic was assigned to accelerate the development of industries necessary for defense. This changed the industrial structure of the region. In Uzbekistan, more than 200 enterprises were switched to manufacturing of munitions; in Kazakhstan, attention was concentrated on coal mining, and its production rose from 30,000 tons of coal in 1930 to 4 million tons in 1937 and 6.3 million tons in 1940. The most important economic development in the entire Central Asian region was the construction of a steel complex near Karaganda, Kazakhstan; however, this steel mill did not have full production cycles and operated on scrap metal and imported pig iron. To increase productivity, in 1938, all institutions and enterprises were working seven days per week with a floating day-off schedule to ensure always having a critical number of employees at work. Also, criminal responsibility was introduced for late arrival at work. Everyone 12 years of age and older who showed up at work 20 minutes later than scheduled was subject to imprisonment for a term of no less than three years.

On June 22, 1941, Hitler's Germany attacked the Soviet Union. During the first five months of the war, German troops occupied the territory with 40 percent of the Soviet population and approximately 70 percent of the nation's economic potential. The survival of the country depended on the ability of the government to evacuate industrial enterprises from European parts of Russia. The scale of the evacuation was unprecedented: 30,000 trains transferred 1,530 large factories and plants to the east between June and December of 1941. More than 200 of them were placed in Kazakhstan, 30 in Kyrgyzstan, 100 in Uzbekistan, and 20 in Tajikistan. More than 300 new enterprises were established in the region employing those who were rescued from the occupying Germans. On the fourth day of war, labor mobilization was declared, which required working 13 hours per day, six days a week; the cancellation of all annual vacations; and prohibition to leave the place of work voluntarily under the threat of an eight-year imprisonment. Food supply was rationed—workers received one pound of bread daily, and nonworking family members received half a pound of bread. There were limits on all other types of food; however, even these norms were rarely met because of inadequate supply.

During the entire Soviet period, Central Asia experienced a shortage of labor needed to build and operate all the enterprises established in the region. With this purpose, the Soviet government forcefully resettled many people from different parts of the country to Central Asia. Sometimes this movement was part of a large ideological campaign aimed to bring volunteers, and sometimes it took the form of criminal punishment. The mass and disorderly forced resettlement of millions of people produced a serious demographic and economic impact in the region. It is estimated that, during the years of Soviet rule, the total number of forced migrants moved to Central Asia amounted to

3 million people, 2 million of whom were placed in Kazakhstan and the rest in other republics. About 700,000 were destined to Uzbekistan and 200,000 to Kyrgyzstan. Tajikistan and Turkmenistan received the smallest number of forced migrants. About 6,000 Iranian Jews were moved from Azerbaijan to Turkmenistan and 2,000 of the so-called traitors and enemy abettors—that is, people accused of collaborating with German troops during their short-term occupation in World War II—were moved from the northern Caucasus region to Tajikistan.[6]

Before World War II, which brought the largest number of migrants, Central Asia had two major waves of settlers. According to a resolution of the Communist Party Central Committee of March 20, 1931, 150,000 households of relatively rich peasants from the European part of the country were relocated to Kazakhstan during the summer of 1931. The deportees were to be employed in mining (for coal, copper, and iron ore) and railway construction. The next wave of resettlers to Central Asia were family members of prisoners of war, prostitutes, and refugees present on the territory of eastern Poland after September 1, 1939 (after it was acquired by the Soviet Union). These people and those who expressed a wish to leave for the territory occupied by Germans but were rejected by Germany were subject to resettlement in the USSR inland. Later they were followed by ethnic Germans and so-called prosecuted people from the northern Caucasus—Chechens, Ingush, Karachai, Kalmyks, Balkars, Meskhetian Turks, and Crimean Tatars. The first and largest transportation was conducted in February 1944 with 400,000 Chechens. In Kazakhstan, they concentrated primarily in Akmolinsk, Pavlodar, north Kazakhstan, the Karaganda provinces, and in Kyrgyzstan in the Frunze and Osh provinces. Most of them were sent to work at the oil fields in western Kazakhstan because they had been employed in the oil industry at home. It appears that Central Asian republics were under strong pressure from Moscow to increase the receipt of special resettlers. For example, in 1944, Uzbekistan agreed to receive only 70,000 Crimean Tatars; however, it later revised its plans and conformed to the figure of 180,000. This required a republican department for special settlements to be established and given the task; 359 special settlements and 97 *komendaturas* (supervision and registration bureaus) were prepared.[7]

The evacuation increased the industrial potential of Central Asia. During the war (1941–1945), the output of machine building grew 653 percent, steel production increased from 11,000 to 119,000 tons, coal output grew from 3,000 to 1,500,000 tons, and electricity production increased from 481 million to 2,679 million kilowatt hours. After the war, geological research revealed that Central Asia had much greater energy resources than previously believed. However, further economic development of Central Asia depended on the effectiveness of the centralized command economy. Using the war victory as evidence that the selected economic model was correct, Stalin's propaganda discarded any possibilities for independent regional development.

Using ideological stereotypes, Soviet leaders refused to restructure the Soviet military economy and continued to develop defense-related industries. In the 1950s and 1960s, Central Asia continued to increase its ability to produce ore, metals, chemicals, and electric power. The largest Soviet hydro power plants were constructed in Tajikistan and Uzbekistan, transforming the region into an important part of the Soviet military industrial complex. Approximately 50 military plants were located in Kazakhstan. In the 1960s, they produced 18 percent of all Soviet armored carriers, 11 percent of artillery systems, and up to 95 percent of navy equipment. The main Soviet rocket and the space science complex was placed in northeastern Kazakhstan with its headquarters in Baykonur. The full cycle of nuclear weapon production from uranium exploration to warhead testing was conducted in Kazakhstan. Since 1949, 487 nuclear explosions (out of 715 conducted in the USSR) were made in Kazakhstan. Twenty-five nuclear missiles were launched and detonated in Kazakh air space as well, but neither the testing nor the damage it caused to the people's health were mentionable before Gorbachev's *glasnost* policy. Other parts of Central Asia were selected as dumping grounds for toxic waste; arsenic wastes were brought from the entire Soviet Union for storage near Tashkent.

At the same time, the production of consumer goods was modest. In 1950, slightly more than 100 textile enterprises existed in the region, most of which had not been reconstructed since the Bolshevik revolution. Despite being the major source of raw material and producing 95 percent of the USSR's cotton, 15 percent of Soviet vegetable oil, 100 percent of machinery and equipment for cotton growing, and more than 90 percent of equipment needed for irrigation, the share of Central Asia in the Soviet clothing, textile, and shoe industries was less than 2 percent. Another major area of government concern was the improvement of services for the population. Government intervention was needed to open a child care facility or bicycle repair shop in a remote town. The service level of public utilities was very uneven; most towns and district centers received gas supplies, but many smaller settlements and villages lacked gas and water supplies. Before the 1970s, some areas of the capital city of Tashkent had inadequate drainage, which caused epidemic diseases.

Governments of the union republics had no real influence over economic decision making regarding their states. They were limited to the preparation of recommendations—not plans—for the development of industries directly managed by federal ministries but located in their territory, and they could only comment on long-term plans that were prepared for them by federal ministries.

Some positive developments occurred in the early 1960s, when Nikita Khrushchev, then the USSR leader, introduced a new system of territorial economic administrations. Between 1957 and 1965, regions were given an opportunity to control their own economies. Initially, each Central Asian republic had its own administration, but in 1962 these were combined to form a single economic territorial administration for the region that integrated republics' economies into a unified economic system. The Central Asian administration defined the distribution of investments and independently managed many spheres of economic activity. In the late 1960s and for the rest of the Soviet period, Moscow completely reversed this policy, denouncing the territorial administration as narrow-minded localism, and returned to centralized management.

In the 1970s and 1980s, all of the industrial development of Central Asia was related to cotton production. The machine manufacturing focused primarily on agriculture and textiles. There were some exceptions—aviation in Uzbekistan, precision instruments in Kyrgyzstan, electric power equipment in Tajikistan, and oil equipment production in Turkmenistan. But the production of machinery for the cotton growing complex, and secondarily for textile manufacturing, predominated. The textile industry provided the most employment. To support irrigation projects needed for cotton production, power plants were actively constructed during this period.[8] In regard to transportation, there was no new construction of railroads, and the development of highways remained very poor. Most of the current routes follow the old tsarist post roads from Tashkent to Almaty; air transport, however, became an important addition. During the Soviet period, airports were built in all major and many minor cities of the region.

Because of the extensive development, all official statistics showed substantial growth. Every five years, approximately 100 new industrial enterprises opened in each republic. In 1985, the year when Mikhail Gorbachev initiated his liberal reforms, the output of industrial production in Central Asia was 21 times more than it had been in 1941. However, all this development was narrowly defined because of the insistence of the federal authorities on development of the cotton monoculture and on transforming the region into a supplier of natural resources for the entire Soviet Union.

Instead of educating the native population and involving them in industrial works, the state brought thousands of specialists from Russia and other areas. This easier short-term solution created numerous social and political problems, including nationalistic conflicts in the long term. Although legal inequalities between the Russian settlers and native people were removed in the mid-1920s, the natives enjoyed equal opportunities in labor (except specific key positions), housing, education, and health care. Local programs similar to affirmative action were introduced in the 1930s. Since then, the Muslim job seekers and college applicants were favored within their own republics. This practice was resented by the non-native population; however, Moscow favored this anti-Russian discrimination, considering it as necessary for reducing Muslim opposition and continuing Soviet presence.

Economic development slowed down in the 1980s. Because of disproportions in industrial development and centralized management, the Soviet Asian economy lost its competitiveness, economic reports were inflated to meet the plans determined by Moscow, corruption and lawlessness increased, and a radical economic reform was required to avoid the coming economic crisis.

AGRICULTURE

Soviet policy was an extension of the tsarist agricultural policy, with an emphasis on growing cotton on gigantic collective farms. As in all other fields, in agriculture, the Soviets started with an immediate property reform, which continued from 1925 through 1929. During the reform, all irrigation systems were nationalized, and land that belonged to beks (peasants who had large herds and hired other peasants to work) was confiscated and redistributed among the poorest locals. During this reform, in 1925, 25,904 households in Fergana, Tashkent, and Samarkand provinces of Uzbekistan suffered from confiscations; 16,490 of households were totally terminated. In 1928, 2,088 households that employed workers were liquidated in Khorezm. In Kyrgyzstan, lands and possessions of approximately 4,000 households were given to the 18,587 poorest families, and, in Uzbekistan, lands of farmers were divided among 94,551 landless peasants. Because these newly created individual farms did not receive anything except land (no seeds, animals, or equipment), they could not survive, and the reform did not achieve its goal of involving poor peasants in agriculture. In Kazakhstan and Kyrgyzstan, the problem was complicated by the policy of forceful settlement of nomadic people, which undermined nomads' traditions and methods of raising herds. Fifty-four thousand animals were confiscated and 277 people were executed for attempts to save their herds between October 1928 and November 1929 in three provinces of Kazakhstan.

In 1928 to 1932, the process known as collectivization started in Central Asia. During this campaign, individual peasants' households were united into collective farms. Privately owned land plots, tools, and livestock animals were transferred to government-owned and managed collective farms, where previously independent farmers became hired employees. As a rule, several neighboring villages were united into a collective farm, which was often the only employer in the area. Typically, all people living on the lands developed by the collective farm were members of that farm—excluding teachers, physicians, police officers, and salespersons, who were employed by institutions directly subordinated to district authorities. Until the mid-1960s, farms were not allowed to have their own heavy machinery; instead, machinery was concentrated at district tractor stations. According to a preliminary approved schedule, all machinery was assigned to perform work for all farms in the district. Each collective farm was uniformly managed by the farm board and by its chairman, who was formally elected by the farmers but actually was appointed by the district party committee. Farm chairmen were controlled by the collective farm party organization and supervised by the party organization and administration of the tractor stations. District departments of agriculture directly supervised collective farms and tractor stations. The executive committee of the district Soviet exercised its authority through village Soviets. The district committee of the Communist Party supervised the work of all of them. The party district committee also approved the allocation of funds, delivery of supplies, fulfillment of production plans by collective farms, and could interfere in all other matters. The district management system was subordinated to provincial institutions, which reported to the authorities in the capital city of the union republic. The republic's leaders were held responsible to their bosses in Moscow.

The policy of collectivization had two major goals: creating large collective farms able to produce and export grain and cotton in large quantities and breaking the unity and will of the peasantry, which the government accused of not keeping in line with the proletariat.[9] Most of the peasants did not support the collectivization and did not want to join the collective farms, but they were forced to do so. To facilitate the collectivization, 8,000 ideologically trusted workers from Central Asian cities and 1,024 activists from Moscow, St. Petersburg, and other major industrial centers in the European part of Russia were sent to Central Asian villages. In January 1930, the party leadership determined districts in different parts of Central Asia for total collectivization, which meant that no peasant would stay outside the collective farms in these areas. The most rapid collectivization occurred in Kazakhstan, where total collectivization was reported in some provinces within a few months. In September 1931, 67 percent of all rural households in Uzbekistan, 56 percent in Turkmenistan, and 49 percent in Kazakhstan were collectivized. Those who joined collective farms lost their property and individual rights. Until the 1960s, passports were not issued to Soviet peasants, and they could not change their employment or place of residence.

Lacking agricultural knowledge and rushing to meet deadlines established by party committees, the collectivization instructors who were often appointed to chair collective farms violated laws and persecuted those who did not join the collective farms by cutting off the water supply, prohibiting peasants from shopping in local stores, increasing taxes, or evicting peasants from their houses and sending them out of the republic. Peasants' resistance to the Bolshevik undertakings, which was widespread and relatively well organized, did not weaken after the famine that followed the reforms. Many party workers were murdered, and bands of Asians burned down farm buildings and killed the collectivized livestock. Only in Kazakhstan, around 80,000 people participated in the approximately 400 popular uprisings between 1929 and 1931. Public disorder was so widespread that Stalin directed regular Soviet army units to fight the revolting peasants using artillery and aviation. Officially, 5,551 individuals were prosecuted in Kazakhstan for opposing the collectivization; 883 of them were sentenced to death.

Many Kazakhs migrated to neighboring republics, where the collectivization proceeded more slowly, or they returned to nomadic life because the collective farms could not provide the necessary food supply. In Kazakhstan, the destruction of lives and property was especially great compared to other regions of the Soviet Union. Approximately 1.5 million Kazakhs lost their lives during the 1930s, and most of them in the period of 1928 to 1932; some Kazakhs continued to die of starvation through 1938. Running away from the difficulties of collectivization, 2 million people fled to Russia and other Central Asian republics, while 200,000 settled abroad in China, Afghanistan, Mongolia, Iran, and Turkey. The lands vacated by these people gradually fell into decay and dereliction. This factor was likely a key reason for the notable concentration of the "special resettlers," collectivization opponents from European Russia and people who resided in the western border area—mostly ethnic Poles, Germans, and Finns—in Kazakhstan and other republics of Central Asia. Later, Koreans, Chinese, and several thousand Harbin repatriates removed from the Far East joined them. The resettlers were faced with cold weather, negligence, and irresponsibility of local authorities. For example, the 4,000 Koreans who arrived on December 31, 1937, in Kustanay, Kazakhstan, spent one week in locked carriages before there was any sign of activity from local authorities.[10] There was a lack of housing, water, food, medicines, and employment. Korean collective farms, the only ethnic-based enterprises, were created to employ the Korean population. They were engaged in rice and vegetable growing, fishing, and, to a lesser extent, cotton production and cattle farming. The resettlement of Koreans in Central Asia continued in the World War II and postwar years. The Koreans demobilized from the Soviet army, and labor battalions were allowed to work in these collective farms only.

The collectivization did not achieve the expected results; even worse, the livestock breeding economy was destroyed and many human lives were lost. The targets of settlement were not met, and only 30 percent of more than half a million people were settled in the 1930s. This failure resulted from the almost total illiteracy of the farm chairmen and the shortage of specialists. According to Martha Olcott, some regions of Kazakhstan averaged 1 accountant for every 12 collective farms and 1 technical specialist for every 50 farms. In June 1930, there were 416 agronomists in Kazakhstan, 4 of whom were ethnic Kazakhs.[11] Before the collectivization, there was hope that a new generation of native leaders loyal to the Communist Party would emerge, but permanent changes in personnel and fear of arrest made it impossible to resolve problems because local officials were made responsible for the party's mistakes. In two provinces of Kazakhstan alone, 100 officials were arrested and 300 were dismissed, and by September 1932, all senior party officials in Kazakhstan and other leaders of the republic had been arrested.

To make collective farming more attractive, some economic incentives were introduced in 1935. Collective farms were freed from required grain and milk deliveries for two years, and the required meat delivery was halved. All collectivized households were exempt from taxation in 1935, and individuals in traditional nomadic regions were allowed to keep a horse and small herds of sheep and goats. A short break in agricultural reforms occurred while the country's leadership was busy developing defense industries and fighting Germany in World War II, but in the early 1950s, new limits were introduced on the size and amount of property that peasants were allowed to possess. For many years, the Soviet Union remained one of the world's largest importers of agricultural products with exhausted land reserves.

In response to this need, Nikita Khrushchev introduced the Virgin Land program in 1954, which was aimed at eliminating grain deficiencies through developing semiarid steppe regions, most of which were located in the northern part of Kazakhstan, by sowing about 100 million of previously unused acres for wheat in an attempt to increase grain production with the least investment of capital. The economic wisdom of this policy is still questioned, because the area lacks adequate rainfall for full-scale farming, whereas it is suited for a pastoral economy. Regardless of mistakes and poor techniques, the sown area increased in Kazakhstan from 24.3 million acres in 1953 to 70 million acres in 1956 and to 72 million acres in 1958.

It is estimated that about 2 million people from other Soviet republics moved to Kazakhstan in the 1950s. Mostly unskilled migrants and former inmates, they soon became disillusioned and dissatisfied with poor living conditions and food supplies. Authorities unfamiliar with the specifics of the region[12] were not able to set appropriate work norms, resulting in hardship and low morale among workers.[13] There was constant personnel and management rotation, and many settlers left Kazakhstan and returned home. Those who remained rioted in 1959 and were suppressed by regular army. The voluntary people's militia units were created to supplement the police force, and, by spring 1960, 4,000 of such units included more than 132,000 individuals.[14]

The main crop cultivated on the virgin lands was grain; however, the production of wheat and cotton increased also. The initial success and substantial harvest increase was temporary because the farms lacked the required amount of equipment and storage facilities. A negative environmental impact of the program decreased its effectiveness. Soil erosion, desertification, and dust storms became common characteristics of the region and led to environmental problems.

Large irrigation projects promoted by the Soviet authorities contributed to the growing environmental problems of the region. The 100-mile-long Great Fergana Canal was built in the summer of 1939 by 180,000 people in 45 days. The canal brought water from the Syr Darya through the Fergana Valley and expanded the possibility of cotton production in the region. This and other canals were built by using unpaid laborers and prisoners. In 1940, about 160 miles of smaller canals were dug by the same method. Canals were built all over the region, and this construction brought great hardship to the local population, who were obliged to turn out in large numbers in shifts for no personal return. Up to 500,000 people were forcefully resettled all across the region in order to secure the needed work force. Irrigation works slowed down during World War II but began with a new speed after the war. In 1947, Soviet authorities approved the construction of the 500-mile Kara Kum Canal from the Amu Darya to Ashgabat, construction of which continued from 1949 to 1962. The canal irrigated 2.5 million acres, although it led to serious wind erosion on the land around the canal. Intensive irrigation channeled water away from traditional water reservoirs and led to the Aral Sea catastrophe.

The transformation of the Aral Sea—the world's fourth largest body of fresh water (slightly bigger than Lake Huron)—into a dead salty remnant that destroyed the fishing industry and ports illustrates how ruthless Soviet exploitation of lands and people resulted in environmental and social catastrophe. To boost the growth of cotton (which the Soviet authorities considered the main strategic Central Asian resource), water from the Aral's two major tributaries—the Amu Darya and the Syr Darya—was channeled into long canals to irrigate the surrounding desert and nourish new cotton fields. As billions of gallons of water were diverted from the Aral Sea, this water reservoir started to shrink. The restructuring of the economy and the application of water conservation techniques was not considered because they would entail a restriction of cotton production. The first signs of trouble became visible in the 1960s. The lake was drying so quickly that, over the next five decades, the lake lost 80 percent its volume. Evaporation and agricultural abuses made the Aral saltier than the ocean, which killed most of the fish. The shores shifted 50 miles to the north and are still receding. The collapse of the fishing industry and other economic problems have displaced as many as 100,000 people.[15] This ecological disaster was acknowledged in the 1970s, and plans to divert the Siberian rivers to Central Asia and build a 1,600-mile-long canal to bring water to desert areas of Kazakhstan and Uzbekistan were drafted. Opposition to these plans was the first publicly voiced antigovernment campaign during Gorbachev's *perestroika;* after the Soviet Union dissolved, these plans were dropped, and independent Central Asian states inherited the disaster.

Cotton specialization transformed the entire country into virtually one great cotton plantation.[16] Uzbekistan at that time was ruled by Sharaf Rashidov (1917–1983), who had been the head of the republic's Communist Party since 1959 until his death. Rashidov represented a new generation of Central Asian leaders who came to power after Muslim communists and Bolsheviks were purged by Stalin. He was among those natives who were recruited to the party career because they demonstrated their readiness to follow party orders, possessed ability to command, and eagerness to learn and succeed. Unlike the first generation of native leaders, who believed in the ideals of communism and revolutionary movement, new leaders knew little about communism and valued the benefits associated with the leadership. They were indifferent to dogmas and were motivated by opportunism and desire for power. Often bribes were paid by the natives in order to be admitted to the Communist Party, which became a club where membership guaranteed career promotion, protection, and welfare. Ideology was irrelevant or nonexistent; the Marxist terminology was memorized and recited like a prerequisite for membership.

Rashidov provided everything the Soviet rulers wanted from a union republic—obedience, law and order, stability, and as much cotton as possible. For the enormous power and relative independence he gained in Uzbekistan, Rashidov paid with the surrender of the Uzbek national will and spiritual and material values to Moscow and a catastrophic destruction of the country's environment and people's health. "In his eagerness to serve his masters, he even outdid their demands, delivering cotton below the price defined by Moscow, and promising even larger quantities of cotton than stipulated by Moscow planners. The ensuing statistics showed that he kept his word,"[17] for which he received the highest Soviet awards and, what was more important, full freedom in running his republic.

In the mid-1970s, it became obvious that the pace with plan targets could not be kept. Under constant pressure from Moscow to increase production at any price, cotton pushed out the other traditional agricultural crops; even the trees around peasants' houses were cut down to make way for cotton. Public schools in rural areas usually operated between January and March because the rest of the year teachers and students were forced to work in the cotton fields. The only thing that mattered was the quantity of cotton delivered to state procurement centers. It was impossible for the producers to fulfill the plan by honest means, and fraud proliferated. Falsification occurred mostly during the delivery. Heads of agricultural enterprises simply bribed the procurement inspectors to inflate the amount delivered, both on the delivery receipts and in reports to their superiors.[18] Another type of deception was to expand the area under cultivation and then to conceal this from the planning offices. Both these practices occurred on a massive scale. The profit for the nonexistent tons amounted to billions of dollars that went directly into the pockets of the republic's administrators. Part of these illicit earnings went for personal consumption, but a significant share was also reinvested to expand the underground business. A considerable part of the profits also were used to buy political protection through bribes paid to high-positioned people in Moscow such as the son-in-law of the Soviet head of state Leonid Brezhnev. In the 1980s, this falsification was rampant. The magnitude of the problem can be illustrated by the case of Akhmadzhan Adylov, the director of a cotton mill who, until his arrest in 1984, reigned for many years like a feudal lord over the town of Gurumsarai and surrounding settlements in the Fergana Valley. Approximately 30,000 people were under his control. According to Boris Rumer,[19] Adylov created his own small sovereign state; no one could enter his territory without permission; its borders were guarded by government police, who were nominally under the jurisdiction of the Uzbek minister of the interior but who were, in fact, in the service and pay of Adylov. This miniature state had its underground prison, which was used to confine and torture residents who demonstrated the slightest independence. Adylov had at his disposal colossal sums for bribing, and his influence was so great that sometimes candidates for a ministerial post in Tashkent came to Gurumsarai for an interview, where they might wait for days in Adylov's reception room. The enterprise under Adylov received millions of investment dollars, of which about half were pilfered.

The scandal had generated investigations and firings, and after 1983 Uzbekistan was swept by a massive wave of arrests. Hundreds of ordinary employees and top figures in the economy, including ministers and party officials, were brought to justice. Moscow's efforts to restore order were unsuccessful, however, and the replacement of officials was not effective. A tried and trusted party official who replaced Adylov was incarcerated within a year and a half for abusing his authority, beating subordinates, and falsifying reports on cotton production. Although the majority of the prosecuted were ethnic Uzbeks, there was nothing ethnically specific in this event. The root cause was not the Uzbeks' cupidity but Moscow's economic policy. Similar problems existed in other Central Asian republics.

POLITICAL AND SOCIAL LIFE

All aspects of social and political life in the Soviet Union were monopolized by the Communist Party, and cultural development was subjected to communist ideology. Historical roots and national specifics were declared signs of backwardness. Russification became a primary element of policies applied by Moscow toward the union republics. Michael Rywkin calls Stalin's nationality policy in the region the "teacher-pupil relationship," because, in 1929, one of the Soviet leaders explained the aims of the Soviet policy in Central

Asia as "teaching the people of the Kyrgyz Steppe, the small Uzbek cotton grower, and the Turkmen gardener the ideals of the Russian worker."[20] Native communists were required to monitor and secure ideological and political conformity, and make sure that the small Uzbek cotton growers joined the collective farm, their sons went to work in the city, their daughters took off the veil, and some of their opportunistic relatives joined the Communist Party. Native activists were supervising their own people while the Russian communists helped them and resolved more important questions, such as the fight against counterrevolutionaries.[21]

Social and cultural reforms started with changes in school policy. The cornerstones of this policy were the opening of new schools; mandatory elementary education for all pupils; the elimination of illiteracy; the expansion of publications in native languages; and the establishment of national theaters, universities, and research institutions. However, all these developments were coordinated with the ideologists in Moscow and were subject to censorship.

In 1926, the government initiated school reform and started to issue permits for opening local private schools. Not ready to prohibit Islam entirely, the government did not explicitly ban the teaching of religion and required that basic sciences be taught as well. The schools were funded by the parents and were supposed to be located in warm, dry, and airy buildings with a sufficient amount of desks. Students under the age of 8 were not admitted. Corporal punishment was forbidden, and the teaching of arithmetic, natural sciences, and native language was obligatory. Students under the age of 10 were permitted to study only for four hours a day, with breaks every 40 minutes, while older students could study up to six hours. It was not permitted for teachers to use students' labor for their personal needs. The students from the Soviet schools were not allowed to attend religious schools. Later, only children ages 14 and above were allowed to enroll in religious classes because the government hoped that antireligious propaganda would make them immune from Islamic influences. To restrict religious education even further, in 1928, the government limited the religious instruction of children to groups of three students. In 1929, such groups were recognized as small religious schools in secret form and were prohibited completely. Teaching religion in any government, social, or private school was forbidden.

The language reform was initiated in Turkistan in 1926. The Latin alphabet and a unified mode of transcription replaced Arabic script. The reform was not completed before 1935, when the second reform changed Latin letters to the Cyrillic (Russian) alphabet. According to official explanations, the 26 letters of the Latin alphabet could not represent all 38 Turkic sounds, and the 33-letter Russian alphabet was better suited for this purpose. However, the main purposes of the reform were the further Russification of Central Asia, penetration of national languages by the Russian language, and the facilitation of the study of the Russian language by the natives. During the first decade after the reform, the percentage of the Russian vocabulary in the languages of Central Asian people rose from 2 to 15 percent.[22] Subsequently, the number of words of Arabic or Persian origin decreased significantly.[23] The reform helped to establish closer cultural ties between Russia and Central Asia and performed an ideological function of making all previously published books, mostly of religious and anti-Soviet content, obsolete and not available to the masses.

This effect of the language reform coincided with the goals of antireligious campaigns that were constantly conducted during the Soviet era. According to Keller, the Soviet government attacked religion because its Marxist-Leninist theory dictated an atheist society and because it could not tolerate any rival for power.[24] In 1927, a total attack on religion began.

Usually, antireligious campaigns were carried out by the secret police; the campaigns physically eliminated most of the clergy and imposed strict punishments on believers. Most of the mosques were closed, so the buildings could be used for other purposes—such as warehouses, sport clubs, or concert halls—or they were disassembled for the building materials. The Religious Organizations Act of 1929 allowed for the construction of new houses of prayer if general technical requirements were observed; however, special conditions set up by police and not specified in the law were almost impossible to meet. This law prohibited all charitable activities of religious groups and introduced the direct supervision of religious activities by a person from a nearest police unit, village soviet, or city council assigned to attend all meetings of the believers. The agent was an observer with no right to participate in discussions or activities; however, he could close meetings and was obligated to do so in case of an outbreak of violence, deviation from the approved program, illegal activities, or upon the request of the meeting participants.

Often, closed mosques were used as court chambers. Muslim courts were not abolished until 1927, although their jurisdiction was gradually narrowed. In February 1924, they were barred from hearing criminal or important civil cases; two years later, they were prohibited from hearing divorce cases, and the People's Commissariat of Justice declared them to be part of a strictly voluntary judicial system. The eradication of Islamic courts did not mean the elimination of Islamic judges who proceeded from religious courts to the people's courts. Because judges were often unfamiliar with the adopted laws and statutes, they made legal mistakes and applied the traditional Islamic Shariah laws.

The liberation of women was one of the principal goals of antireligious campaigns aimed at eliminating traditional practices of veiling, polygamy, bride payments, and prearranged child marriages. In Central Asia, the emancipation of women contrasted with the norms of traditional society. Women were veiled and secluded from all aspects of social, political, and economic life and were treated as everything from humans to chattel, depending on how their families and villages and they themselves interpreted religious and social traditions.[25]

Although the Islamic reformist movement has promoted the adoption of European family structures since the early twentieth century, the veil was one of the most important symbols for Central Asian women. A few educated and brave Uzbek women unveiled themselves in the early 1920s, although they had no followers. In the late 1920s, a strong unveiling campaign began. Forceful attempts to liberate women had disastrous results and caused much bloodshed. In 1928, 104 cases of murder connected with the unveiling of women who had been victimized by their husbands' families were reported. The campaign had some positive results, too. In 1939, female students made up 42 percent of the urban school population and 41 percent of the rural school population. The position of women significantly improved during the Soviet rule. At the end of the Soviet era, 99 percent of women in the region were literate, and women accounted for almost half of all students in higher and secondary professional educational establishments. Women made up approximately 45 percent of all government and party officials. However, this statistic did not reflect the fact that most of the native women were employed in predominantly unskilled positions. The disparity between men and women was great in the field of science. Over one-third of the researchers were women, but women formed only one-tenth of the professors, PhD holders, and high-ranking academicians.[26] However, these figures do not imply discrimination. For many women, low-skilled jobs were a matter of preference because such positions provided the opportunities to have a shortened working day and to work near their houses in order to have ample time for domestic chores. Paradoxically, despite all the policies implemented, women in Central Asia remained the most conservative, religious, and tradition-bound component of the society.

Because child marriages or the practice of older men marrying pubescent or prepubescent girls (often as second or third wives) was an important local tradition, the Bolsheviks strongly enforced child protection laws and imposed severe punishments on violations. As compensation for the restrictions on women, it became acceptable in Central Asia for adolescent boys to take on the role of public sexual objects for men. These boys would dance suggestively in public gathering places and were sometimes acquired by wealthy patrons for sexual services. After the total sovietization of Central Asia, this practice was criminalized and eventually banned. In 1927, Turkmenistan and Uzbekistan started to regulate private sexual behavior in compliance with the new Russian Family and Marriage Code. Such activities as sexual relations with a minor, compulsion of a person to enter sexual relations, and even bride payments were criminalized. Because of the deep roots of local customs, polygamy was not considered a crime in Uzbekistan until 1931, although it was outlawed by the Russian Criminal Code in 1928, which was applicable in Uzbekistan.

The fight against Islam in Central Asia coincided with a cultural revolution aimed at freeing people from superstition and making them believe in the power of science and the ability of the Soviet state and Communist Party to lead the citizenry toward higher stages of economic and cultural development. For this purpose, pilots took peasants on airplane rides to prove that there was no God in the sky, while doctors used modern pharmaceuticals to demonstrate that germs caused diseases. The provision of biomedical services was one of the principal elements of Stalin's cultural policy, because it kept industrial workers healthy.[27] Between 1927 and 1937, in Kazakhstan, the number of physicians grew from 452 to 1,571, and the number of hospital beds increased from 3,767 to 16,290.[28]

The effectiveness of government efforts to undermine Islam was minimal. Forced mosque closings created outrage, the unveiling campaign injured or killed more women than it helped, and sending activists to the mosques on Muslim holidays occasionally resulted in murders followed by state reprisals. A secular society in Central Asia was created by modern development, industrial building, and the opening of universities and other educational institutions, which opened new opportunities for local people. Those who wanted to succeed had to play according to the rules of the twentieth-century industrial and widely nonreligious society. Nonreligious and (at least) bilingual urban elites were created in all five Soviet Central Asian republics. In the rural areas, which were much less affected by economic and social development, the enforcement of Soviet values was weaker and Islamic traditions were stronger. All over the region, Islam provided the population with the organizational, ideological, and institutional help to preserve the national culture, identity, and traditional way of life. The Central Asian party members who worked against Islamic institutions were probably motivated more by power politics than communist ideology and remembered Islamic traditions learned in their childhood. The next generations of officials did not have personal negative associations with the clergy but, dependent on the Communist system, they expressed at least superficial support to anti-Islamic campaigns. Behavior of those officials was dualistic, and those who closed down a mosque one day might hire a mullah to perform the funeral of a relative the next.

Stalin was afraid that national traditions hid opposition to the Soviet Union, and he accused native leaders who preserved national traditions of opposing Communist policies, which was a crime punishable by death. Despite the fact that almost all former Central Asian nationalists switched to the Soviet regime, almost all of them were accused of anti-Soviet activities and executed, while their family members were sent to prison camps in Siberia. Approximately 110,000 people were murdered in Central Asia between 1929 and 1953.

In Kazakhstan, 17 percent of all party members were purged and eventually sentenced to imprisonment. In Uzbekistan, during the period of 1937 to 1953, almost 100,000 people were tried, and 13,000 of them were executed. Arrests affected all levels of the society, especially the nations' clerisy and people who received their education abroad or who participated in revolutionary movements outside of the Bolshevik Party.

In February 1956, Soviet leader Nikita Khrushchev, who was trying to distance himself from the mass terror of the Stalin era, accused Stalin of political crimes and initiated the rehabilitation of individuals illegally prosecuted during Stalin's show trials. In Uzbekistan, in October 1956, the first secretary of the Communist Party, Nuriddin Muhitdinov, took the first step toward the rehabilitation of the purged Uzbek intellectual elites and announced the rehabilitation of some Uzbek writers. Muhitdinov stated that only certain Uzbek writers and poets, such as Abdulla Qodiriy, who had few ideological "mistakes and shortcomings" should be rehabilitated by the republication of what he called their "most valuable works." He thus excluded those Uzbek writers and poets who had "hostile intentions" and had been against the Soviet government during the early Soviet period.[29] Since Muhitdinov failed to mention any other Jadid writers by name besides Qodiriy, local neo-Stalinists ignored this proposal of rehabilitation. The full rehabilitation started only in the late 1980s, when Soviet president Mikhail Gorbachev announced his policy of *glasnost*.

On March 14, 1959, Sharaf Rashidov was elected the first secretary of the Central Committee of the Uzbekistan Communist Party, the highest post in the republic and one he held until his death in 1983. Later he turned his appointment into an unrestricted personal rule synonymous to lawlessness and exploitation of the people. Rashidov in Uzbekistan and his Kazakh counterpart, Dinmukhamed Kunaev—who was at the top of Kazakh authorities since 1942 until his dismissal in 1986—proved that the extreme centralization and uniformity of the Soviet system was largely a myth in regard to the implementation of policies in some Central Asian republics and in the areas where the center chose not to exert its power. Reports of confusion and nonimplementation of federal legislation in these republics often appeared in mass media. Traditional methods of feudal and tribal relationships were used by communist bosses in their practical activities. While these traditional relations were blessed by Islamic doctrine, the most outrageous forms of corruption, lawlessness, and oppression in Central Asia were carried out by local authorities disguised as Islamic traditionalists. Adylov, one of the leading figures in the cotton scandal, explained his cruelty by saying that he was a descendant of Timurlane.

Because Islam was not destroyed by repressions, Rashidov, Kunaev, and other local leaders assured federal authorities that Central Asian Islam presented no danger to Bolshevik rule. In reality, local elites were actively involved in destroying Islam, seeing its representatives as potential contenders to local political power. The local party elite replaced the regular clergy with local clergy who were willing to follow the directives of local party committees and the secret police. Although most of the population avoided any alliance with the discredited clergy, these people were viewed with some respect by the people of Central Asia because they knew Arabic, could read the Koran, and pilgrimaged. While traveling throughout the Muslim community abroad, they promoted a positive image of the Soviet Union. The parallel existence of official and underground Islam in Central Asia continued to the end of the 1980s.

The Afghan war initiated by the Soviet leadership in December 1978 impacted the re-Islamization of Central Asia. An almost immediate response to this invasion was the pan-Islamic jihad against Soviet intervention. This unified response brought about 35,000 Islamic mercenaries from many countries of the Islamic world to join the Afghan guerillas. Within this number were hundreds of ethnic Uzbeks, Tajiks, and representatives of other Muslim minorities of the Soviet Union who defected from the Soviet troops in Afghanistan or clandestinely crossed the southern border. Many of the young Soviet Muslims crossed the border to Afghanistan to strengthen their radical Islamic ideas in Pakistani religious schools. Eventually, the Soviet government understood how risky it was to use military servicemen recruited from the Muslim population of the country to fight their brethren in Afghanistan and stopped sending them to war.

In the 1980s, Central Asia—and especially the republic of Uzbekistan—became the center of crime and corruption in the Soviet Union. Despite the fact that 26,000 officials in Islamic provinces were fired and prosecuted between 1982 and 1985, federal authorities were getting weaker in their ability to force Central Asians to follow the course. Open cases of disobedience among Central Asian Muslims emerged in the early 1980s. During this time, Kyrgyz authorities openly ignored Moscow's demands to reprimand criminal officials, and Uzbek Communist Party leader Sharaf Rashidov was buried according to Islamic rituals at his widow's insistence, contrary to the strong opposition from the authorities due to the political visibility of the case.

While the Soviet Union entered the economic and political crisis, Communist parties of the national republics were acquiring more independence. In the mid-1980s, party membership was open to persons aged 18 and older and varied from 6.7 percent of the population in Kyrgyzstan and Tajikistan to 7.2 percent in Turkmenistan and to 8.1 percent in Kazakhstan and Uzbekistan. The variation was due to the urban-rural profile of the republic, the level of education, employment, nationality structure, sex ratio, and other factors. Very young and very old party members were relatively rare; the great majority consisted of middle-aged men. Titular nations were represented moderately, and a large part of the party consisted of non-Asians, especially non-Russian non-Asians. Another Communist Party paradox was that, despite officially being the party of the working people, party members were about six times as numerous among nonmanual labor group as among the groups of manual workers and collective farm peasantry. At the end of the Soviet period, only 1 in 30 members was a worker. All people in the leading and managerial positions were party members. The tendency to recruit those persons who were academically best qualified demonstrated the intent of party leaders to improve the intellectual quality of the party and the desire of the intellectually advanced individuals to obtain better professional positions, which were available with party membership only. That is why membership seems to be concentrated in the functions of management and direction rather than among the well-educated professional groups, such as teachers or physicians. Ordinary workers and laborers did not rush to join the party because admission to the party did not affect their daily lives. They did not receive any material benefits from being a party member (except for those who used the party for advancing their careers), and they were required to attend long and boring party meetings after work and pay party dues.

THE LAST SOCIALIST REFORM

In March 1985, Mikhail Gorbachev became the secretary general of the Communist Part of the Soviet Union (CPSU) Central Committee, immediately initiating the unprecedented program of reforms that became known as *perestroika* (rebuilding) and *glasnost* (openness). The goal of the reforms were to speed up the country's development and converge the ideas of socialism with basic principles of the market economy and social democracy. Without any real competition and a democratic political system, all changes remained illusionary, and the reforms did not bring the expected results. Because of the campaign against heavy drinking and the ongoing economic crisis, the federal budget shrunk, and the GDP of the Central Asian countries decreased in 1989 by 1 to 1.5 percent compared to 1985. The freedom of the mass media provoked public discussions about the future of the socialist society, ideological pluralism, and the national rebirth of the union republics. In Central Asia, local elites no longer feared Moscow's comrades and came forth to defend their national heritage and remind Russia of its colonial conquest and domination.

When Mikhail Gorbachev came to power, the government's anti-Islamic policy intensified. In November 1986, Gorbachev met with the members of the Central Committee of the Uzbek Communist Party, and, according to witnesses' accounts, he expressed so much hostility toward Islam in his instructions to local communists that his speech was not reported in the Soviet newspapers.[30] Later, Gorbachev's reforms brought the first relaxation to the religious lives of Soviet Muslims; the restoration of mosques was allowed, and the first political rise of Islamic self-consciousness was tolerated.

In the late 1980s, the ideas of sovereign state development became especially popular among national elites and intellectuals. In 1989 and 1990, all five republics adopted laws regulating the status of national languages, which were recognized as official state languages. The study of native languages was initiated and, together with the publication of previously prohibited books of national authors, it became a factor in the growing national self-consciousness. Informal social, political, and religious organizations were established. At first, these nongovernmental organizations focused on studying national traditions, culture, history, and environmental concerns, but many of them had overtly nationalist agendas. Later, these groups were transformed into political parties, which continue to play active roles in political processes today.

The growing gap between rising expectations and government promises of better life on one hand and worsening living conditions of the population on the other stimulated ethnic conflicts in the republics. The first ethnic conflict in the USSR, which was reported by the Soviet mass media, occurred on December 17–18, 1986, in Almaty, Kazakhstan. It started with the firing of Dinmukhamed Kunaev, the dogmatic and corrupt Communist leader of Kazakhstan, who ruled the republic for many years. Kunaev had been ousted largely because the economy was failing. Although Kazakhstan had the third-largest GDP in the Soviet Union, by 1987, labor productivity had decreased 12 percent, and per capita income had fallen by 24 percent. By that time, Kazakhstan was underproducing steel at an annual rate of more than a million tons. Agricultural output also was dropping precipitously.

The conflict between generations of Kazakh leaders began in January 1986, when the chairman of the Kazakh government, Nursultan Nazarbaev, harshly criticized Askar Kunaev, the head of the Academy of Sciences, at the sixteenth congress of the Communist Party of Kazakhstan for not reforming his department. Dinmukhamed Kunaev, Nazarbaev's boss and Askar's brother, deeply angered and feeling betrayed, went to Moscow and demanded Nazarbaev's dismissal while Nazarbaev's supporters campaigned for Kunaev's dismissal and Nazarbaev's promotion. Firing Kunaev, Mikhail Gorbachev ignored requests to promote the young and ambitious Kazakh Prime Minister Nazarbaev, and replaced Kunaev with Gennady Kolbin, an ethnic Russian who had no previous experience of working in Kazakhstan. Although the firing of Kunaev was expected because he was under official attack for cronyism, mismanagement, and malfeasance, the announcement of Kolbin's appointment provoked spontaneous street demonstrations by the Kazakhs.

About 3,000 youths, angered by the decision to replace the Kazakh leader with an outsider, participated in riots on December 17 and 18, 1986. Cars and food stores were burned, trees on main city squares were broken, and ethnic Russians were attacked and insulted. It is believed that, despite the fact that the riots were provoked by Kunaev's dismissal, their roots were in the popular resentments resulting from assertions of local party bosses that Kazakhstan was the bountiful provider of meat, bread, and steel for the rest of the country, with the implication that it was getting too little in return.[31] The demonstrators shouted slogans such as "Kazakhstan for Kazakhs!" and attacked non-Kazakhs on the street. A student and a policeman were killed, and an additional 200 people were injured. About 100 demonstrators were detained, and 12 of them were sentenced. This event was the first nationalist outbreak in the Soviet Union and the manifestation of deeply hidden nationalist feelings among native people of Central Asia. Fearing the spread of nationalist revolts, central Soviet authorities quickly punished local officials who failed to prevent these events. The former republic's leadership was criticized for inefficiency, corruption, nepotism, and high living. Scores of officials were purged, including those responsible for education.

While attempting to conciliate the Kazakh population with promises, Kolbin also conducted a purge of pro-Kunaev activists, replacing hundreds of republic-level and local officials. Although officially nationality-blind, Kolbin's policies seemed to be directed mostly against the Kazakhs. The downfall of Kolbin, however, was the continued deterioration of the republic's economy during his tenure. Agricultural output had fallen so low by 1989 that Kolbin proposed to fulfill meat quotas by slaughtering the millions of wild ducks that migrated through Kazakhstan. The republic's industrial sector had begun to recover slightly in 1989, but credit for this progress was given largely to Nursultan Nazarbaev, an ethnic Kazakh who had become chairman of Kazakhstan's Council of Ministers in 1984. By 1989, Moscow surrendered, recalled Kolbin, and replaced him with Kazakh Nursultan Nazarbaev.

Following Almaty riots in 1986, nationalist protests became more violent across the Soviet Union. By June 1989, when Kolbin was already scheduled for rotation back to Moscow, riots in Novy Uzen—an impoverished western Kazakhstan town that produced natural gas—lasted nearly a week and claimed at least four lives. In March 1989, an unusual and unsanctioned event took place in the Uzbek capital city of Tashkent. Thousands of demonstrators, mostly students, gathered in front of the city's main mosque carrying signs reading, "There is no truth if there is no religion." They called for a religious revival; demanded the removal of Central Asia's chief mufti, the leading spokesman for Soviet Islam who was accused of being too intimate with the Kremlin; and urged making Uzbek the official local language. Gorbachev responded by returning to the Uzbek religious leaders an ancient Koran that had been taken from the area by tsarist troops during the colonization. This act demonstrated a political turn toward Islam and Muslims.

The Osh ethnic conflict in Kyrgyzstan in the summer of 1990 was one of the largest and most violent riot-type conflicts on the territory of the former USSR. Osh is one of the most industrialized provinces. Almost all Kyrgyz oil and gas extraction is carried there. The conflict spread to nearby cities and villages, and attempts were made to expel the Uzbek population. During the week-long conflict, 120 Uzbeks, 50 Kyrgyz, and 1 Russian were killed, and more than 5,000 crimes were committed (including murder, rape, assault, burning of houses, and pillage). Violence was stopped by imposing martial law and sending army troops into the zone of conflict. According to some research, the conflict was related to an economic mafia's activities and an imbalance in the power structures of the republic, which represented major regional clans.[31] This conflict was the only conflict in the former Soviet Union that was followed by court investigations; most active participants of the unrest were identified and sentenced.

Following these conflicts, Gorbachev called for the creation of popularly elected legislatures and for the loosening of central political control to make such elections possible. For the newly elected legislations, the future of the Soviet Union became one of the most important issues. During 1990 and 1991, leaders of the Soviet Union and the Central Asian republics discussed and developed major principles for reforming the union; some republics started to change their political systems and elected their own presidents. On August 20, 1991, nine Soviet republics were supposed to sign a new treaty aimed at preserving the Soviet Union. On the eve of this treaty, however, a coup was staged by conservative generals and politicians in Moscow to destroy the creation of a new union entity and cancel freedoms brought by the Gorbachev reforms. Instead of preserving the Soviet Union, the coup, which collapsed in a few days, sped up the dissolution of the USSR. Kyrgyzstan and Uzbekistan declared their independence and secession from the Soviet Union on August 31, Tajikistan on September 9, Turkmenistan on October 27, and Kazakhstan on December 16, 1991. National and territorial units that were administratively created by Communist officials in the mid-1920s became independent and sovereign states.

NOTES

1. Union republics never had their own armed forces, because the Soviet authorities decided all military issues uniformly. During World War II, national Uzbek and Kazakh military units were formed, but they were dissolved and outlawed after the war. In the 1980s, Central Asian republics supplied the largest share of draftees for the Soviet army, which was built according to

Russian prerevolutionary traditions. The presence of non-Russians with various religious, cultural, and language specifics created problems and complicated Soviet military capabilities.

2. In Kazakhstan, the criminal code was adopted in July 1959. The code decriminalized national customs and traditions, making such acts as offering bride money or arranging a marriage no longer an offense. At the same time, penal sections were provided for acts such as nonfulfillment of economic plans and failure to support old parents or a wife incapable of working.

3. Mary McAuley, "Party Recruitment and the Nationalities in the USSR," *British Journal of Political Science* 10, no. 4 (October 1980): 462.

4. The most economically prosperous year of the Russian Empire before World War I, traditionally used for comparison by Soviet statistics.

5. Boris Rumer, *Soviet Central Asia: A Tragic Experiment* (Boston: Unwin Hyman, 1989), 104.

6. Pavel Polian, *Against Their Will: The History and Geography of Forced Migration in the USSR* (Budapest, Hungary and New York: CEU Press, 2004), 124.

7. Polian (2004), 152.

8. Because Central Asia has a high rate of seismic activity and suffers from frequent, occasionally powerful, earthquakes, nuclear power plants were not constructed in the region, and two-thirds of the existing power plants were based on hydropower.

9. Martha Olcott, "The Collectivization Drive in Kazakhstan," *Russian Review* 40, no. 2 (April 1981), 131.

10. Polian (2004), 257.

11. Olcott (1981), 141.

12. During the virgin land campaign in Kazakhstan, territories designated for land development were taken out from the jurisdiction of Kazakh authorities and subordinated directly to Moscow. Leaders of these territories were appointed by Moscow and were mostly Russian. This practice was cancelled after the campaign ended.

13. Roy Laird and John Chappell, "Kazakhstan: Russia's Agricultural Crutch," *Russian Review* 20, no. 4 (October 1961): 336.

14. Richard Stone, "Coming to Grips with the Aral Sea's Grim Legacy," *Science* 284, no. 4 (1999): 31.

15. Rumer (1989), 146.

16. Soucek (2000), 254.

17. Rumer (1989), 160.

18. For a number of years, the reports on cotton production were systematically inflated by 1 million tons per year.

19. Rumer (1989), 166.

20. Rywkin (1990), 111.

21. Ibid., 93.

22. Most of the Russian words that entered native languages are technical or political terms or modern Soviet or international acronyms and expressions. These words usually keep their original Russian transcription but retained endings and other grammatical forms traditional for native languages. Presently, Turkmenistan is the only Central Asian nation that switched its alphabet back to the Latin transcription. All other countries continue to use the Russian alphabet.

23. Shoshana Keller, *To Moscow, Not Mecca: The Soviet Campaign against Islam in Central Asia, 1917–1941* (Westport, CT, and London: Praeger, 2001), 18.

24. Keller (2001), 23.

25. Nancy Lubin, "Women in Soviet Central Asia: Progress and Contradictions," *Soviet Studies* 33, no. 2 (April 1981), 197.

26. Paula Michaels, "Medical Propaganda and Cultural Revolution in Soviet Kazakhstan, 1928–1941," *Russian Review* 59, no. 2 (April 2000), 162.

27. Michaels (2000), 165.

28. Patrick Bascio and Evgueny Novikov, *Gorbachev and the Collapse of the Soviet Communist Party: The Historical and Theoretical Background* (New York: Peter Lang, 1994), 83.

29. Adeeb Khalid, *The Politics of Muslim Cultural Reform* (Berkeley: University of California Press, 1998), 273.

30. James Jackson, "What Really Happened in Alma-Ata," *Time,* March 2, 1987, 17.

31. Valery Tishkov, "Don't Kill Me, I'm a Kyrgyz!": An Anthropological Analysis of Violence in the Osh Ethnic Conflict, *Journal of Peace Research* 32, no. 2 (May 1995): 138.

representatives proved to be able to monitor the presidents, their administrations, and governments. Presidents of these republics obtained unlimited power far exceeding the power they had had as Communist Party leaders.

Strong presidential systems in these states have hampered the emergence of political parties and effective legislatures. The presidents either feel themselves to be above politics, or they head or support dominant communist-type parties. Several presidents altered their constitutions to enhance their powers relative to their legislatures. Demonstrating a concern with at least appearing democratic, Central Asian leaders have not usually canceled elections—except in Kazakhstan, Turkmenistan, and Uzbekistan, where referendums on extending presidencies were held to circumvent competitive elections. Some presidents have delayed or forced early elections, such as legislative elections in Kazakhstan and Kyrgyzstan.

In Central Asian presidential republics, legal and bureaucratic systems have been adjusted to suit the interests of the presidents, and the political process reflects the strong role of clans, which have penetrated formal political institutions, divided economic resources, and defined electoral results.[2] These states share common legacies and are based on similar authoritarian principles; however, they pursue their own interests and design their own political, social, and economic policies. Table 8.1 summarizes the various democracy-building efforts of the five Central Asian republics.

Kazakhstan is an important power in Central Asia by virtue of its geographic location, large territory, ample natural resources, and economic growth. President Nursultan Nazarbaev was appointed by the legislature in 1990 and won an unopposed popular election in 1991. A 1995 referendum extended his rule. He was reelected in 1999 and 2005, and, in 2000, legislation granted him some official powers for life. In April 1992, President Nazarbaev announced his strategy of political and economic development of the country. This strategy declared Kazakhstan the state of the self-identified Kazakh nation, stimulating emigration of non-Kazakh people.

The first constitution of independent Kazakhstan, passed in 1993, balanced the authorities of the president with significant powers of the legislature. In December 1993, the presidential administration initiated the self-dissolution of the Supreme Council of Kazakhstan, which, before its dismissal, had given President Nazarbaev additional authorities not provided for in the constitution—including the right to make laws. The first elections to the Kazakh Parliament were held in March 1994; they were rigged and conducted with serious violations of law. In less than a year, the Parliament was dissolved upon a suit filed with the Constitutional Court. The latter was also dismissed and abolished soon afterward. Taking advantage of the Parliament's absence from March through December 1995, an extraconstitutional 327-member People's Assembly composed of cultural and ethnic leaders initiated

8

Post-Soviet Transformation

When the Soviet Union disintegrated in 1991, all Central Asian states began the same process of a sudden decolonization, independence, and political transition. Despite the proclaimed goals of adopting market economies and secular, democratic political systems, Central Asia seemed to be the least likely region in the former Soviet Union to become democratic.[1] The high monopolization of power in the hands of party officials inherited from the former USSR was the main reason that, in all five Central Asian states, a strong presidential rule was established. Former Communist leaders automatically became presidents of the newly independent republics, transforming Communist Party apparatuses into presidential administrations, although all these republics formally disavowed communism.

BUILDING OF STATE INSTITUTIONS

The new independent states professed intentions to democratize and to uphold human rights. These assurances were given when they joined the United Nations, the Organization for Security and Cooperation in Europe, and many other international and regional organizations. As shown by subsequent developments, super-presidential republics heavily dominated by the executive branch of power were created. Neither the people of these republics nor their

Table 8.1. Democracy Building in the Central Asian States

Criterion	Kazakhstan	Kyrgystan	Tajikistan	Turkmenistan	Uzbekistan
No civil war, separation is not a threat	Yes	Y–	No	Yes	Yes
Democratic constitution approved	Yes	Yes	Yes	No	Y–
Free and fair presidential election	No	Y–	Y–	No	No
Free and fair parliamentary election	No	Y–	N+	No	No
Multiple political parties operate freely	Y–	Yes	Yes	No	No
No extremist threat	Yes	Y–	No	Yes	Y–
Legislature is a powerful body	No	Yes	Yes	No	No
U.S. assistance under Freedom Support Act (FY2006), in millions of dollars	24.8	29.0	23.8	5.0	17.8

Note: N+ = No with some improvements; Y– = Yes with deviations from international standards.
Source: Supporting Human Rights and Democracy: The U.S. Record 2006 (Washington, DC: U.S. Department of State Department, 2007).

two national referenda, which extended President Nazarbaev's authorities until the year 2000. The assembly also adopted a new Kazakh constitution, under which most of the power was concentrated in the presidency, giving it substantial control over other branches of government. A Constitutional Council, which replaced the Constitutional Court in 1995, has three of seven members appointed by the president; the regional governors are appointed by the prime minister, but they serve at the discretion of the president, who also has the power to annul their decisions.

The bicameral legislature consists of a popularly elected 77-member lower chamber (the Majilis) and an upper chamber (the Senate), whose 39 members are indirectly elected by regional assemblies or by the president. The legislature cannot initiate changes in the constitution, exercise oversight over the executive branch, nor control the budget. The president may dissolve the legislature, while the legislature has highly limited power to remove the president. Most legislative activities occur behind closed doors, and ties with constituents are nonexistent. In late 1998, the legislature extended the president's term from five to seven years and enabled Nazarbaev to call an early presidential race for January 1999; he won against three other candidates with 79.8 percent of the votes.

President Nazarbaev won another term with 91 percent of votes in a five-man race on December 4, 2005. Many observers credited economic growth in the country and promises of increased wages and pensions as bolstering his popularity. Political in-fighting became public in February 2006, when Kazakhstan's police announced that it had detained the top aide to the speaker of the Senate and accused him of involvement in the abduction and murder of the opposition party's leader.

Kyrgyzstan seemed to be the most determined proreform state in the region when, in the summer of 1990, the Kyrgyz Supreme Soviet chose physicist Askar Akaev as the republic's first president. Akaev began pushing for political and economic liberalization even before the Soviet Union's collapse, commenting in a 1991 interview that, "although I am a Communist, my basic attitude toward private property is favorable."[3] In December 1991, shortly after obtaining independence, Akaev was reelected by a free and fair popular election. He led a political and economic shock-therapy program designed to democratize the new state. Kyrgyzstan was the first former Soviet country that introduced its own currency, adopted a Western-style civil code, a and a modern legal and regulatory framework, liberalized prices, privatized industry, adopted an open political system, and became the largest recipient of foreign aid. It was the first former Soviet country to join the World Trade Organization. The constitution was modeled on that of the United States, and other pieces of democratic legislation were adopted. During the early years of the transition, Kyrgyzstan experienced basic freedoms of speech, press, and assembly; the creation of an independent judiciary and a representative legislature; and legal protection of property rights. Without outbreaks of ethnonationalism and military coups, Kyrgyzstan had become a semiliberal democracy.

Dissatisfied with the constitution that he thought was idealistic, former President Akaev orchestrated in 1994 the dismissal of a legislature he found difficult to work with and accepted legislative power pending new elections. He initiated constitutional referendums to enhance his power in 1994, 1996, and 1998, creating a weak bicameral legislature called the Jogorku Kenesh (Supreme Assembly). This legislative body gave the president more power to veto legislation, dissolve the legislature, and appoint almost all officials, including local officials. However, he could not appoint a prime minister without legislative confirmation. It was more difficult to impeach the president, and it restricted his legislative power over bills involving the budget or other expenditures. Despite these changes, the legislature continued to display a degree of independence by passing many bills and overriding some presidential vetoes. The most recent referendum, in February 2003, re-created a unicameral legislature of 75 members and eliminated party list voting.

In 1995, the Constitutional Court was sworn in, and Akaev's distant kinswoman Cholpon Baekova was named to chair the Constitutional Court. Although she was a democratic reformer and most of her decisions were impartial, Akaev relied on her kin loyalties and other informal means of leverage when he needed judicial support during crises. Her 1998 judgment supported the constitutionality of Akaev's bid for reelection, allowing him to run for another term as allowed by the 1993 constitution. This decision disregarded his election in 1991 under a previous constitution and cost him popular legitimacy. Judicial reforms began in 1996, though the judiciary remains under the influence of the executive branch. Political parties are weak, and, although nearly 25 are registered, some are inactive. Less than half of the members of the legislature claim party affiliation, and voting rarely takes place along strict party lines.

Tajikistan was the least prepared and least inclined toward independence. In September 1992, a loose coalition of nationalist, Islamic, and democratic parties and groups tried to overthrow the government inherited from the Soviet period. Kulyabi and Khojenti regional elites, assisted by Uzbekistan and Russia, launched a successful counteroffensive that had resulted in 20,000 to 40,000 casualties and up to 800,000 refugees and displaced persons.[4] In 1993, the Commonwealth of Independent States (CIS) authorized peacekeeping in Tajikistan, consisting of Russian, Kazakh, Kyrgyz, and Uzbek troops. After the two sides agreed to a cease-fire, the UN Security Council established a small UN Mission of Observers in Tajikistan (UNMOT) in December 1994. In June 1997, Tajik president Rakhmonov and the late rebel leader Seyed Abdullo Nuri signed a comprehensive peace agreement. Benchmarks of the peace process were largely met, and UNMOT pulled out in May 2000. The current president of Tajikistan. Emomali Rakhmonov. rose to power as a representative of the Kulyab regional elite. In 1988, he became a state farm director in the Kylyab region, and, due to his links to a local warlord, he became chair of the Kulyab regional government in 1992. Weeks later, he was elected chair of Tajikistan's legislature and proclaimed head of state. He won presidential elections in 1994, 1999, and 2006 according to the 1994 constitution, which was adopted in a questionable referendum.

The constitution created a strong president with broad powers to appoint and dismiss cabinet members and other officials. The first presidential race was held at the same time as the constitutional referendum, and opposition was excluded from the electoral, constitution-drafting, and referendum processes. The legislative election of 1995 was marred by many irregularities—such as voter intimidation and ballot box stuffing—that precluded the election of an independent legislature. A significant movement toward ending the civil war was marked by the signing of a comprehensive peace accord in June 1997 and the inauguration of a National Reconciliation Commission. This commission has proposed a coalition government and has named several oppositionists to ministerial posts; however, the legislature, dominated by former communists, refused to confirm them. It has also violated provisions of the peace accords by banning religious parties, aimed against the oppositionist Islamic Revival Party. This ban created widespread protests that led to amending the law.

The 1994 constitution created three branches of power, including a legislature with usual parliamentary powers. In 1999, the legislature rubber-stamped constitutional changes proposed by Rakhmonov creating a seven-year presidential term and a two-house legislature[5] and legalizing religious parties. In 1999, the opposition again boycotted the election, alleging that the government prevented the opposition candidates from registering, so that Rakhmonov emerged as the only approved candidate. Rakhmonov won with 96.9 percent of votes. Seeking to avert renewed war, the opposition agreed to respect the electoral outcome in return for a pledge by Rakhmonov to allow fair legislative elections scheduled for 2000. New legislative electoral law was approved in 1999.

Five candidates ran in the presidential election in Tajikistan held on November 6, 2006, including incumbent President Rakhmonov. All four challengers praised Rakhmonov and campaigned little. The opposition Democratic and Social-Democratic parties boycotted the race, claiming it was undemocratic, and the Islamic Renaissance Party chose not to field a candidate; Rakhmonov officially received 79.3 percent of votes with a nearly 91 percent turnout.

Turkmenistan has made little progress in moving from a Soviet-style government to a democratic system. According to the U.S. State Department, during the late President Niyazov's rule (died December 21, 2006), Turkmenistan was the most authoritarian of the Central Asian states.[6] Corruption and nepotism were rife, and Niyazov's Ahal-Tekke tribe dominated cultural and political life.

On January 13, 1990, Turkmen Communist chief Saparmurat Niyazov was elected chairman of the Supreme Soviet, then the national legislature. In six months, the Supreme Soviet adopted the Independence Declaration and announced Turkmenistan a sovereign state. The presidency in Turkmenistan was introduced in 1990 as well, even before this institution was proclaimed by the constitution. Then the nation's leader, Saparmurat Niyazov, was elected president by 98.3 percent of voters.

The 1992 constitution calls Turkmenistan a secular democracy and provides for the separation of powers, but in actuality the president has absolute power and Turkmenistan remains a one-party state. It created a presidential republic in which the president is also the prime minister; he has the power to appoint all executive, judicial, and regional officials; and has wide authority to rule by decree and to control the legislative process. The government is silent on how the legislature (Mejlis) initiates and approves laws and on relations between the Mejlis and the quasi-legislative Khalk Masilkhaty, a 2,466-member People's Council with mixed executive and legislative powers consisting of members of the Mejlis, ministers, judges, regional executives, 60 unpaid people's representatives, and others.

Following the adoption of the constitution, Niyazov suggested conducting new elections, and he was reelected president in an uncontested race with an official tabulation of 99.5 percent of a vote that was widely viewed as fraudulent. In 1993, the former Communist Party, which was renamed the Democratic Party of Turkmenistan, recommended to extend the term of Niyazov's office until 2002. In January 1994, 99.99 percent of the voters supported this idea on a national referendum and confirmed his adopted moniker Turkmenbashi the Great, which means the Father of All Turkmens. In December 1999, the People's Council of Turkmenistan proposed to abolish term limits for the president, and, in 2002, the same People's Council made Niyazov president for life. Niyazov's portraits were printed on every piece of currency, and gold-plated monuments to him were erected all over the country. The 200-foot monument in the center of Ashgabat, the capital, rotated with the sun so his visage always faced the light. It is not clear in what direction Turkmenistan will develop under new president Berdymukhamedov, who was elected in February 2007.

Uzbekistan is a potential regional power by virtue of its relatively large population, energy resources, and location in the heart of the region. It has made scant progress in economic and political reforms, and its human rights record remains poor. President Islam Karimov was elected to the newly created presidency by the Uzbek Supreme Soviet in 1990. In December 1991, he was popularly elected president of Uzbekistan, winning 86 percent of the vote against opposition Erk Party candidate Mokhammed Solikh. In 1995, he won support by 99.6 percent of 11.25 million voters in a referendum to extend his presidential term until the year 2000. He has extensive decree powers, primary authority for drafting legislation, and control of virtually all government appointments. The dominant party is the People's Democratic Party (PDP) of Uzbekistan—the renamed former Communist Party—and most government officials belong to the PDP. Legislative races were limited to candidates from the PDP and several other progovernment parties.

In January 2002, Karimov orchestrated a constitutional referendum to create a bicameral legislature and to extend his term to December 2007. The new legislature (Oliy Majlis, or Supreme Assembly) consists of a 120-member, directly elected lower chamber and a 100-member upper chamber composed of 16 members appointed by the president; the rest are selected by local legislatures. The lower chamber has most of the responsibility for drafting laws, and the Senate confirms the prime minister and other top officials. Constitutional amendments approved in April 2003 established that—after the next presidential election—the prime minister will exercise greater power. Explaining his constitutional goals, Karimov in January 2005 proclaimed that he aimed to create three powerful branches of government, to correct a situation where "everything now depends on me."[7]

REGIONAL TENSIONS AND CONFLICTS

The legacies of the comingled ethnic groups, convoluted borders, and emerging national identities pose challenges to stability in all Central Asian states. Emerging national identities compete with those of the clan, family, region, and Islam. Central Asia's borders fail to reflect ethnic distributions and are hard to police. Ethnic Uzbeks make up sizeable minorities in the other Central Asian countries and Afghanistan. More ethnic Turkmen reside in Iran and Afghanistan (over 3 million) than in Turkmenistan. Sizeable numbers of ethnic Tajiks reside in Uzbekistan, and 7 million reside in Afghanistan. Many Kyrgyz and Tajiks live in China's Xinjiang province. (See Table 8.2 for comparative statistics on the ethnic composition of the five republics.)

Ethnic tensions were behind the civil war in Tajikistan (1992–1997) and many other violent conflicts in the region. In July and August 1999, several hundred Islamic extremists invaded Kyrgyzstan. Juma Namangani, the co-leader of the Islamic Movement of Uzbekistan (IMU), headed the largest guerrilla group. They seized hostages and several villages, allegedly seeking to create an Islamic state in south Kyrgyzstan as a springboard for a jihad in Uzbekistan. With Uzbek and Kazakh air and other support, the Kyrgyz army forced the guerrillas out in October 1999. Dozens of IMU and other insurgents again invaded Kyrgyzstan and Uzbekistan in August 2000. Uzbekistan

Table 8.2. Comparative Ethnic Groups in the Central Asian Republics

	Kazakhstan		Kyrgyzstan		Tajikistan		Turkmenistan		Uzbekistan	
	1989	2005	1989	2005	1989	2005	1989	2005	1989	2005
Total population (in millions)	16.5	15.2	4.3	5.2	5.2	7.3	3.6	5.0	20.1	27.3
Titular nation (%)	40	53	52	65	62	80	72	85	71	80
Russians (%)	38	30	21	12	8	1	9	4	8	5.5
Largest minority (%)	German 6	Uzbek 3	Uzbek 13	Uzbek 14	Uzbek 24	Uzbek 15	Uzbek 9	Uzbek 5	Tajik 5	Tajik 5
Other (%)	16	14	14	9	6	4	10	6	16	9.5

provided military assistance, but Kyrgyz forces were largely responsible for defeating the insurgents by late October 2000. In the summer before September 11, 2001, the IMU was involved with Osama bin Laden in a Taliban offensive against the Afghan Northern Alliance, and that prevented further IMU invasion into Central Asian states. About a dozen alleged IMU members invaded Kyrgyzstan from Tajikistan in May 2006 but were soon defeated.

A series of explosions in Tashkent in February 1999 were among early signs that the terrorist threat in the region is real. By various reports, the explosions killed 16 to 28 and wounded 100 to 351 people. During the trial, 22 suspects, 6 of whom were sentenced to death, revealed that they belonged to the IMU and were trained in Afghanistan, Tajikistan, Pakistan, and Russia. The aftermath involved wide-scale arrests of political dissidents and others deemed by some observers as unlikely conspirators. In September 2000, the State Department designated the IMU as a foreign terrorist organization, stating that the IMU, aided by Afghanistan's Taliban and by Osama bin Laden, resorts to terrorism, actively threatens U.S. interests, and attacks U.S. citizens. The "main goal of the IMU is to topple the current government in Uzbekistan,"[8] the State Department warned. IMU forces assisting the Taliban and Al Qaeda suffered major losses during coalition actions in Afghanistan, and IMU's leader Namangani was probably killed. On March 28 through April 1, 2004, a series of bombings and armed attacks were launched in Uzbekistan, reportedly killing 47 people. An obscure Islamic Jihad Group (IJG) of Uzbekistan, a breakaway part of the IMU, claimed responsibility. On July 30, 2004, explosions occurred at the U.S. and Israeli embassies and the Uzbek prosecutor-general's office in Tashkent. The IMU and IJG claimed responsibility and stated that the bombings were aimed against Uzbek and other "apostate" governments. Several IJG members were apprehended in Kazakhstan in late 2004.

The largest public unrest occurred in Uzbekistan on May 13, 2005. Dozens or perhaps hundreds of civilians were killed or wounded after Uzbek troops fired on demonstrators in the eastern town of Andijon. The night before, a group stormed a prison where businessmen accused of supporting terrorist groups were held and released hundreds of inmates. The freed inmates then joined the mob in storming government buildings and gathered thousands of people on the main square to demonstrate against the trial on terrorists. President Karimov flew to the city to direct operations and restore order. Reportedly, 100 or more individuals have been arrested and sentenced, including some Uzbek opposition party members and media and nongovernmental organization representatives. During the trials, the accused all confessed and testified that they aimed to overthrow the government; however, many observers criticized the trial as appearing stage-managed. The international community accused the Uzbek government of the indiscriminate and disproportionate use of force in Andijon and for the obstruction of an independent inquiry, which was rejected as violating the nation's sovereignty.

DEMOCRATIZATION EFFORTS

Several Central Asian leaders have declared that they are committed to democratization. Despite such pledges, no peaceful and democratic transition of power has occurred. Until recently, the only Soviet leader in Central Asia who had been replaced was the Tajik leader; he was ousted in the early 1990s during the civil war. The remaining leaders stay in power by orchestrating extensions of their terms, holding suspect elections, eliminating possible contenders, and providing emoluments to supporters and relatives. After this long period of leadership stability, President Rakhmonov of Tajikistan replaced the former Communist leader of the republic and became the formal head of this state in 1992, after Tajikistan declared its independence; President Akaev of Kyrgyzstan was toppled in a coup in 2005, and President Niyazov of Turkmenistan died in late 2006, marking the passing of three out of five Soviet-era leaders from the scene. Kazakhstan's president was reelected in 2005. A presidential election is scheduled for December 2007 in Uzbekistan.

In Kyrgyzstan, President Akaev was overthrown in March 2005, after tainted legislative elections. Government corruption contributed to the success of the protestors also.[9] Despite Akaev's promise to step down from power after his final term would expire in 2005, there was a possibility of a dynastical succession after his children won parliamentary seats in February 27, 2005, elections. These elections resulted in opposition candidates winning less than 10 percent of the seats, although there reportedly were many close races. Protests broke out in southern cities of Osh and Jalal-Abad with protesters occupying government buildings and the Osh airport. The protestors called for a new election and Akaev's resignation. Akaev refused to resign but pledged not to use force to end the protests. When the protesters stormed the presidential offices in Bishkek on March 24, 2005, Akaev fled the country with his family, escaping first to Kazakhstan and then to Russia. He submitted his resignation to a delegation of members of the Kyrgyz parliament visiting him in Moscow.[10] The Kyrgyz Parliament accepted the resignation after stripping him and his family members of immunity and privileges that had been granted to him by the previous parliament. In the following presidential elections, opposition politician and acting president Kurmanbek Bakiev received 88.71 percent of the votes.

A conflict between the executive and legislative branches over the balance of powers resulted in the passage of constitutional amendments in December 2006. The amendments established a mixed voting system for a new legislature to be elected in 2010, with half of the members elected by party lists and half in single-member constituencies. The legislature would be increased from 75 to 90 seats, and the body would have more influence over budget legislation. The majority party in the legislature would nominate the prime minister and cabinet.

Another power succession occurred in Turkmenistan in 2006, after President Niyazov's death. Because the late president was the prime minister of Turkmenistan as well, the chairman of the legislative body was supposed to become the acting president. However, the same day, news of the president's death was announced, and the speaker was accused of state treason and put in jail. Deputy Prime Minister Kurbankuly Berdymukhamedov, who, by some observers, was named as an illegitimate son of the deceased president, became an acting president. Because under law the acting president could not run for the vacant office, the constitution was immediately amended, and a new election law was passed. Previously, the country did not have the law on presidential elections because Niyazov, who ruled Turkmenistan for 21 years, was declared president for life, and all possible contenders were eliminated in 2002, after an assassination attempt on the president's life. Reportedly, gunshots were made in the direction of the president's cavalcade from a near passing truck. No one was injured during the incident; however, a number of influential cabinet members were named responsible for this act of terrorism and were sentenced to life in prison. Repressions against the opposition were initiated also.

During President Niyazov's rule, a new calendar was introduced with months and days renamed after the president and his late relatives. Also, the opera, the ballet, the philharmonic orchestras, and circus performances were banned because, in the president's opinion, they were not native to the Turkmen people. With the same justification, all books in the nation's libraries were substituted by a two-volume Book of Spirit—*Rukhnama* in Turkmen—which contained Niyazov's philosophical and historical thoughts and his own collections of poetry.

The Rukhnama book, published in 2001, was considered to be the nation's code of morality and culture. Since then, the study of Rukhnama became mandatory in all schools, universities, and enterprises. The knowledge of this book was required for professional attestation of each person working in Turkmenistan and for graduation from a university. About 1 million copies in 30 languages have been published. In 2004, President Niyazov published the second volume of the Rukhnama book, which contains instructions to the future generations. In a televised address to the nation, President Niyazov told his compatriots that he has made an agreement with Allah that those who will read this book for three hours every day will be admitted to heaven. Among other bans were prohibitions to use radios in cars, to have dental crowns made from gold, and to use mountain stream water for anything but drinking. Foreign university diplomas and degrees were not recognized in Turkmenistan, and the use of Russian language was suppressed as part of efforts to build a national identity.

In regard to governing the country, all cabinet members were required to participate in annual 20-mile runs, and often Niyazov interrupted government meetings to read his poems aloud. Although Turkmenistan was the only former Soviet republic that allowed dual citizenship of Turkmenistan citizens, foreign-born individuals were discriminated against. In the atmosphere of fear, educated elites—particularly Russian speakers—fled the country, and state structures began to break down because there was no one competent to run them. People still in positions of nominal authority were afraid to make decisions.

The first Turkmen Law on Elections of the President was published on December 28, 2006. According to the new document, the election of the president shall be conducted by popular voting, and the winner has to receive more than 50 percent of votes; the president is elected for an unlimited number of five-year terms. International and domestic observers and mass media representatives were allowed to monitor the elections and ballot count. Elections and individual campaigns of the candidates are financed from the national budget. Candidates are selected by the People's Council, and they need to receive two-thirds of the votes of council members to be registered. The People's Assembly had chosen six candidates for the elections scheduled for February 11, 2007—one from each region and all of whom were government officials and members of the ruling Democratic Party. Kurbankuly Berdymukhamedov was elected with 89.23 percent of the votes. In his inaugural address on February 14, Berdymukhamedov pledged to continue to provide free natural gas, salt, water, and electricity and subsidized bread, gasoline, and housing to the populace and to uphold the foreign policy of the previous government.

In Uzbekistan, the legislature initiated a political reform in November 2006, amending the nation's constitution and Political Parties Act. As of the next election cycle, which is scheduled for 2008, a proportional electoral system will be established in the country, and the lower chamber of the legislature will consist of political parties' factions, granting each party's leader the position of a chamber's vice speaker. To strengthen political party discipline, members of the legislature are not allowed to change the party or cancel their party affiliation. Regarding the scope of political activities of the parties and their eligibility to be included in the national ballot, the law states that parties' programs and platforms shall depend on the course and tasks of the government. This provision is interpreted differently by legal analysts. Some say that it prohibits any party activities that contradict the main government policy; others, however, believe that it allows for the discussion of those issues, which are within the realm of government activities. In case the legislature does not agree with the president, the new constitution gives the president the right to dissolve the legislature. In an attempt to project an image of parliamentary control over government activities, the Parliament and its individual factions were given the right to petition the president with a recommendation to dismiss the prime minister. The prime minister also may be dismissed by the president without parliamentary involvement.

SECURITY ISSUES

Crime, corruption, terrorism, drug and human trafficking, and ethnic and civil strife jeopardize the security and independence of all the new states of Central Asia, although to varying degrees. Kazakhstan has faced the potential of separatism in northern Kazakhstan where ethnic Russians are dominant, although this threat appears to have diminished in recent years with the emigration of hundreds of thousands of ethnic Russians. Tajikistan faces the still-fragile peace that ended its civil war and possible separatism, particularly by its northern Sogd (formerly Leninabad) region. Kyrgyzstan has faced increasing demands by its southern regions for greater influence in the central government that has been met in part through power sharing between a president from the south and a prime minister from the north. Turkmenistan faces clan and provincial tensions and widespread poverty that could contribute to instability in the transition period after the December 2006 death of long-time president Saparamurat Niyazov. Uzbekistan faces escalating civil discontent and violence from those whom President Islam Karimov labels as Islamic extremists, from a large ethnic Tajik population, and from an impoverished citizenry.

Border Tensions

Borders among the five Central Asian states, for the most part, were delineated by 1936 along linguistic and ethnic lines. The borders were ill defined in mountainous areas and extremely convoluted in the Fergana Valley, which is divided between Kyrgyzstan, Tajikistan, and Uzbekistan and contains about one-fifth of Central Asia's population. Over a dozen tiny enclaves add to the complicated situation. Some in Central Asia have demanded that borders be redrawn to incorporate areas inhabited by coethnics. Caspian Sea borders have not been fully agreed upon, mainly because of Iranian intransigence, but Russia and Kazakhstan have agreed on delineations to clear the way for exploiting their seabed oil resources. In late 2006, Turkmenistan indicated some willingness to negotiate the ownership of undersea oil and gas resources.

Kazakhstan, Kyrgyzstan, and Tajikistan largely settled their border conflicts with China by compromising on many of the disputed territories, which are usually in unpopulated areas. Popular passions were aroused in Kyrgyzstan after a 1999 China-Kyrgyzstan border agreement ceded about 9,000 hectares of mountainous Kyrgyz terrain. Kyrgyz legislators in 2001 opened a hearing and threatened to try to impeach then-president Akaev. Akaev arrested the leader of the impeachment effort, which led to violent demonstrations in 2002 calling for his ouster and the reversal of the border agreement. Dissident legislators appealed the border agreement to the Constitutional Court, which ruled in 2003 that it was legal.

The borders problem has been an important source of concern to Russia and Kazakhstan, since northern Kazakhstan still has a large concentration of ethnic Russians. In 1998, Russia established border patrols along its 4,200-mile border with Kazakhstan for security reasons. By the late 2004, most of the Russian-Kazakh border had been delimited. To dilute the influence of ethnic Russians in the north, Kazakhstan reorganized administrative borders in northern regions, established a strongly centralized government to limit local rule, and moved its capital northward.

Uzbekistan has had contentious border talks with all the other Central Asian states. As of early 2007, there were still disputed border areas between Uzbekistan and Kyrgyzstan where legislators protested a border delineation agreement with Uzbekistan reached by the two prime ministers that ceded a swath of the Kyrgyz territory allegedly to improve Uzbek access to ethnic Uzbek enclaves in Kyrgyzstan. The Kyrgyz government proposed to draw the boundary on the basis of work carried out by a parity commission in 1955. The commission had defined the border between two countries according to actual use of lands by economic entities, while Uzbekistan insists on delineation of the border on the basis of documents prepared for national-territorial demarcation in 1924 to 1927.

In the late 1990s, Uzbekistan unilaterally attempted to delineate and fortify its borders with Kazakhstan. In September 2002, the Kazakh and Uzbek presidents announced that delineation of their 1,400-mile border was complete, and some people in previously disputed border villages began to relocate if they felt that the new borders cut them off from their homeland. However, many people continued to ignore the new border or were uncertain of its location, which led to several shootings of Kazakh citizens by Uzbek border troops. The Uzbek and Tajik presidents signed an accord in October 2002 delimiting most of their 720-mile joint border.

Besides border claims, it has not been decided whether borders are open or closed. Open borders in the Central Asian states after the breakup of the Soviet Union were widely viewed as fostering trafficking in drugs and contraband and free migration, so border controls have been tightened in all states. During 2001, Kazakhstan joined Turkmenistan and Uzbekistan in imposing a visa regime on cross-border travel, while Kyrgyzstan has softened its visa requirements on U.S. and Western European travelers. Uzbekistan mined its borders with Kyrgyzstan and Tajikistan in 1999 with the intent to protect against terrorist incursions, but the mining led to many civilian Kyrgyz and Tajik casualties. Kyrgyzstan has demanded that Uzbekistan clear mines along the borders, including some allegedly sown on Kyrgyz territory, but the Uzbek Foreign Ministry in March 2003 asserted that it would maintain the mine fields to combat terrorism. The status of Bokhara and Samarkand is not resolved and contributes to political instability in the region. Tajiks regard both cities as historic centers of Persian culture lost to Uzbekistan in the Moscow-directed process of state and boundary creation during the 1920s. Dushanbe, Tajikistan's capital, is seen as poor compensation.

Islamic Extremism

As soon as the Soviet ideology was discarded, Central Asian rulers turned to Islamic doctrines and declared themselves genuine defenders of Islam, which was viewed by them as a part of the greater ethnic idea. Pointing at Tajikistan's civil conflict, where the issue of Islam in political life contributed to strife, Central Asian leaders attempted to preserve the secular nature of their states and prevent radicalization of religion. Different countries of Central Asia interpret their secular status differently. In Uzbekistan, not a single mullah was elected to the Parliament, and none have run for office since it was prohibited by the constitution. This prohibition is unlike the old Soviet constitution, which tolerated the nominal presence of Islamic clerics in the elected bodies. In Turkmenistan, Islam is under complete control of the government, which controls even career promotions of the clergy. In Kazakhstan, because of the nomadic origin of the population, Islam has some superficial forms. It coexists there with the Russian Orthodox Church that the Russian settlers brought with them. Islam, which is tolerated in Kazakhstan, is mostly for rituals and has not developed any significant political coloration.[11] Askar Akaev, who was the president of Kyrgyzstan between 1991 and 2005, appeared to be the most tolerant of all the Central Asian leaders to the different forms of religion in his country. Parallel to the Islamic boom, there also has been an explosion of diverse religious denominations and sects from Protestants to Hare Krishnas. Because the Muslim faith is the dominant religion in Kyrgyzstan, President Akaev paid special attention to it, believing that Islam is a culturally cohesive force that can play an important role in the process of post-Soviet nation building. Present Kyrgyz leadership follows the same ideas and has proclaimed religious freedom as a part of the democratic transformation of Kyrgyzstan.

Most of Central Asia's Islamic population appears to support the concept of secular government and does not have a deep knowledge of Islam, but interest in greater observance is growing. This interest is exploited by newly formed religious parties. Calls for government to be based on Shariah law and the Koran are supported by small but increasing minorities in most of Central

Asia. All over the region, Islamic forms of justice are replacing the legal system established by the Soviet Union. Ad hoc courts are set up in mosques by Muslim enthusiasts who insist on their own form of justice. Much of the attraction of Islamic extremism in Central Asia is generated by poverty and discontent.[12] Radical groups in Afghanistan, Pakistan, Saudi Arabia, and elsewhere foster Central Asian extremism providing funding, education, training, and manpower to the region. Some of these ties were at least partially disrupted by the U.S.-led coalition actions in Afghanistan.

The Central Asian states impose several controls over religious freedom. All except Tajikistan forbid religious parties[13] and maintain Soviet-era religious oversight bodies, official religious administrations, and approved clergy. The governments censor religious literature and sermons. Officials in Uzbekistan believe that it is increasingly vulnerable to Islamic extremism. Thousands of alleged Islamic extremists have been arrested and sentenced, and many mosques have been closed. Restrictions were tightened with the adoption of the Freedom of Worship Act in 1998, which banned all unregistered faiths, censored religious writings, and made it a crime to teach religion without a license. Public expressions of religiosity are discouraged; women in religious clothes and young men who wear beards face government harassment and intimidation. Some bloody incidents instigated by Islamic radicals occurred recently in several republics. On the southern border of Kyrgyzstan, a group of Uzbek radicals invaded several remote villages in the mountains and declared the formation of an Islamic republic, demanding a free passage through Kyrgyz territory to the Fergana Valley of Uzbekistan. The Kyrgyz government managed to resolve the conflict through negotiations.

Military Cooperation and Post-9/11 Developments

The Operation Enduring Freedom conducted by the U.S.-led coalition in Afghanistan decreased terrorist threats to Central Asia. Kyrgyzstan became a critical regional partner of the coalition, providing bases for U.S. and coalition forces at Manas (in mid-2006, these troops reportedly numbered about 1,100). Uzbekistan provided a base for U.S. operations at Karshi-Khanabad (before the pullout in 2005, U.S. troops reportedly numbered less than 900), a base for German units at Termez (in early 2006, German troops reportedly numbered about 300), and a land corridor to Afghanistan for humanitarian aid via the Friendship Bridge at Termez. Tajikistan permitted the use of its international airport in Dushanbe for refueling and hosted a French force (there were reportedly 400 troops there in mid-2006). Kazakhstan and Turkmenistan provided overflight and other support.[14]

In 1999, U.S. Central Command became responsible for military engagement and cooperation with Central Asian states. All these states, except Tajikistan, joined the North Atlantic Treaty Organisation's (NATO) Partnership for

Peace program by mid-1994; Tajikistan joined in 2002. Central Asian troops have participated in periodic military exercises in the United States since 1995, and U.S. troops have participated in exercises in Central Asia since 1997. After disagreements about the 2005 Andijon events, Uzbekistan sharply reduced its participation in international military programs, and the U.S. base in Karshi-Khanabad was closed in November 2005. Perhaps indicative of the reversal of U.S. military-to-military ties, former pro-U.S. defense minister Qodir Gulomov was convicted of treason and sentenced to a seven-year imprisonment, later suspended. In contrast to Uzbekistan's participation, Kazakhstan's progress in military reform enabled NATO in January 2006 to elevate it to participation in an Individual Partnership Action Plan.

Russia attempts to play an important role in regional affairs and lead collective security efforts within the CIS. In May 2001, CIS members authorized the formation of a Collective Rapid Deployment Force (CDRF). One year later, Kazakhstan, Kyrgyzstan, Russia, and Tajikistan with Armenia and Belarus decided to create a Collective Security Treaty Organization (CSTO), which transformed the CDRF into a standing force with a small multinational staff and a mobile command center. Moscow allowed CSTO members to purchase Russian-made defense equipment and supplies for their CDRF components at the same price paid by the Russian military. The Russian Ministry of Defense also subsidizes the cost of training officers from CSTO militaries.[15] In October 2003, Russia established its first regional military base at Kant, Kyrgyzstan, which lies only 20 miles from the U.S. base. Another Russian military facility in southern Kyrgyzstan is supposed to open in 2007.[16] In October 2004, Tajikistan granted Russia's 201 Motorized Infantry Division a permanent base near Dushanbe. A year later, Tajik and Russian officials announced that Russia would also obtain a new air base near Dushanbe, with housing available for 6,000 military personnel. In 2005, Russia and Uzbekistan signed a Treaty on Allied Relations that pledged mutual military assistance in the event that either becomes a victim of aggression.

Drugs and Trafficking

Central Asia is a major player in the drug trade and is ranked fourth internationally among the main producer regions. Opium poppy and wild hemp are grown on 11 million acres of the Chui Valley situated in Kazakhstan and Uzbekistan, where all major cities located near the valley serve as distribution centers. Most Central Asian drugs are aimed at sales in Russia, which, according to Russian estimates, amount to US$100 million annually. Since the Soviet time, Central Asia has been used as a circuitous route to deliver drugs from Afghanistan to Iran and some Western countries. Drugs also are sold along the way in Uzbekistan and Tajikistan. According to the UN Office on Drugs and Crimes (UNODC), up to 7 percent of the gross domestic product of the population from nomadic to settled because it was easier to govern the latter.

WAR AGAINST KHANATES

The tsar told von Kaufman to avoid further conquests regardless of how attractive and easy they would seem. The purpose of Russian politics in the area was declared as subordinating the neighboring khanates to Russia's moral influence, establishing peaceful trade relations with them, and eliminating robberies in the Russian territories. Local military leaders and administrators, however, were better informed about the development in the area than government officials and often conducted their independent policies without confirming their actions with officials in St. Petersburg. The accession of Samarkand in 1868 was a complete surprise to the tsar, who initially opposed this move but had to accept it.

After concluding the peace treaty with the khanate of Kokand in 1868, General von Kaufman concentrated all of his troops against the Bokharan emir, who was defeated during the battle at Samarkand in May 1868. After that, the Bokharan army of 50,000 men attempted to retake the city and outflanked the Russians. The attacked Samarkand was defended by a garrison of 658 men. The emir of Bokhara lost his army in this attack and had no choice but to ask for peace. On June 12, 1868, General von Kaufman wrote to the emir of Bokhara, explaining his position: "I have never intended nor desired to destroy the khanate of Bokhara; I repeat now what I have said previously, that the peace and tranquility of Russia's neighbors constitute the goal of my labors and even of my wars. When I can secure peace, I terminate hostilities."[10] On July 18, 1868, the emir of Bokhara was forced to sign a peace treaty, which gave the Russians Khojent, Dzhizak, and other cities; Samarkand also was ceded to the Russians. Being unhappy with the conditions of the peace treaty, the emir beheaded one of the two Persians who brought this document to him on behalf of the Russians and threw the other into a pit before signing the treaty. The treaty was a commercial convention providing for the opening of Bokhara to Russian traders on an equal footing with native merchants and did not limit the emir's sovereignty. The treaty defined the Russo-Bokharan boundary and imposed an indemnity on Bokhara. Despite the fact that the treaty did not mention the Russian protection of Bokhara, the state lost much of its independence in practice. For example, in 1872, following Russian protests, Emir Muzaffar of Bokhara agreed to renounce his right to communicate with foreign heads of state without the previous knowledge of the governor general of Turkistan.

After securing his powers in the central areas of Turkistan, von Kaufman started offensives against Khiva and Turkmen tribes as ordered by the War general of Turkistan. The various temporary statutes under which Turkistan was controlled gave von Kaufman almost unrestricted authority and a great deal of latitude in policy. All military, civil, judicial, and political powers were concentrated in his hands. Initially, von Kaufman was allowed to carry out negotiations with neighboring states on his own account, establish and oversee the expenditures of the budget, set taxes, and establish the privileges of Russian subjects in the province. He also had the power to confirm and revoke death sentences passed on from the Russian military courts. Nowhere else in the Russian Empire did a military governor general have so much independence from central control. Administratively, the newly occupied lands were organized according to the traditional Russian administrative system, which did not reflect historic, economic, and national specifics of the region. The introduced government system was called military-people's government, because elected local officials complemented the military administration. In Tashkent and other large cities, the government was brought in accordance with the Russian self-government standards. The city council in Tashkent was formed in 1877. The native population elected one-third of the members (24 delegates), and two-thirds of the delegates were elected by the Russians. Russian Turkistan consisted of between two and five provinces (the number was constantly changing). The governor general and military governors of the constituent provinces were appointed by the tsar. Only initial conquests were incorporated into the Russian Empire directly. To save some expenditures associated with administering the new territories and minimize British concerns about Russian expansion, the existing khanates were preserved.

Russian administrative policies were different for Turkistan and Kazakhstan, which was not included in the Turkistan governorship system. Turkistan had some geographic and political unity, but Kazakhstan was divided into three parts that more or less followed the previous division into hordes. The provinces, which were created here, were run from the neighboring Siberian cities and were subordinate to the Ministry of Interior.

In 1867, a wagon tax was imposed on the Kazakh population, and, in 1891, the tax was transformed into a residence tax and levied on all residential dwellings. Additionally, the Kazakhs were charged with the duty to transport mail and supply carriages for the Russian army. In 1868, all of Kazakhstan was declared the state property of the Russian Empire, and lands belonging to nomads were seized and distributed among the resettlers from the European parts of Russia who received up to 100 acres of land upon their arrival in Kazakhstan. If local people wanted to become farmers, their land plots had to be apportioned by their communes. At the end of the nineteenth century, native people lost about 9 percent of their lands. The nomads were prohibited to go outside the specified area, and tax privileges for the settled peasants were introduced. The government expedited the transformation of and pointed out that Tashkent lay far beyond the frontier, which Prince Gorchakov had defined in his memorandum on Russia's southern limits. Britain stated that the seizure of Tashkent was "scarcely consistent with the professed intention of the Russian government to respect the independence of the states of Central Asia."[6] But no one seriously expected that Russia would withdraw from Tashkent. Chernyaev openly refused to return previously taken possessions. Since the Asians, under his view, respected only force, he believed that with "the slightest concession Russia would not be respected and feared, but would also risk losing all that it acquired earlier and would have to reconquer everything."[7]

After the defeat at Tashkent, the khanate of Kokand was reduced to a valley where it had originated many years ago. The attack on Kokand was also initiated without the emperor's approval, and St. Petersburg, which was far away from the war theater, had to accept the governors' independent actions. The absence of direct communications (it took more than a months for mail to be delivered from St. Petersburg to Tashkent) untied hands to the Russian military stationed along the Asian borders. In September 1866, Alexander II called a new meeting on Central Asian policy and emphasized his desire to stop the accession of new lands, preserving the independence of Kokand and Bokhara although under Russian influence. A commercial treaty of 1868 left Khan Khudayar as a Russian vassal, yet free to continue building his lavish palace by squeezing more taxes from a shrunken population. In Kokand—a city of 80,000 people, 600 mosques, and 15 schools teaching 15,000 students—the Russians did not touch the native administration and justices. American diplomat Eugene Schuyler described in 1873 that

> When a criminal was to be put to death he is taken through the streets of the bazaar, the executioner following behind him, while the crowd hooted and pelted him with stones. Suddenly, without a word of warning, when the executioner thought the spectacle has lasted long enough, he seized the criminal by the head, thrust the knife into his throat and cut it, and then the body sank to the ground, where it was left for some hours before it was carried away and the blood was covered with sand.[8]

COLONIAL ADMINISTRATION

In 1867, Tashkent became the military and administrative headquarters of a new governorate-general of Turkistan and the official place of residence of the governor general.[9] Turkistan was governed by a temporary statute promulgated in 1867 and a permanent one after 1886. General Konstantin von Kaufman, one of the best Russian administrators, was appointed the governor

RUSSIAN COLONIZATION
(1865–1917)

RUSSIA

MONGOLIA

1830's

Astana

1803

1853

1824

Aral
Sea

Caspian Sea

1854

Bishkek • Almaty

1865

Tashkent

1873

1875

1895

1885

Dushanbe

Ashgabat

IRAN

PAKISTAN

CHINA

AFGHANISTAN

Russian Colonization (1865–1917) Russian territorial acquisitions in the nineteenth century (the shaded area reflects Uzbek khanates not included in the Russian Turkistan province).

the region is derived from drug trafficking. The UNODC warns that funds derived from drug trafficking destabilize the state by supporting crime, corruption, and terrorism and compromise legitimate investment and economic growth. UNODC also estimates that about 1 percent of Central Asia's population is addicted to drugs, with the percentage addicted to opiates being higher than that in Europe.[17]

Nonproliferation of Weapons of Mass Destruction

Central Asia has nuclear research and power reactors, uranium mines, milling facilities, and associated personnel. After declaring independence, President Nazarbaev of Kazakhstan ordered the removal of all Soviet nuclear warfare stored on the territory of this republic to Russia regardless of calls from many mostly Arab states to keep these arsenals to establish the first Muslim nuclear state. Kazakhstan is reported to possess one-fourth of the world's uranium reserves, and Kazakhstan and Uzbekistan are among the world's top producers of low enriched uranium. Today, Kazakhstan's nuclear resources include the Ulba fuel fabrication facility, which provides nuclear fuel pellets to Russia and other former Soviet states, and a fast breeder reactor at the Caspian port of Aktau, the world's only nuclear desalinization facility. Nuclear fuel cycle facilities are often minimally secured and staffed by poorly paid personnel, creating targets of opportunity. Low enriched uranium is also produced in Uzbekistan and Kyrgyzstan. Kazakhstan and Uzbekistan also hosted major chemical and biological warfare facilities during the Soviet era, raising concerns about possible proliferation dangers posed by remaining materials and personnel.

ECONOMIC AND SOCIAL DEVELOPMENT

All the states of the Central Asian region possess large-scale resources that could contribute to the region becoming a "new silk road" of trade and commerce. The Kazakh and Turkmen economies are dependent on energy exports. Uzbekistan's state-controlled cotton and gold production rank among the highest in the world, and much is exported. It also has moderate energy reserves. Kyrgyzstan has major gold mines and strategic mineral reserves, is a major wool producer, and could benefit from tourism. Tajikistan has one of the world's largest aluminum-processing plants and is a major cotton grower. Despite the region's development potential, the challenges of corruption, inadequate transport infrastructure, punitive tariffs, border tensions, and an uncertain respect for contracts discourage major foreign investments—except for some in the energy sector.

The vast majority of people in the Central Asian states suffered steep declines in their quality of life in the first few years after the dissolution of the

Soviet Union. Social services such as health and education, inadequate during the Soviet period, declined further. In the new century, however, negative trends in poverty and health have been reversed in Central Asia, although the quality of life remains far below that of Western countries. Defining poverty as income levels of less than $2.15 per day, a World Bank report found that the poverty rate in 2001 was 21% in Kazakhstan, 70% in Kyrgyzstan, 74% in Tajikistan, and 47% in Uzbekistan (data for Turkmenistan was not available).[18]

Central Asia remains largely a rural society, and the daily life of ordinary people is usually monotonous and depends on how much work is available on one's plot of land. It consists of

> waking up at dawn and beginning daily chores; men milk the cows and women clean the house. Breakfast consists of tea and bread. If the weather is good and work needs to be done, men spend the day working on the farm. Women spend their day cleaning, cooking, and tending to babies and animals. Lunch and dinner consist of eggs from people's own chickens, and soup, heavy with potatoes and fat. Throughout the course of the day, neighbors stop by, come in for tea and talk about neighbors, weddings, farming, and politics. If there are enough hands around the farm to perform the labor, older men drink large quantities of cheap vodka starting early in the morning. Mothers work especially hard to find suitable husbands for their daughters, beginning in the girl's late teens, seeking someone with a decent source of income and whose family they know. The crime rate is extremely low because nobody is anonymous in the village and there is little of value worth stealing; animal theft is the most common crime.[19]

The labor market situation has deteriorated in all five states because the number of jobs offered has diminished after the breakup of the USSR. The worst year was 1995, when the region's measured gross domestic product was 63 percent what it was 1989, a level not regained until 2005. Because the informal economy is proportionately larger now than it was under the Soviet regime, the region's overall output in goods and services has now surpassed the 1989 level, and occupation in informal-sector jobs has softened the labor market impact of recession.[20] With high rates of poverty associated with agricultural overpopulation, nonfarm job creation is a key development priority. Urban unemployment also exacerbates poverty and would be higher if not for emigration.

Russia's comparatively higher standard of living pulls millions of mostly illegal migrants from Central Asia into the Russian labor market. Their remittances make an essential contribution to the gross national products of their countries of origin, remove potentially dissatisfied social elements from these states, and give Central Asian governments another reason to stay on Moscow's good side. The 300,000 Tajiks working abroad remit some US$500 million annually to home, a sum more than the entire trade deficit. About 320,000 Kyrgyz are working in Russia, remitting some US$150 million home annually. This figure is also comparable with the nation's trade deficit.[21] Emigration of many not of the titular nationality—notably, Russians from Kazakhstan and Kyrgyzstan, Germans from Kazakhstan and Tajikistan, and Crimean Tatars and Meskhetians from Uzbekistan—improved the balance between job seekers and employment opportunities.[22] South Korea became a surprising destination for migrants from Uzbekistan; a bilateral agreement of 2005 established an annual quota of 1,000. Migrants may include descendents of Koreans who were forcibly relocated to Uzbekistan from the Soviet regions north of Korea on the eve of World War II when an invasion was expected by Japan from occupied Korea; or they may include North Koreans, who, after that war, were sent by their government to work in the USSR as payment of a recurrent trade deficit. Migration balances the demographic, labor, and economic situation as the populations continue to increase. The highest fertility rate in newly independent Central Asia is among the Tajiks and is about five children per woman.[23] The lowest rate is in the most modernized state of Kazakhstan, near three children per woman.

After 16 years of independence, these new states provide evidence that official governmental declarations of sovereignty do not necessarily imply absolute freedom, autonomy, and welfare. Although the years of post-communism witnessed massive changes in Central Asian societies, the Central Asian states find that their involvement in international trade is highly limited and conditional; that the markets they have created are highly distorted, and that the political institutions and processes that have come into being since independence are authoritarian and dominated by many of the same interests and practices that governed the institutions of the old system.

However, all of them have good prospects. Turkmenistan's oil and gas wealth could contribute to its long-term stability, Uzbekistan's large population and many resources could provide a basis for its stable development and security, and Kyrgyzstan's emerging civil society could facilitate entrepreneurial activity. The Muslim population in all these republics professes the most moderate and tolerant version of Islam. Even though regional cooperation is minimal today, theoretically it can be enhanced by affinities among the current elites. Many of the officials in the states learned a common language (Russian) and received similar Soviet-era ideological training that stressed authoritarianism. In addition, many were Communist Party members, which is why President Nazarbaev's April 2007 suggestion to unite all five republics into one powerful state is not groundless.

More than ever, the role of Central Asia in the world, its involvement in market relations, and the speed of social changes domestically depend on the extent that Central Asian societies take advantage of the opportunities provided by greater international cooperation and foreign presence while preserving what is culturally important to them.

NOTES

1. Jim Nichol, *Central Asia: Regional Developments and Implications for U.S. Interests,* U.S. Library of Congress, Congressional Research Service, CRS Report RL33458 (2007), 3.

2. Kathleen Collins, "Clans, Pacts, and Politics in Central Asia," *Journal of Democracy* 13, no. 3 (November 2002): 137. Ethnographic evidence indicates that clans today range in size from 2,000 to 20,000 members—much smaller than the large tribal confederations of the nomadic period.

3. Askar Akaev, "All of a Sudden I Became a President," *Christian Science Monitor,* January 10, 1991, (archive edition), http://www.csmonitor.com/1991/0110/o1kir1.html.

4. Jim Nichol, *Tajikistan: Recent Developments and U.S. Interests,* U.S. Library of Congress, Congressional Research Service, CRS Report 98–559 (2007), 4.

5. In the bicameral legislature, the upper chamber—the National Assembly representing regional interests—consists of 34 members (25 members are selected by indirect voting by local council assemblies, 8 members are appointed by Rakhmonov, and 1 is reserved for the former president); the lower chamber—the Assembly of Representatives—has 63 members (22 are elected by party list and 41 in single member districts).

6. U.S. Department of State. *Country Reports on Human Rights Practices for 2006,* at http://www.state.gov/g/drl/rls/hrrpt/2006/78845.htm.

7. Jim Nichol, *Uzbekistan: Recent Developments and U.S. Interests,* CRS Report for Congress, No. RS 21238 (2007), 6.

8. U.S. Department of State, *Foreign Terrorist Organizations,* updated September 25, 2004, http://www.state.gov/documents/organization/41055.pdf.

9. Allegedly, former President Akaev and his family had skimmed off Kyrgyz state assets, including U.S. payments for use of the Manas air base.

10. Reportedly, he now works as a physics professor at the Moscow State University.

11. Collins (2002), 147.

12. Evgueny Novikov, *Tolerant Islam in the War of Ideas* (Washington, DC: American Foreign Policy Council, 2006), 12.

13. Tajikistan's civil war settlement included the legalization of the Islamic Renewal Party.

14. Nichol (2007), 3.

15. Richard Weitz, "The CIS Is Dead. Long Live the CSTO," *Central Asia-Caucasus Analyst,* February 8, 2006, http://www.cacianalyst.org/view_article.php?articleid = 3989.

16. Erica Marat, "Reports Suggests Moscow Wants New Base in Kyrgyz-stan," *Eurasia Daily Monitor,* May 24, 2005, at www.rferl.org.

17. U.N. Office on Drugs and Crime, *Illicit Drugs Situation in the Regions Neighbouring Afghanistan and the Response of the ODCC* (Vienna, Austria: UNODC, 2002).

18. See World Bank, *World Development Report 2000/2001: Attacking Poverty* (Washington, DC: World Bank, 2001).

19. Scott Radnitz, "Networks, Localism, and Mobilization in Aksy, Kyrgyz-stan," *Central Asian Review* 24, no. 4 (December 2005): 424.

20. Michael Kaser, "Labour Market Policies and Central Asia," *Central Asian Survey* 24, no. 4 (December 2005): 363.

21. Kaser (2005), 365.

22. One-half million ethnic Germans annually migrated from the transition countries to Germany between 1990 and 1994. The flow subsequently dropped to about 280,000 annually, according to IOM 2005 World Migration Report, http://www.iom.int/jahia/Jahia/cache/offonce/pid/1674?entryId=932. Of nearly a million Germans in Kazakhstan at the time of independence, only one-third of them remain.

23. Robert Turner, "Tajiks Have the Highest Fertility Rates in Newly Inde-pendent Central Asia," *Family Planning Perspectives* 25, no. 3 (1993): 141.

9

Political and Legal Thought of Central Asia

Despite the facts that Central Asia was traditionally a land of literate people and book making was always considered a form of art there, study of regional legal and political thought, especially of earlier periods, is complicated because of an almost total absence of original sources. Constant wars and invasions destroyed most of the written documents located in Central Asian cities. Later, the rulers of local states and the clergy eliminated all traces of contradictory ideas or views of their political enemies. Suppression of dissent was common in Central Asian traditions, and therefore it is difficult to study works created by local intellectuals.

ANCIENT VIEWS ON LAW AND STATE

The oldest and most complete source of legal and political thought in Central Asia, which evidences that 30 centuries ago a great culture existed on this territory, is the Zoroastrian Avesta. Most researchers translate this word as *law,* so this document was considered a codification of basic religious, behavioral, and ritual principles. Originally, the Avesta consisted of 21 books, but only 4 are known to researchers now. The best preserved part of the Avesta is Videvdat, translated into Persian in fifth to fourth centuries B.C. The list of crimes and related punishments contained in this book reveals a close-knit society, busy with cattle breeding and led by clergy interested in population growth. The law always favored married people over a singles and fathers over childless men. The Avesta divides prosecuted crimes into six groups: crimes against religion (heresy, atheism, marriage with the follower of another religion); crimes against an individual (threats, assaults, harm caused by a physician, abortions, crimes against a woman's health during pregnancy); crimes against animals, especially against dogs; property crimes (stealing, plundering, fraud, and greed, which was also considered a crime because, according to the book, those who decline just requests are actually thieves illegally possessing the requested thing); crimes against morality (homosexuality—the only crime in the entire code punishable by death—prostitution, masturbation, and marital infidelity. However, marriages between family members with mother, sisters, or daughters—though rare—were not punished and even encouraged by the priests); and crimes against natural forces (earth, fire, flora, and water).

The first known people's movement on the territory of Central Asia occurred in the late fifth to early sixth centuries A.D. It was called Mazdakism after its leader Mazdak, who used traditional Manichean ideas of conflicts between good and evil and light and darkness and preached for a reduction of the importance of religious formalities. Some called him the first socialist philosopher because he believed that all conflicts have social roots. Mazdak explained the reason for social inequality was that the rich and powerful had acquired common property, which should not belong to them because material things such as fire and air shall belong to everybody. Declaring private property to be a form of evil, he called for capturing, sharing, or destroying property that belonged to rich people. He viewed the inequality in property distribution as the reason for social disorders, crime, wars, and mutual hatred. Social equality achieved through violent actions was the main idea of Mazdak's movement. The movement attracted many followers, who, despite the concepts of good conduct, raided the palaces and harems of the rich, removing valuables to which they believed they had equal rights. Because of his great popularity, Mazdak was appointed the chief priest of Iran. He was hanged three years later, in 524 A.D., and most of his followers were massacred by the Persian king. Small pockets of Mazdaki societies survived and settled in remote areas; they were, centuries later, eventually absorbed by Central Asian Buddhism.

Mazdakism influenced further political movements in Central Asia, and its ideas were used by the participants of a mass anti-Arab and anti-Islamic revolt in Sogdiana in 776. The leader of the revolt, Khashim ibn Khakim named Mukanna, declared himself a prophet and incarnation of God, fighting against the spiritual enslavement of Central Asians by Islam. He found many supporters in all parts of the country. When the uprising was suppressed by invading Arabs, he was executed by the Arabs. The suppression of the revolt

entailed the destruction of Mukanna's hometown of Kesh, located not far from present-day Tashkent; the town was comparable to Bokhara in size and importance in the eighth century.

ISLAMIC STUDIES AND MEDIEVAL UTOPIAS

Developments of Central Asian political thought can be analyzed by the treatise *On Views of the Citizens of the Virtuous City* written by Abu Nasr al Farabi (870–950). Interpreting the ideas of Plato and Aristotle, Farabi rejected the concept of divine origin and predestination and theorized about an ideal state, showing what effect correct or incorrect thinking could have. According to al Farabi, the state was a union of people who wanted to progress toward the true human end. The natural needs of people were the real reason for the establishment of a state. For him, a virtuous state is one that cares about all its citizens and where all the people help each other. Of course, Farabi realized that such a society was rare and would require a very specific set of historical circumstances to be realized. The presence of a good ruler was a necessary condition for the existence of such a good state. A despotic regime of violent and uneducated rulers was strongly criticized by Farabi because ignorant rulers deceived and misguided societies, failed to comprehend the purpose of human existence, and supplanted the pursuit of happiness for another goal—whether this be wealth, sensual gratification, or power. Whether al-Farabi intended to outline a political program in his writings remains a matter of dispute.

The expansion of Islam in the early medieval period resulted in the expulsion of customary laws of settled tribes and nomads traditional to the Turkic khanate and Euphtalite state and their replacement by the norms of Muslim law, which developed through interpretations of Koranic dogmas instead of legislation. The main feature of Central Asian law was its religious nature. Laws and other legal acts, which could provide for equal legal treatment of private individuals regardless of their religion, were not allowed. There are no known substantial legal acts and documents that were in force in the Central Asian states before the Russian colonization. The Koran and other sources of Muslim law did not allow the issuance of legal acts that could establish equal rights for private individuals regardless of their religious beliefs. However, some Central Asian state rulers' acts, which did not contradict dogmas of Islam and undermine the legal superiority of Muslim population, were recognized as obligatory legal acts. All Muslim law was based on dividing people into *fidels,* who were Muslims, and *nonfidels,* non-Muslims.

Central Asia had provided the Muslim world with significant volumes of legal and religious literature. Activities of Central Asian Muslim clerics had not only regional but Islam-wide importance. Al-Biruni (973–1048), one of the

greatest Muslim scholars in Central Asia from Khorezm, wrote on comparative religions, including Judaism and the faith of the Samaritans. Al-Biruni
mentioned his contacts with Jewish teachers in his book *Chronology,* where he
quoted the Old Testament frequently. Biruni mentioned religious festivals of
other faiths as well, and described some sects of his time, such Rabbinic Jews,
Miladites, Maghribis, Alfaniya, and Karaites.

Abu Omar al-Jauzjani (b. 1193) wrote about the history of religious struggle
in Samarkand under the Mongols in his historical works. According to him,
Christians and Muslims of Samarkand, who were involved in religious strife,
tried to gain Mongol support against each other. The Mongol Berke Khan accepted Islam and then helped Muslims to fight against Christians in 1259. As
a result, the Christians were oppressed and Berke was praised by al-Jauzjani
for his Muslim zeal.

The most influential orders of Sufism, a mystical movement in Islam that
emphasized the development of personal spirituality and an internal comprehension of divinity, originated in Central Asia as well. Sufism appeared first in
the seventh or eighth centuries A.D. (there are disagreements about the precise
dating). Sufi scholars and spiritual leaders played an important role in spreading Islam among the nomads of Central Asia. Major teachings of Sufism were
popular among Central Asian peasants because they refused the solemn and
complicated rites of orthodox Islam and the presence of clergy and proposed
belief in asceticism, internal contemplation, identification of nature with God,
and nonparticipation in public social life. In the late eleventh and early twelfth
centuries, Sufism was legalized in Sunni Islam.

POLITICS IN POETRY

The Islamic renaissance in Central Asia was characterized by the development of humanitarian ideas in the framework of a religious poem. Mahmud
al-Kashgari (1029–1101) and Zhusup Balasaguni (b. 1015) were the best representatives of scholars and thinkers of that time. Their works influenced further
development of the Kyrgyz people and affected our knowledge about relations
within the Kyrgyz and Kazakh society in the eleventh century. Both authors
lived in Kashgar, the capital of Eastern Turkistan, but studied and worked in
all major cultural centers of Central Asia—Bokhara, Samarkand, and Baghdad. Al-Kashgari's major work is his *Dictionary of Turkic Language,* which is
an encyclopedia of Turkic people and the only original contemporary source
describing their tribal organization, traditions, customs, economy, and geographical surroundings. The dictionary, which was intended for use by the caliph of Baghdad, the new Arabic leader of the Turks, included the first known
map of the areas inhabited by Turkic people. The map—different from all other
maps attributed to this region and time period due to the changing size of the

depicted localities—was centered on the Turkic-speaking areas of Central Asia, the area between present-day Kyrgyzstan and the Chinese province of Xinjang. The map is oriented with east at the top, has a scale that becomes smaller as one gets closer to the edge of the map, and color keys of gray for rivers, green for seas, light yellow for deserts, red for mountains, and yellow for cities and towns. Today, this map is kept at the National Library in Istanbul.

Kashgari's dictionary consisted of epic poems written in all genres known to people at that time. Kashgari's expressed his ethical views through reflections of other tribe members. Kashgari viewed work, friendship, and intellect as the basis for the moral improvement of humans, and words that described these concepts were of special importance for him. Kashgari thought that positive traits were acquired by people in the process of work; therefore, labor was the necessary form of human existence and a factor in the social value system. The first among Central Asian scholars who expressed the idea that an individual shall be valued by his or her work and contribution to society and not by property or social status, Kashgari established direct relations between good work results and knowledge possessed by an individual. For him, learning and science were two major tools that could help a person achieve personal goals and ultimate goals defined for him or her by providence. This applied to ordinary individuals as well as to the rulers. Kashgari wrote that leaders should obtain knowledge not for their own interest but to help those in need, and he evaluated rulers according to the welfare of their subordinate people.

Zhusup Balasaguni was another encyclopedic author and thinker whose work impacted Kazakh and Kyrgyz people. His major work, which was a collection of didactic poems entitled *Blessed Knowledge*, was written between 1067 and 1070 and brought Balasaguni wide recognition and an appointment to a ministerial position at his khan's court. The book was a philosophical and political treatise written in Turkic and presented the ideals of justice, knowledge, and human life. *Blessed Knowledge* reflected the Qarakhanid state during the period of establishing Islam and the transition to a sedentary agriculture. The main idea of the book was that knowledge was the highest social value, and education was the main instrument of development. The book, three copies of which were found in 1913 and partially published in 1925, reveals information about the local political system and the place and role of social groups, rules, and traditions. Balasaguni stated that the purpose of each individual regardless of his or administrative position was to make other people happy. This specifically applied to those whose decisions affected the lives of many people. According to Balasaguni, chiefs should rule with politeness and modesty cultivated by good education.

After the Uzbek state was created in the fifteenth century, the great educator, politician, mystic, thinker, poet, and founder of the Uzbek literature Alisher

Navoi (1441–1501) transformed the Turkic language—traditionally regarded by men of letters as uncouth and plebeian—into a recognized and graceful medium for poetry and prose of the highest order. Navoi was close to the Sultan, and he believed that the most glorious duty was performing service to the people. He expressed his outrage with greedy feudals and supported the idea of an enlightened monarch. According to him, an ideal state was one with a centralized monarchy where the ruler cared about the well-being of his subjects.

In the seventeenth and eighteenth centuries, Central Asian khanates were feudal societies ruled by despotic leaders where Shariah laws and customary norms regulated social relations. Legal and political ideologies were represented by two schools—clerical and progressive. Clerical ideology was formed by mullahs, court poets, and historians who defended the idea of the God-given power of the ruler, justified all the ruler's actions, and promoted the idea of his total control over the subjects. According to the clerical ideology, any critique of the existing public order was a critique of religion and thus was punishable as a crime against the faith. The progressive ideology interpreted religion in a historic content, as an instrument for establishing equal relations among the believers. In Central Asia, political thoughts and philosophical ideas were expressed not in treatises but in poems read in public teahouses and markets. Most of these poems expressed a desire for a ruler who could distribute goods wisely and equally among the people.

Turdy Farogi (d. 1700) was one of the best-known critics of the existing legal and political institutions, condemning the oppression and opulence of the bureaucrats and merchants. Farogi criticized the rulers of the country who were not concerned about the daily life of the population. He requested change in the forms and methods of government through the establishment of an enlightened monarchy with a fair ruler at the top. Such a ruler would feed the hungry, clothe those in need, establish peace, and involve wise men in the government. For Farogi, the creation of a large centralized state instead of numerous divided khanates is the appropriate response to the question of how to get rid of corrupt officials.

Sayido Nasafi (d. 1807) was the poet of Tajik craftspeople, describing their difficult life and emphasizing the moral superiority of working people. In a time of economic crisis, Nasafi objected to land and real estate being transferred to the hands of clergy and noted that the country became like a plundered village. Of interest are Nasafi's ideas regarding the relations between the ruler and his people; he was the first in Central Asia who said that a ruler's power is based on the people. Because the existence of rulers is impossible without the people, he argued that, if a ruler wanted to hold his power firm and make it last longer, the main concern should be the welfare of the people and the prosperity of the country. For Nasafi, all problems are concentrated in the state officials whose pleasures were earned by the blood and sweat of simple people suffering from feudal wars initiated by the officials. He urged people to stop wars, which slow down the development of culture and economy, and suggested to fight the officials because it would be meaningless to wait for their favors.

Mirza Abdulkadyr Bedil (1644–1721) greatly influenced the development of Central Asian political thought and philosophy. Although he was born and lived in India, Bedil was well known in Central Asia because the language style and expressions used in his poems were more comprehensible for Tajiks (among whom he is almost a cult figure). His views on the state were expressed in a book entitled *Ifron* (Knowledge), in which Bedil advocated the enlightened monarchy as the best form of government. Following his contemporaries, Bedil believed that rulers who seek advice from scientists can provide fairness and guarantee the nation's development. In regard to social development, Bedil divided human history into several stages. During the first stages, there was no division of labor, no rich and poor, no oppressors and oppressed, nor rulers and subjects. Later, when land that had originally belonged to the peasants was taken by the rich, the fair system failed. Bedil insisted that that was the reason why the country became subordinated to one ruler. Although the creation of a strong state led to stronger peace, this did not improve the lives of peasants, who, according to Bedil, were the foundation of the society because they feed the nation.

Dovletmamed Azadi (1700–1760) expressed the political views of the Turkmen people. His views did not differ essentially from those of his contemporaries in other parts of Central Asia. He also divided the society into poor and rich, believing that the rich depend on the poor and deprive them of the respect they deserve. Azadi's political concept was based on the views of the oppressed. For Azadi, the khan should protect and defend the interests of the people from plunderers and invaders. He insisted that, because almost everything in the state depended on the personal features of the ruler, a good ruler should be just, fair, generous, and humane. The idea that the ruler is God's shadow on Earth was very popular in Central Asia, and Azadi elaborated these views, stating that only just rulers fulfill the mission to represent God. According to him, tyrants do not stand up to their mission. Similarly, Azadi divided all states into just and unjust. All states that he knew about were unjust because the rulers conducted their policies not in the interest of the people. A just state is an ideal model, which can be created if the ruler would punish robbers, judges' rulings would be fair, physicians would treat those in need, and there would be enough water for everyone. Mutual assistance, independence, legality, peace, friendship, and caring are the basic principles on which a just state should be built. The idea of a just state was closely associated with Azadi's idea of uniting all Turkmen tribes into one centralized state, which would have eliminated conflicts between the tribes, defended them from foreign aggressions, and created favorable conditions for the political and cultural development of Turkmen people. Azadi's ideas were highly valued and supported by his contemporaries and followers Andalib (1710–1770) and Shabende (1720–1800). Developing Azadi's antifeudal ideas, these Turkmen poets criticized the rulers and the clergy, accusing the government of ravaging the people, and demanded social justice.

Another antigovernment Central Asian thinker of the second half of the eighteenth century was Azadi's son Makhtumkuli Fragi (1734–1790). He is considered the father of Turkmen literature, and Fragi's words are held in greater reverence than those of the Koran. His inclusion of street wisdom in classical forms and his simplicity of language contributed to Fragi's popularity with traveling bards. In regard to politics, Fragi developed the concepts of state and individuality. He believed that all people are different because their behavior, personal features, and views are different. Because of their differences, peoples' acts do not always coincide and sometimes escalate and result in conflicts. Fragi thought that when people focus on self-preservation, they head toward a catastrophe of destroying each other. According to him, the state and state rulers were created with the sole purpose of avoiding such a catastrophe, preventing fights between the people, and securing peace in the country. However, in daily life, the philosopher saw different realities, and the state he observed followed completely opposite policies. Rulers arbitrarily and violently conducted aggressive wars, and Fragi criticized his state—mostly because people in this state depended on their property status. Criticizing the state bureaucracy, Fragi was not favorable toward the clergy either and unmasked its role in the state apparatus. He denied all wars except the war for independence or unification of the country conducted by armed people. Fragi had no particular suggestions regarding the future political and social systems, and his works *Future of Turkmenistan, Our Prayers,* and *Turkmen Fortress* contained general descriptions of a country ruled by wise men where friendship and fairness govern. At the end of his life, all his works were confiscated by the Persians; Fragi personally witnessed how the camel on which his manuscripts were loaded fell into a river and was swept away.

The political thought of the Kyrgyz people is associated with the names of Asan-Kaigy (d. 1465) and Tolubai-Synchi (lived in the fifteenth century). Their views did not differ from those of their contemporaries, and these men traditionally accused those who govern of lacking respect and compassion to the population. Although they justified destroying the power of such people by force, they did not call for resistance to such power. Believing in mutual love and compassion, they suggested that people get rid of such authorities by relocating. Tolubai-Synchi specified that peace and friendship between people could be achieved if the country is ruled by wise men with an understanding of what is good and bad. The first Kyrgyz theorist who made open statements against the power of the khan was Sanchi-Synchi (late sixteenth to early seventeenth centuries), who advocated overthrowing the power if it is based on violence and deception.

Political thought of Kazakhstan developed after the Kazakh khanate was created in the middle of the fifteenth century. Kazakh statehood consolidated Kazakh ethnos, and at the end of the fifteenth century and early into the sixteenth century, tribes united into three major groups called hordes. Works attributed to Bukhar-Zhirau (1693–1787), a poet at the court of Khan Ablai, are examples of political thought expressed in Kazakh folklore, which was the only form of knowledge dissemination known to the Kazakhs. According to Bukhar-Zhirau, the world was created by God. Bukhar-Zhirau called for his audience to follow all Islamic rites and rituals and argued for the preservation of existing relations. Bukhar-Zhirau idealized the khan and praised the khan's officials while writing patriotic verses. He called people to unite and fight against Jungur feudals and promoted the idea of creating a strong centralized khanate that would unite all thee hordes. Bukhar-Zhirau also defended the idea of peaceful relations with Russia.

The ideas of people's happiness and welfare were central in the songs of *akyns,* the performers of folklore. Shal-Akyn, Zhiembet-Zhirau, and Margaski-Zhirau are the eighteenth-century *akyns* whose names were preserved by history. Traditionally, they criticized the immoral behavior of the rich, condemned the oppression of local administrators, idealized a just ruler, and promoted patriotic feelings of their tribesmen. Shal-Akyn disputed some norms of the Shariah law, expressing doubts about the tradition of polygamy.

ENLIGHTENMENT AND EDUCATION

In the second half of the nineteenth century, the ideology of enlightenment and education became especially popular in Central Asia. Chokan Valikhanov (1835–1865), a famous scholar, was an outstanding educator in Kazakhstan. A grandson of the last great khan of the Kazakh Middle Horde and personal friend of Russian novelist Fyodor Dostoyevsky, Valikhanov took part in several expeditions in unexplored areas of Central Asia. In 1860, he was elected a member of the Russian Geographic Society while working on an Asian map collection for the Russian armed forces in St. Petersburg. His political ideas were strongly influenced by Russian revolutionary democrats. Valikhanov was a strong proponent of close ties between Kazakhstan and Russia and strongly defended the necessity of the Europeization of Kazakhstan, believing that the local aristocracy was the main barrier to Kazakhstan's progress and accusing the tsarist administration of supporting regressive anti-Western forces in Kazakhstan. Valikhanov also believed that the Russian government would eventually understand that "it needs people and not sultans because mathematically 100 is much more useful than 10."[1] Being under the influence of Russian democrats, he tried to find some traces of peasants' communities in Kazakhstan, which, according to him, should be a nucleus of the future ideal state. Valikhanov declined any attempts to use Islam for progressive reforms, thinking that no reformation would be possible within the Muslim religion.

Works of Abai Kunanbayev (1845–1904) were based on ideas of enlightenment as well. His main contribution to Kazakh culture was his poetry, which expressed nationalism and grew out of Kazakh folklore. Before Kunanbayev, most Kazakh poetry was oral, echoing the nomadic habits of the Kazakh steppe's people. In his poems, Abai Kunanbayev exposed the problems arising from the remaining patriarchal property relations and condemned conflicts among the tribes; he thought these disputes slowed the implementation of progressive economic methods. Being patriotic, Kunanbayev criticized those who called for the transformation of Kazakhstan into a Muslim caliphate under a Turkish sultan.

Central Asian political scholar Ahmad Donish (literary name of Ahmad Mahdum, 1827–1897) visited St. Petersburg three times as secretary of the Bokharan embassy and used his knowledge of Russia and its culture in his works. Donish often compared Russia and Bokhara and promoted friendship between these states. Donish was probably the first Central Asian scholar who did not assess political developments from a theological point of view and believed in the social contract theory. Initially, he was a proponent of reforms from above, and he hoped that the rule of law instituted by the emir of Bokhara would stop lawlessness. However, his proposals were not accepted by the emir and, in the 1870s, he overcame his reformist illusions. In an 1870 essay, Donish advocated a European-style representative body consisting of people from all walks of life who would meet in the presence of the emir and debate issues and vote on matters pertaining to public welfare. All governmental concerns, after having been debated and voted on, would be approved by the emir. To curtail the emir's authority even more, Donish included the office of the *wazir*, an equivalent to the head of executive government. This two-pronged assault on the emir's powers, Donish thought, would not only introduce order into the government but would allow for a system of checks and balances. The emir rejected Donish's suggestions and, further, did not allow reform of the traditional educational system nor of the institution of European-style courses. Upon his return from his third trip to St. Petersburg (1883–1884), Donish was assigned to Bokhara's most remote district as a judge. His critique of the Bokharan public system became more acute, and he justified the legality of a public uprising against oppressors and religious authorities. Highly influential in rousing the people, Donish's works rallied the emir, the court, and the clergy against him. Donish was singled out as an irreligious and unprincipled person, and his books were deemed anti-Islamic.

Turkmen poets of the nineteenth century remained under the influence of stereotypes and hoped for a just ruler who would improve the living conditions of the regular people. Political ideas of the Kyrgyz people were expressed by Toktogul Saltylganov (1864–1933), an *akyn* who went away from traditional beliefs in a just ruler to denial of social justice under the political system that existed through the nineteenth century in the Kyrgyz lands. His fame reached a high point in the Soviet era, when his prerevolutionary works were interpreted as reflecting the class struggle; however, modern interpretations suggest that they had more to do with clan rivalries. Saltyganov welcomed the Bolshevik revolution and glorified its leaders in his poems.

RADICAL ISLAM AND REVOLUTIONS

As in many parts of the Muslim world, the late nineteenth and early twentieth centuries witnessed the emergence of a radical Islamic movement in Central Asia. A school of thought called Jadidism was established as a Central Asian response to challenges of the European reform movements. The term *jadidism* came from the new method of teaching the Arabic alphabet that was popular among Muslims of the Middle East and European Russia. Although part of the group favored religious and social reform to meet the Western challenge, the movement became part of a wider pan-Turkist and pan-Islamist Muslim cultural and political movement aimed at establishing an Islamic state without borders. One of the founders of the Jadidism movement was Furkat (1858–1909). Together with another Uzbek educator Mukimi (1851–1903), Furkat criticized both the Russian administration and the local clergy, who used the 1898 uprising in Andizhan to raise anti-Russian sentiments for reestablishing feudal institutions and submit Turkistan under dependency from the Turkish sultan. Unlike Furkat, Mukimi did not believe in the possibility of peaceful reformation from the leaders, because he was sure that the governing authorities did not consider peoples' interests.

There were different schools within the Jadidism movement. Understanding that further development was impossible without political, social, and cultural reforms, one group of Jadids developed the idea of national independence. Looking back at the nation's history, the Jadids explained all negative developments by the loss of national independence and statehood. Behbudi (1875–1919), one of the movement's leaders, believed that, because the khanates had been disconnected from the world during the last 50 years, local people lost access to the civilization's achievement and became colonized. The colonial system, according to him, forced Turkistanis to live under European laws and standards, which were unknown and unfamiliar to the population.

Behbudi concluded that education was the only opportunity for people to defend their rights and national interests from the government. Behbudi also thought that native professionals could bring help to their nation while working at courts and other government institutions of the Russian Empire.

In accordance with their reformist agenda, the Jadids attempted to create new literature through which they conducted their religious education of the peoples of Central Asia. They claimed that classical literature failed to fulfill these demands because it was fundamentally artistic. The Jadids wanted to create a committed or engaged type of literature that would help to awaken the community. Insisting on the didactic aspect of imaginative literature, the Jadids used literature to introduce new ideas and criticize nontraditional social and political values and institutions. In 1906, the first newspapers were published and circulated in Tashkent under various Russian auspices. Three of the newspapers were dedicated to literary and scientific discussions, but none of them lasted for long. During World War I, a small jadidist theater group toured throughout Turkistan, presenting plays filled with poetry and polemical dialogues written by the reformers and raising funds for the cause. The first permanent theater in Tashkent was founded in 1913. Jadids' ideas were not spread widely because most of the Turkistanis could not read, and theater was viewed with suspicion by the conservative clergy.

The older generation of Jadids—represented by Abdul Vohid Burkhanov, Usman Khojaev, Mukhitdin Rafoat, Sadriddin Ayni, and others—were correct in estimating their role in the society. Because Jadids were not a strong force, they had no influence on the majority of the population. The Jadids were very careful in their reforms and advocated nonviolent struggle and phased reforms, because people followed the traditional clergy, which could initiate anti-Jadid actions at any moment. The two groups could not find common ground.

The main part of the Jadids' theory was the idea of unity among all Central Asian people. The absence of solidarity among the people and the educational backwardness were viewed by Jadids as reasons that native people of Central Asia were colonized. Educational activities of the Jadids were characterized by the opening of new schools and the publishing of journals and newspapers. Jadids followed the Russian political process and established relations with Russian political parties. They did not, however, accept Russian social democratic ideas, believing that these norms contradicted Muslim traditions. In 1907, Jadidism was declared illegal by the Russian authorities, and numerous teachers who propagated local reforms were prosecuted. At the end of World War I, Jadidism became a political force once again; it advocated for the creation of a constitutional democracy with a local legislature in Tashkent directly elected in Central Asian localities and charged with the adoption of laws applicable to the region. The Jadids hoped that these reforms would lead to better relations with the Russian administration. The democratic revolution of February 1917 gave Jadids hope that Turkistan would have autonomy in the new state. Disappointed with the policies of the provisional government, the Jadids declared Turkistan's independence and the creation of a Central Asian federation as their goals.

After the Bolshevik revolution of 1917, Jadidism was transformed into a secularized political movement that sought the creation of native discourses and political liberation from foreign domination. A group of Jadids who were interested in a political rather than a cultural reform separated from the movement and were led by a descendant of the Khivan royalty, Mustafa Chokaev (1890–1941). He criticized the policies of local communists and recommended opening the grain market, restricting the export of grain from the regions, and canceling price fixation and the restrictions against private bakeries. In regard to military policy, the Jadids argued for a voluntary army. Certain Jadid leaders initially associated themselves with the Bolsheviks in hopes that this would help them to advocate for the national rights of the native people, including political and cultural autonomy from Soviet rule. Eventually, they transformed themselves into Muslim communists and essentially dominated the political life of Central Asia until 1924–1925.

SOVIET RULE AND POLITICAL THOUGHT

Native intellectuals of the revolutionary period in Turkistan aimed to unite the Muslim people of Central Asia and struggled for their independence from colonial Russian-Soviet rule. Writers Cholpan (1897–1938) and Fitrat (1886–1938) were active in promoting and reforming Uzbek language and literature. In his poems, Fitrat expressed pessimism and a wish for an end to Soviet domination of his native land. His dramas reflected fundamental issues and a crisis of the Central Asian society. Written in the early 1920s, Fitrat's plays dealt with the British domination in India and the indigenous reaction to this foreign control. Even though the plays reflected the picture of foreign domination in India, they indicated a similar situation in Soviet Central Asia under the Russians. Cholpan's poetry, written during the same period as Fitrat's plays, exhibited many similarities to literary works of writers from other Eastern countries under colonialism. Cholpan expressed anticolonialist and patriotic views in his writings to encourage people to fight against colonialist aggression. During the Soviet rule in Central Asia, the Soviet government integrated literary activities into the state structure, attempting to eliminate potential opposing literary trends and their representatives—including Choplan and Fitrat, who were accused of nationalism and later murdered during the Stalin purges.

After Stalin's death, there was no physical repression of writers, but the Soviet government continued to prohibit the emergence of any literary ideology or activity it deemed contradictory to the Marxist-Leninist foundations of its rule. Soviet socialist realism thus remained the only permitted literary and artistic method until the dissolution of the Soviet Union.

With the social and political transformation initiated by the Gorbachev government in the second half of the 1980s, national history and ideas of statehood development, ethnic identification, and religious influence were reconsidered. The first alternative elections in 1988 and anti-Russian riots in Kazakhstan in 1986 and in Uzbekistan in 1989 were the turning points in public discussions about the place of Central Asian republics in the Soviet Union and their historic heritage and perspectives. Growing national consciousness and patriotism required ideological and theoretical justifications, which were supported by newly created governments, national elites, and progressive national writers. The development of such national symbols as a coat of arms, a flag, and an anthem was not only a subject of hot debates but enhanced historical studies and furthered the ideas of national independence aimed at overcoming the identity crisis inflicted by the Marxist-Leninist ideology.

NATIONAL INDEPENDENCE IDEOLOGY

In 1991, all Central Asian states declared their sovereignty and independence. The formation of a national independence ideology became the main subject of discussions in government think tanks and among local philosophers and historians. It was a common conclusion that a national spiritual revival would be impossible without building a democratic state based on the rule of law principles. Local legal and political scholars popularized Western values and major human rights principles. In all of these republics, drafters of the national legislation attempted to connect Jeffersonian ideas with national traditions and meet local leaders' requests to justify keeping power in their hands. In Kazakhstan, for example, academicians in Almaty were united in explaining that political developments are secondary to economic achievements, and they justified human rights abuses by the necessity to build a strong, stable, and prosperous society. According to them, only a country where people are well off may allow itself the luxury of political competition. Regarding legal development, scholars all over the region are unanimous in defending a secular state with a strong presidential system of government.

In a search for national ideas, politicians and intellectuals turned to traditional ideas expressed in folklore and preserved in the peoples' memory. In Uzbekistan, Said Ahmad, a popular writer, was one of the authors of the national independence ideology. Said Ahmad suggested paying more attention to spiritual education, which would secure a moral revival of the nation. He wrote that the "world culture is decorated by Uzbek spirituality"[2] and hoped that a highly publicized, government-sponsored Enlightenment against Ignorance campaign would help to eliminate public fear, ideological instability, lack of independent thinking, and spiritual dependence. The panacea for preventing vulgarity and cynicism among the populace was seen in creating a happy, peaceful, and prosperous life based on pride in national history, respect to great ancestors, and traditional tolerant religious values. Recognizing religion as part of a national historic heritage, all Central Asian republics declared major religious festivals national holidays. In Kyrgyzstan, the folkloric epos *Manas* was used as a source for national ideas. Principles of the unity of the nation, friendship among the people, patriotism, tolerance, hard work and study, harmony with the nature, and defense of the Kyrgyz statehood promoted in the epos became the fundamentals of the presidential ideological program Kyrgyzstan Is Our Common House. Similar ideas were expressed in the *Rukhnama* (Book of Spirit), written by the late president of Turkmenistan, Saparmurat Niyazov, in 2001. In the author's opinion, the *Rukhnama* was supposed to substitute for all other books in the country and provide historical, political, and cultural accounts of the Turkmen nation. Linking the fate of the nation, state, and individuals, this book reviewed the history in a way that optimistically showed the eternal victory of life over evil and inertia.

The status of a national language was one of the first serious issues discussed in the search for national ideas. As soon as Kazakhstan and Uzbekistan became independent, local languages were given the status of official state languages—an important issue because of a multiethnic population and a real threat to the existence of local language skills. Local languages were poorly studied in schools and, under a strong Russian domination, were not needed for those who wanted to advance their careers. All over the region, native languages were usually spoken only on the periphery, and their use was a sign of backwardness. Famous Kyrgyz writers Genghis Aytmatov and Tugolbai Sydykbekov created the Committee for Defense of the Mother Language and initiated the adoption of a Language Act in the Kyrgyz legislature. Debates associated with the passage of this law were important for raising national self-awareness among the people living in the region and increased interest in their own history as a factor of a growing national self-identification. The revival of historic geographic names and pompous celebrations of historic dates and anniversaries served this purpose as well.

Problems of ethnic genesis and national history were reviewed and reconsidered during numerous scholarly gatherings, and problems of historical development became of interest to specialists and to the general public. According to research reports recently published in Kazakhstan and Kyrgyzstan, the state formations of nomadic tribes that moved to the region were attributed to much earlier periods than was considered under the Soviet historiography. Relations with Muslim societies, which remained on the Chinese territory, were reevaluated also. Reforming views were applied to the analysis of the Russian colonization and Soviet history, and the role of religious factors in Central Asian history also was reconsidered. Uzbek scholars revived the Jadids whose names and works had been deleted from the Soviet textbooks and reexamined their views on the combination of a secular education with an Islamic culture, recognizing them as responsive to modern challenges.

The study of centuries-old events and ideas is relevant today because it appears to be analogous to present-day ideological and political transformations taking place in the sociopolitical life of this region. Like the Jadids, most of the current reformers are representatives of the local intelligentsia and relatively young people with the best education, connections, and opportunities; they enter local politics and cooperate with the Russian elites to achieve their political, rather than religious, goals.

NOTES

1. Chokan Valikhanov, *Sobranie Sochinenii* [Collection of Works] (Almaty, Kazakhstan: Kazakh Savet Entsiklopediasy, 1985), 124.

2. Said Ahmad, *Sobiq Ughri: Hikoi a Lar* (Tashkent, Uzbeckistan: Ezuvchi, 1991), 16.

Notable People in the History of Central Asia

Chinghis Aitmatov (1928–), most famous Kyrgyz writer, whose works synthesize national mythology in the context of contemporary life, interweaving human lives with the lives of animals. In the 1990s, he served as the Kyrgyz ambassador to the European Union, the North Atlantic Treaty Organization, and Belgium.

Askar Akaev (1944–), Kyrgyz physicist, who, in 1990, was selected by the Kyrgyz legislature to serve as the president of Kyrgyzstan. He won uncontested presidential elections in 1991 and remained the Kyrgyz president until he was overthrown during public revolts in 2005.

Al-Farabi (870–950), thinker who created a unique system of knowledge that combined logic, astronomy, mathematics, theory of music, ethics, psychology, and law. He also established a Koran-based pantheistic study of social development that rejected the dominance of orthodox Islam.

Toshkhodji Asiri (1864–1915), Tajik poet and educator, who worked as a stone cutter declining the offer to become a judge. Created and publicly read his poems of social content in a teahouse outside of a central mosque in Khojent. The main idea of his works was the propaganda of secular education and science, contemporary technological developments, and a disapproval of local religious leaders.

Sadriddin Ayni (1878–1954), prominent member of the Jadid movement, publisher, educator, and writer; one of the founders of modern literature in Uzbek and Tajik.

Mahmud Hoja Behbudi (1874–1919), first Central Asian playwright, essayist, publisher, and bookseller; a leading figure in the enlightenment movement and champion of new methods in literacy education.

Biruni (973–1048), astronomer, historian, poet, geographer, pharmacologist, and mineralogist. He proposed—500 years before Copernicus—that the Earth rotates around the sun, estimated the distance to the moon and the radius of the Earth, and explained solar eclipses. He also helped ibn-Sina steal dead bodies for medical experiments.

Borombay Bekburat (?–1858), leader of northern Kyrgyz tribes, colonel of the Russian army, founder of military fortresses, and initiator of Kyrgyz accession to Russian citizenship in 1855.

Mustafa Chokaev (1890–1941), secretary to the Muslim faction at the Russian legislature; he was a leader of the independence movement and chairman of the Turkestan Central Council of Muslims, a regional government body in 1917, and he established the Provisional Autonomous Government of Turkestan in Kokand. In 1920, he escaped to Paris, where he became a leading expert on the history of Central Asia.

Abdulkhamid Cholpan (1897–1938), Uzbek poet who initially adopted a positive attitude toward the Bolshevik revolution, but his later works indicated a sense of betrayal and dissatisfaction with Soviet rule. Died as a victim of the Stalinist purges after false accusations of being a German spy.

Arthur Conolly (1807–1842), British intelligence officer, explorer, and writer. He participated in many reconnaissance missions in Central Asia and coined the term The Great Game to describe the struggle between the British and Russian Empires for domination over Central Asia. In 1841, he undertook a single-person rescue mission to free his fellow officer Charles Stoddart; he and Stoddart were later executed on charges of spying for the British Empire.

Dzhambul Dzhabaev (1846–1945), traditional folksinger and an expert in Kazakh music; he sang to the accompaniment of a plucked string instrument. He was a highly awarded author of primitive-style flattering odes to Stalin.

Abdurauf Fitrat (1886–1938), active member of the Jadid movement, poet and playwright, propagandist of the Young Turks political movement ideas in Uzbekistan, and minister of education in the Soviet Bokharan government. His dramas reflected his desire to stop the Soviet domination and the crisis of Central Asian societies. He was executed during the Stalin purges.

Mikhail Frunze (1885–1925), Soviet general born in Bishkek, commander of the eastern front during the Russian Civil War (1920–1921). Established Soviet control in Russian Turkistan and organized suppression of public resistance and the Basmachi movement.

Islam Karimov (1938–), president of Uzbekistan since March 1990; he came to power as the Communist Party's first secretary in Uzbekistan in 1989 and declared Uzbekistan's independence in 1991.

Konstantin von Kaufman (1818–1882), Russian general and the first governor general of Russia's Turkistan province. He led most of the military campaigns and diplomatic efforts aimed at Russia's territorial expansion in Central Asia.

Junaid Khan (1857–1938), commander of the Basmachi movement in Turkmen lands, usurper of power in the Khiva khanate in 1918, and organizer of anti-Soviet resistance in Central Asia until 1931; escaped to Afghanistan, where he led anti-Soviet emigrations.

Faizulla Khojaev (1896–1938), prime minister in the first Soviet government of Uzbekistan and an active member of the Bolshevik movement in Central Asia; he conducted the autonomous policy and opposed Stalin's measures to impose a cotton monoculture on the republic. In 1937, he was accused of being a nationalist and a separatist and was tried at a Moscow show trial. He was executed in 1938, and his family was exiled to a prison camp in Siberia.

Dinmukhamed Kunaev (1912–1993), first secretary of the Kazakh Communist Party Central Committee, leader of the republic in 1960 to 1986, and member of the highest Soviet political and state institutions. A dogmatic communist, he was accused of corruption and was removed from office by Mikhail Gorbachev.

Kurmanzhan Manatbay (1811–1907), first woman who led the mountainous Kyrgyz tribes to their independence after her husband, the ruler of the Alai province, was killed. In 1876, she joined Russia with all her people; the tsar awarded her with the rank of army colonel.

Mollamurt (1879–1930), founder of Turkmen modern poetry. He created popular patriotic songs and wrote poems in support of Soviet authorities and their policies advocating the need for social changes and pacification of Turkmen tribes. He was killed by anti-Bolshevik guerillas.

Alisher Navoi (1441–1501), prominent statesman and founder of the Uzbek literary language and literature.

Nursultan Nazarbaev (1940–), president of Kazakhstan since the fall of the Soviet Union (elected December 1, 1991). Before, he worked as the leader of the Communist Party of Kazakhstan (1989–1991) and chairman of the Kazakh government (1984–1989).

Saparmuart Niyazov (1940–2006), the last Communist leader and the first president of independent Turkmenistan, who ruled the country for 21 years. He established a totalitarian regime with his personality cult and secured personal fortune through uncontrolled access to the nation's gas reserves.

Emomali Rakhmonov (1952–), president of Tajikistan since 1994; in November 2006, he was reelected for his third seven-year term.

Sharaf Rashidov (1917–1983), leader of Soviet Uzbekistan for 33 years. In 1950, he was elected chairman of the legislature and, in 1959, was promoted to be the head of the Uzbek Communist Party. His tenure is synonymous with corruption, nepotism, and lawlessness. Building his power base on feudal traditions, he and his mafia network falsified figures to earn about $2 billion in profit for cotton that was never grown. Recently, he has reemerged as a national hero.

Abu Ali Ibn-Sina (Avicenna) (980–1037), the sultan's personal physician and curator of the best library in the Islamic world. He wrote the philosophical encyclopedia, translated Aristotle into Arabic, and his Medical Canon explained the positions of the main internal organs and the circulatory system. When translated into Latin in 1543, it became a textbook for Western medicine until the nineteenth century.

Charles Stoddart (1806–1842), British colonel and diplomat. He was sent to Bokhara in 1838 by the East India Company to forge an alliance with the emir against the Russians advancing into Central Asia. He was captured by the emir and was tortured for over three years. He was publicly beheaded in the central market square of the city, where he was ordered to dig his own grave.

Olzhas Suleimenov (1936–), leading Kazakh writer who, during the Soviet era, was accused of glorifying feudal nomadic cultures; he advocated the closing of nuclear testing sites in Kazakhstan. After Kazakhstan's independence, he became speaker of the Parliament until 1994 and then accepted several ambassadorial positions.

Timur (Tamerlane) (1336–1405), military and political leader, founder of the modern Uzbek nation, the last nomadic emperor. He succeeded as a warrior in the Mongol army and became lord of Transoxiana after political and military maneuvering. He personally led his mounted archers to battles and conquered more territory than any other single ruler. His death from tuberculosis prevented a clash with Ming China. In the last years of his life, he divided his empire among his descendants, and his empire did not survive him.

Nazir Turiakulov (1893–1937), journalist, diplomat, and the first Soviet ambassador to the Kingdom of Saudi Arabia in 1928–1936; the only Kazakh on the highest level of the Soviet diplomatic service before World War II.

Ulugbeg (1394–1449), Timur's grandson, who, at the age of 15, was made viceroy of Samarkand. His love of mathematics, history, theology, medicine, poetry, and music gave the city a reputation for learning and culture that drew the best scholars and artists to Samarkand. In 1429, the first Asian observatory, which also served as a library, was built for him. Ulugbeg determined coordinates for 1,018 stars, devised rules for predicting eclipses, and measured the stellar year to within one minute of modern electronic calculations. He was arrested and beheaded by his son.

Chokan Valikhanov (1835–1865), Kazakh historian, ethnographer, geographer, economist, and traveler who published books on the roots of Kyrgyz ethnicity and religion. He prepared the first complete edition of Asian maps while serving as a Russian army officer.

Glossary of Selected Terms and Concepts

akyn: performer of improvised traditional folk songs or epics in Kazakhstan and Kyrgyzstan

arzbegi: official in the Timurid Empire responsible for receiving complaints from the citizens

batyr: strong man, hero, or professional warrior

bek: originally, a governor of a territory in the Turkic khanate (sixth century); later, a tribal leader or representative of nobility with administrative functions over the local population

Bolsheviks: faction in the Russian Social Democratic Workers' Party, which led the socialist revolution of 1917 and became the Communist Party of the Soviet Union

Commonwealth of Independent States (CIS): intergovernmental regional organization encompassing 12 former Soviet Union republics and aimed at enhancing cooperation of the member states in political, economic, environmental, cultural, and other areas

cotton affair: most notorious corruption case during the Soviet period, when Uzbek officials around 1978 to 1983 misused up to US$2 billion by inflating reports on amounts of cotton delivered to the state

emir: warlord, commander, head of state in Bokhara in the seventeenth to twentieth centuries

Hanafi: school of Islamic jurisprudence in Sunni Islam founded in the seventh century and popular among the Central Asians; is known for its laxity in ritualistic issues

horde: state-like union of Kazakh tribes

indigenization: Soviet policy of promoting native people to high-level government positions

Jadidism: progressive educational, literary, and political movement in the late nineteenth to early twentieth centuries that advocated enlightenment of local people through modernizing traditional Islam

jizya: tax levied on followers of non-Muslim but permitted religions

khan: title of feudal rulers in early medieval state formations, chief of a tribe

khanate: state formation ruled by a khan

makhalla: Jewish quarter in a Central Asian town

manap: leader of a Kyrgyz tribe

masterly inactivity: British policy of guiding the countries included in the British sphere of influence but leaving to them the power of decision making. This policy prevented British military assistance to the Central Asian khanates facing Russian threats

paranja: black robe that covered a woman's body, accompanied by a smaller face veil. The extent of covering was determined by local customs and economic status of a woman

perestroika: policy of political and economic reforms initiated by Mikhail Gorbachev in 1985 to 1991

protectorate: form of colonial dependency under which a colonized state preserves some independence in internal affairs, while foreign affairs, defense, and other important issues are regulated by the metropoly

Red Army: pro-Bolshevik military units, which served as a foundation for the Soviet armed forces

registan: main square in the capital city of a Central Asian state, usually the location of the emir's palace

satrap: provincial governor appointed by Persian kings during the Akhaemenid Empire in the sixth to fourth centuries B.C.

soviet: council, a representative government body on all levels of Soviet administration

Sufism: mystical movement in Islam that emphasizes the development of personal spirituality and internal comprehension of divinity through the refusal of rites of orthodox Islam; includes beliefs in asceticism, internal contemplation, and nonparticipation in public social life

Supreme formal legislative body of the USSR and each union republic Soviet:

titular nation: people belonging to the same ethnicity; a designation that was used by the Soviet authorities for establishment of a national republic in Central Asia—for example, Uzbeks in Uzbekistan, Kazakhs in Kazakhstan

ulus: administrative component of the horde; original meaning of the word is nation

vizier: chief minister or adviser to the head of a Central Asian state

White Army: former tsarist military units that fought against the Red Army during the Russian Civil War (1918–1920)

1842 (Osnabrueck, Germany: Biblio Verlag, 1969), and difficulties of traveling there are described in Ella Christie, *Through Khiva to Golden Samarkand* (Philadelphia: Lippincott, 1925). A report on journeys and studies in Bokhara by the secretary of the Royal Danish Geographical Society and the commander of the first Danish Pamir expedition, O. Olufsen, entitled *The Emir of Bokhara and His Country* (London: William Heinemann, 1891) is a classic example of detailed reporting on geography, economy, religion, and culture in this emirate based on firsthand interviews with government officials and the native population. Numerous maps and illustrations create a visual image of life in this state in the late nineteenth century.

For the history of Central Asian states' formation, the standard work remains Rene Grousset's *The Civilizations of the East* (London: H. Hamilton, 1931–1934). The ethnic riots of the people in these states are traced in David Law's *From Samaria to Samarkand: The Ten Lost Tribes of Israel* (New York and London: University Press of America, 1992). For the earliest periods of the region's history, a good introduction is written by David Childress, *Lost Cities of China, Central Asia, and India: A Traveler's Guide* (Stelle, IL: Adventures Unlimited Press, 1985), which is a review of cultures preceding and then surrounding Central Asian societies. An informative, although sometimes technical, reading on the history of invasions and military developments is prepared by Erik Hildinger, *Warriors of the Steppe: A Military History of Central Asia, 500 B.C. to 1700 A.D.* (New York: Sarpedon, 1997). External relations of medieval Central Asian states are the subject of essays collected and edited by Richard Frye, *Islamic Iran and Central Asia (7th–12th centuries)* (London: Variorum Reprints, 1979). His other book—Richard Frye, *Bukhara: The Medieval Achievement* (Costa Mesa, CA: Mazda Publishers, 1996)—tells the biography of this most influential Central Asian city.

Many studies are dedicated to a particular historical period or an individual. The Arab invasion is examined in Hamilton Gibb, *The Arab Conquest in Central Asia* (London: The Royal Asiatic Society, 1923), which has been many times reprinted since its first publication. The post-Timurid history is discussed in Mansura Haidar, *Central Asia in the Sixteenth Century* (New Delhi, India: Manohar, 2002). A good contribution to the scholarship on Mongol domination in the region are Jack Weatherford's *Genghis Khan and the Making of the Modern World* (New York: Crown Publishers, 2004) and Beatrice Manz's *The Rise and Rule of Tamerlane* (Cambridge, England and New York: Cambridge University Press, 1999). These persons are studied as the founders of nomad conquest dynasties and as supremely talented individuals. Intellectual life of the region in the early medieval period is subject of books by Edward Browne, *A Literary History of Persia: From the Earliest Times to Sadi* (London: T. F. Unwin, 1902) and *A History of Persian Literature under Tartar Dominion (1265–1502)* (Cambridge, England: University Press, 1920). Browne's books are surpassed by other works but are still useful for the original texts provided. Among the research on the cultural history of the region, one of the most complete studies is Shirin Akiner's *Languages and Scripts of Central Asia* (London: School of Oriental and African Studies, University of London, 1997); however, this book lays disproportionate emphasis on twentieth century. Events of the nineteenth century and efforts of British and Russian governments to establish control over the region are reviewed in the very well-written book of Peter Hopkirk, *The Great Game: The Struggle for Empire in Central Asia* (New York: Kodansha International, 1992).

Many works focus on the history of Russian colonization. Seymour Becker's *Russia's Protectorates in Central Asia: Bukhara and Khiva, 1865–1924* (London and New York: Routledge Curzon, 2004) examines the Russian conquest of the ancient khanates of Bukhara and Khiva in the 1860s and 1870s and the relationship between Russia and the territories until their extinction as political entities in 1924. The colonization from the security perspective of the Russian General Staff concerned with actual and potential regional wars is reviewed by Alex Marshall in *The Russian General Staff and Asia, 1800–1917* (London and New York: Routledge, 2006). How and to what extent have the presence and control of outsiders Russified Central Asian life and how much have Central Asians relinquished their sense of ethnic differentiation are evaluated in the collection of essays edited by Edward Allworth, *Central Asia: 120 Years of Russian Rule* (Durham, NC, and London: Duke University Press, 1989) and in Elisabeth Bacon's, *Central Asians under Russian Rule: A Study in Culture Change* (Ithaca, NY: Cornell University Press, 1980), both of which are suited for general readers. A very scholarly study of political ideas that became popular among Central Asian intellectuals is Khalid Adeeb's *The Politics of Muslim Cultural Reform: Jadidism in Central Asia* (Berkeley, Los Angeles, and London: University of California Press, 1998). On the economic development of the region during the colonization period, Steven Marks's *Road to Power: The Trans-Siberian Railroad and the Colonization of Asian Russia, 1850–1917* (Ithaca, NY: Cornell University Press, 1991) is a thorough chronicle of industrial changes.

Despite Central Asia having a long, full, and eventful history, it has been researched unevenly, and specific periods receive much more attention than others. The literature on the transformation of Central Asia into Bolshevik society and the incorporation of the region into the Soviet Union is abundant. Among the best recent works are the research performed by Francine Hirsch, *Empire of Nations, Ethnographic Knowledge & the Making of the Soviet Union* (London and Ithaca, NY: Cornell University Press, 2005) on the development of national ideas by the people of Central Asia and intricacies of the national state-building process initiated by the Soviets in 1924 and a fascinating review of early Soviet politics aimed at forming satellite communist states in Central Asia in Peter Hopkirk, *Setting the East Ablaze: Lenin's Dream of an Empire in*

Asia (New York: Kodansha International, 1995). Jeremy Smith, *Bolsheviks and the National Question* (New York: St. Martin's Press, 1999) discloses how the Russian Bolsheviks dealt with the problems posed by a multinational state and created a system that allowed the nationalists of the old Russian Empire to flourish and develop. Michael Rywkin provides a concise historical survey of social and political changes brought to the region by the Russian Bolshevik revolution in *Moscow's Muslim Challenge: Soviet Central Asia* (Armonk, NY: M. E. Sharpe, 1990). A prolific author and a knowledgeable specialist in central Asian affairs, Shirin Akiner focuses on *The Formation of Kazakh Identity from Tribe to Nation-State* (London: Royal Institute of International Affairs, 1995). How individual people were affected by the Bolshevik revolution is researched in the book written by a famous Kazakh diplomat, Tair Mansurov, *Ambassador Turiakulov: Diplomat, Politician, Man of Honor* (Moscow: Real Press, 2004). The impact of Soviet political developments on prosecution of religion in Uzbekistan and independent Central Asian states after the 1917 Bolshevik revolution is analyzed in Shoshana Keller's, *To Moscow, Not Mecca: The Soviet Campaign against Islam in Central Asia, 1917–1941* (Westport, CT, and London: Praeger, 2001). How antireligious campaigns affected women is examined by Douglas Northrop in *Veiled Empire: Gender & Power in Stalinist Central Asia* (Ithaca, NY: Cornell University Press, 2004). A good recent addition to the scholarship of this subject is well-documented Marianne Kamp's *The New Woman in Uzbekistan: Islam, Modernity, and Unveiling under Communism* (Seattle: University of Washington Press, 2006). Although most authors study the impact of dramatic political events on the area in general, a few books follow the historic path of smaller nations. A detailed and well-argued study of Central Asian peoples who were forced to migrate to China is Eberhard Wolfram's *China's Minorities: Yesterday and Today* (Belmont, CA: Wadsworth, 1982). Colin Mackerras's *China's Minorities: Integration and Modernization in the Twentieth Century* (Hong Kong and New York: Oxford University Press, 1994) looks at the status of the Uighur people in China throughout the twentieth century. The pioneer work of Michael Shterenshis, *Tamerlane and the Jews* (New York and London: Routledge Curzon, 2002), regardless of its limiting title, appears to be the most comprehensive research on the Jewish history of Central Asia. Pavel Polian's *Against Their Will: The History and Geography of Forced Migration in the USSR* (Budapest and New York: CEU Press, 2004) is the only book on the history of settlers and is based on recently declassified Russian archival materials. Divisions within each national grouping—which were not eliminated during the Communist rule—are subject of the analysis in John Glenn's, *The Soviet Legacy in Central Asia* (Houndmills, NY: Palgrave, 1999).

Several good books document the period of Soviet collapse and the transition of the Central Asian states to independence. Jack F. Matlock, who served as U.S. ambassador to the Soviet Union during the Gorbachev period, provides a knowledgeable analysis of the struggle of national republics within the context of the Soviet breakup in *Autopsy of an Empire* (New York: Random House, 1995). *Gorbachev and the Collapse of the Soviet Communist Party: The Historical and Theoretical Background* (New York: Peter Lang, 1994) by Patrick Bascio and Evgueny Novikov, describes political events in Central Asia that led to the dissolution of the USSR and the establishment of independent governments. Economic factors behind this collapse and the personalities involved are discussed Jeremy Smith, *The Fall of Soviet Communism 1985–1991* (Houndmills, Basingstoke, Hampshire, NY: Palgrave Macmillan, 2005). Formation of new states in the region is evaluated by Clifford Bosworth in *The New Islamic Dynasties* (New York: Columbia University Press, 1996). Clear and intelligent analysis of political developments during the first years of the transition to independence—emphasizing the distinctions of the Central Asian states from the political upheavals in the Russian Federation—is provided in Shereen Hunter's *Central Asia since Independence* (Westport, CT: Praeger, 1996) and in Dilip Hiro's *Between Marx and Muhammad: The Changing Face of Central Asia* (London: HarperCollins, 1994). The institutional design of electoral systems in the newly independent states is examined in Pauline Luong's *Institutional Change and Political Continuity in Post-Soviet Central Asia* (Cambridge, England: Cambridge University Press, 2002).

One of the most popular topics in contemporary Central Asian studies concerns religious issues and the fight against radical Islam. Evgueny Novikov, in *Tolerant Islam in the War of Ideas* (Washington, DC: American Foreign Policy Council, 2006), contributes to better understanding of the language, arguments, discussion methods, theological sources, images, allegories, and examples being used by Central Asian governments in their struggle against radical Islam. Major trends in the Central Asian Islamic movement are evaluated in the book *Islam and Central Asia: An Enduring Legacy or an Evolving Threat* (Washington, DC: Center for Political and Strategic Studies, 2000) compiled by Susan Eisenhower and Roald Sagdeev. The role of Islam and its impact on the nation-building process are reviewed in Oliver Roy, *The New Central Asia: The Creation of Nations* (New York: New York University Press, 2000). Ahmed Rashid's *Jihad: The Rise of Militant Islam in Central Asia* (New York: Penguin Books, 2003) investigates connections between Islamic organizations of Central Asia with fundamentalist religious centers abroad. Interesting examples of militant religious propaganda are given in Vitalii Naumkin's *Radical Islam in Central Asia: Between Pen and Rifle* (Lanham, MD: Rowman & Littlefield, 2004). Gregory Gleason attempts to answer the question, what kind of Islam would define the further transformation of the Central Asian states and how it will affect their economic development in *Markets and Politics in Central Asia: Structural Reform and Political Change* (London: Rutledge Press, 2003). Clans—which are informal political actors critical to understanding regional politics, their roots, political role, and transformation during the Soviet and post-Soviet periods—are researched by Cathleen Collins in *Clan Politics and Regime Transition in Central Asia* (Cambridge, England and New York: Cambridge University Press, 2006).

Scholars pay attention to the use of substantial energy reserves of these countries. Lutz Kleveman analyses the impact of newly discovered oil reserves on foreign policy of the Central Asian states, especially on relations with the neighboring states in *The New Great Game: Blood and Oil in Central Asia* (New York: Atlantic Monthly Press, 2003). Ahmed Rashid draws parallels between economic and religious factors in *Taliban: Militant Islam, Oil, and Fundamentalism in Central Asia* (New Haven, CT: Yale University Press, 2000). The oil rush and the redistribution of wealth and prosperity among foreign multinationals, regional powers, and local populations are discussed in the immensely readable *The Caspian: Politics, Energy and Security* (London and New York: Routledge Curzon, 2004) by Shirin Akiner. The collection edited by Richard Auty and Indra de Soysa, *Energy, Wealth & Governance in the Caucasus & Central Asia: Lessons Not Learned* (New York: Routledge, 2005), draws on the experience of the developing market economies to understand the practical consequences of both well-managed and ill-managed deployment of the energy revenues in the region. Of special interest is Richard Pomfret's *The Central Asian Economies since Independence* (Princeton, NJ: Princeton University Press, 2006), which provides a concise and up-to-date analysis of the huge changes undergone by the economies of all countries in the region since 1991. With separate chapters on each country and chapters analyzing their comparative economic performance, the book highlights similarities and differences.

The new pattern of security concerns of the Central Asian successor states is analyzed in Arne Haugen's *The Establishment of National Republics in Soviet Central Asia* (Houndmills, Basingstoke, Hampshire, NY: Palgrave Macmillan, 2003). The main contention of the book is that the security problems of these newly independent states—where subnational, supranational, and national loyalties frequently override a population's loyalty to the state—are similar to those that were faced by other colonial countries shortly after they attained independence. The roles that diaspora communities play in the forming of national identities are explored in the collection of high-quality articles edited by Touraj Atabaki and Sanjyot Mehendale for *Central Asia and the Caucasus: Transnationalism and Diaspora* (London and New York: Routledge, 2005). They conclude that the loyalties of these communities are divided between their countries of residence and those states that serve as the homelands of their particular ethnocultural nation, particularly Russia and China. Because of the multiethnic nature of these states, the researchers pay special attention to the role and status of Russian language and culture. The most recent book on this subject is David MacFadyen's *Russian Culture in Uzbekistan: One Language in the Middle of Nowhere* (New York: Routledge, 2006). This book examines the predicament of Russian culture in Central Asia, looking at literature, language, cinema, music, and religion, and argues that Russian people—formerly perceived as progressive and engaging with Europe—are now confronted by the erasure of their culture as local ethnic cultures become much stronger. Russia's policy toward Afghanistan and the four key states that surround it—Tajikistan, Uzbekistan, Turkmenistan, and Kyrgyzstan—and Russia's position in regard to new security challenges of the region and increased foreign engagement are examined by Lena Jonson in *Vladimir Putin and Central Asia: The Shaping of Russian Foreign Policy* (London and New York: I. B. Tauris, 2004).

For individual country studies, books authored by Martha Brill Olcott, *Kazakhstan, Unfulfilled Promise* (Washington, DC: Carnegie Endowment for International Peace, 2002) and by Frederic Grare, *Tajikistan: The Trials of Independence* (Surrey, England: Curzon Press, 1998) can be recommended. For many other aspects of Central Asian historical and contemporary development, publications in *Central Asian Survey* and *Europe-Asia Studies* published by Routledge are of interest.

Index

About the Author

PETER L. ROUDIK is Senior Foreign Law Specialist at the Directorate of Legal Research of the Law Library of Congress. His research extends to all aspects of legal and political development in the former Soviet states.

Press, 2002) provide information on the modern history of these nations, defining the leading figures, institutions, political parties, and organizations. The people who make up the society, their origins, dominant beliefs and values, and their common interests and the issues on which they are divided are analyzed in Peter Ferdinand's *The New States of Central Asia and Their Neighbours* (New York: Council on Foreign Relations Press, 1994).

One of the most thorough studies on the region's history that covers the period from the earliest times until the middle of the nineteenth century is Ahmad Dani's (Ed.) *History of Civilizations of Central Asia* (Paris: UNESCO Publishing, 2003). A great introduction to the subject is the classic work of Lawrence Kraderer, *Peoples of Central Asia* (Bloomington: Indiana University Press, 1996). An accessible introduction to the history of the region, which begins with the arrival of Islam and includes a modern history of the region (which expands to include Mongolia and Xinjiang) is Soucek Svat's *History of Inner Asia* (Cambridge, England and New York: Cambridge University Press, 2000). This book is supplemented with many useful maps, charts, and illustrations. A definitive history of Central Asia from prehistory to the contemporary machinations of the Russian Empire is Francis Skrine and Edward Ross, *The Heart of Asia: A History of Russian Turkistan and the Central Asian Khanates from the Earliest Times* (London and New York: Routledge Curzon, 2004). Originally published in 1899, this book is valuable not only because of the quality of the historical work on the early period, but also because of the unique picture that it gives of contemporary views on the potential for Anglo-Russian conflict at a time when the Russian Empire was Britain's closest rival for Asian hegemony.

For those interested in exploration of Central Asia, Kenneth Wimmel's *The Alluring Target: In Search of the Secrets of Central Asia* (Fairfax, VA: Trackless Sands Press, 1996) is a well-researched story of Western expeditions to Central Asia from ancient voyages to 1935. Reports on archeological and anthropological discoveries made during such expeditions can be found in R. Pumpelly, *Explorations in Turkistan, Expedition of 1904: Prehistoric Civilizations of Anau* (Washington, DC: Carnegie Institution of Washington,1908); Fredrik Hiebert, *A Central Asian Village at the Dawn of Civilization, Excavations at Anau, Turkmenistan* (Philadelphia: University of Pennsylvania Museum of Archaeology and Anthropology, 2003); and Gregoire Frumkin, *Archaeology in Soviet Central Asia* (Leiden, The Netherlands: Brill, 1970). Reports and diaries of travelers to this remote area describe the people and places. One of the first foreign visitors was Chinese official Chang Kien, whose report dated to the second century B.C. is thoroughly analyzed by Friedrich Hirth, "The Story of Chang Kien, China's Pioneer in Western Asia," *Journal of the American Oriental Society* volume 37 pps. 89–152 (1917). The court of the Bokharan emir is pictured in Alexander Lehmann, *Reise nach Buchara und Samarkand in den Jahren 1841 und*

Bibliographic Essay

The long and fascinating history of Central Asia is reflected in numerous books written on different aspects of political, economic, and cultural developments of the region. Independence, which these states acquired after 1991, and their geostrategic importance were the reason for the abundance of recently published studies, varying from simple reference books to multivolume scholarly research. One of the most comprehensive sources of background information is by Glen Curtis (Ed.), *Kazakhstan, Kyrgyzstan, Tajikistan, Turkmenistan, and Uzbekistan: Country Studies* (Washington, DC: Federal Research Division, Library of Congress, 1997), which describes political, economic, social, and national security systems and institutions and examines the interrelationships of those systems and the ways they were shaped by historical and cultural factors. Reliable sources of general information are books published in 2005 by the Mason Crest in Philadelphia. They give a dynamic portrait of each Central Asian nation. They are: William Habeeb, *Turkmenistan*; Collen O'Dea, *Tajikistan*; Joyce Libal, *Uzbekistan*; Daniel Harmon, *Kyrgyzstan*; and Jim Corrigan, *Kazakhstan*. Historical dictionaries written by Rafis Abazov, *Kyrgyzstan* (Toronto, Ontario, Oxford, England, and Lanham, MD: Scarecrow Press, 2004); and *Turkmenistan* (Toronto, Ontario, Oxford, England, and Lanham, MD: Scarecrow Press, 2005) and by Kamoludin Abdullaev and Shahram Akbarzadeh, *Historical Dictionary of Tajikistan* (Toronto, Ontario, Oxford, England, and Lanham, MD: Scarecrow